Yukio Mishima

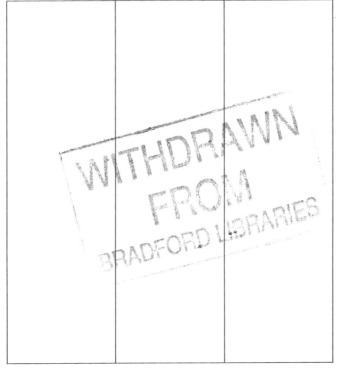

Please return/renew this item by the last
date shown. Items not required by other
customers may be renewed by calling
01274 430094 or at:
http://capitadiscovery.co.uk/bradford

Titles in the series Critical Lives present the work of leading cultural figures of the modern period. Each book explores the life of the artist, writer, philosopher or architect in question and relates it to their major works.

In the same series

Yukio Mishima

Damian Flanagan

REAKTION BOOKS

For Karen

Published by Reaktion Books Ltd
33 Great Sutton Street
London EC1V 0DX, UK

www.reaktionbooks.co.uk

First published 2014

Printed and bound in Great Britain by Bell & Bain, Glasgow

A catalogue record for this book is available from the British Library

ISBN 978 1 78023 345 1

Contents

Mishima, in Shield Society uniform, addressing the crowd, 25 November 1970.

1

Japan in the Age of Mishima

When one comes to write of Yukio Mishima, Japan's first internationally renowned literary superstar, nearly always one starts with death. With any other subject, birth would be as good a starting point as any, but with Mishima, it is as though time is reversed and refluxed, and the final dramatic day is not just the summation of the life, but also the day the Mishima story achieves apotheosis and, in an orgy of blood, becomes eternally reborn.

At death, this was a man still at the peak of his powers and possessed of a steely will, determined to carry out an act of tremendous daring. At 11 a.m. on the cold, bright Wednesday morning of 25 November 1970, Mishima led four members of his private army, the Shield Society, into the Eastern Headquarters of the Self-defence Forces in Ichigaya, Tokyo, for a prearranged meeting with General Kanetoshi Mashita. The unwitting general probably thought that Mishima had come to discuss arrangements for members of the Shield Society to train with Japan's official (though paradoxically non-constitutional) military forces and little suspected that he was about to become a pawn in one of the most outlandish and spectacularly shocking events in post-war Japanese history.

Mishima began innocently enough by showing the general his prized Seki no Magoroku sword, but then, without warning, Mishima's men suddenly took the general hostage and gagged and tied him up in his office. Fierce scuffles broke out as officers repeatedly forced entry into the office, but Mishima narrowly managed to drive them out again by slashing at their arms with the sword. Mishima then demanded that the entire army assemble beneath the office balcony to hear him speak, threatening to kill the general and commit suicide if the demand was not acceded to. By noon around a thousand men had quickly assembled beneath the balcony. One of the world's greatest living writers, dressed bizarrely in what could easily be mistaken for a bell boy's uniform, wearing white gloves and a headband with a rising sun and the words *Shichisho Hokoku* (Seven Lives for the Nation!), was pacing back and forth on the balcony and, gesticulating wildly, began hectoring the soldiers with his prepared speech. Banners proclaiming Mishima's intentions were draped over the balcony and leaflets containing Mishima's 'Declaration of Protest' were scattered as media helicopters circled overhead.

What was the message Mishima was trying to get across? According to the polemic which Mishima distributed that morning and requested be printed in full in the newspapers after his death, the Shield Society, while feeling profound kinship with their brothers in the Self-defence Forces (SDF), had been forced into today's extreme act because they could no longer tolerate the deceit that the SDF represented. Article 9 of the American-imposed constitution of 1947 proclaimed that Japan renounced forever aggression and the right to have its own military, but according to Mishima such foolish idealism had soured into rank hypocrisy with the creation of the SDF, which was the Japanese Army in all but name.

For too long, Mishima passionately believed, Japan's glorious samurai traditions, its manliness and heroism, had been suppressed as something of which to be ashamed. Instead, the so-called Peace Constitution had turned Japan into an effeminate, anodyne, culturally barren society. Only by overthrowing the Peace Constitution could a new Japan, at one with itself and in tune with its noble history and traditions, be reborn. It was up to the SDF to lead the way, to no longer accept the hypocrisy which forced Japanese soldiers to hide behind a mask, pretending to be something different from what they really were. His words rang out:

What is the meaning of having a military? It is to defend Japan! What does defending Japan mean? Defending Japan means defending the cultural and historical traditions that centre on the emperor! . . . In the midst of economic prosperity, Japan has fallen asleep and become a spiritually empty husk. Do you all understand that? . . . If the Japanese don't stand up, if the SDF don't stand up, constitutional reform won't happen. You will all end up being nothing more than soldiers of America . . . Aren't you samurai? Aren't you samurai? If you are samurai, why do you defend a constitution that rejects you? Why, for the sake of a constitution that denies you, do you go along with a constitution that denies you? So long as that's the case, you will never, ever be saved . . . You pretend you are constitutional, but the SDF are unconstitutional. The SDF are unconstitutional. You too are unconstitutional![1]

Mishima, however, was not addressing a remotely sympathetic crowd. Irritated with having to interrupt their lunch breaks, bored with hanging around and bewildered by Mishima's latest antic, when he asked dramatically: 'Is there not one amongst you who will stand up with me?', the soldiers heckled him with: 'Fuckwit!', 'Shit for Brains!' Mishima responded:

So, not one of you! Now it is certain I will die. Since you won't stand up for constitutional reform, my dream for the SDF is over. Now I will cry out '*Tenno heika banzai!*' [Long live the emperor!].[2]

With that, Mishima knelt and faced the imperial palace, reciting '*Tenno heika banzai*!' three times. But his voice was drowned out in a sea of: 'Shoot him!', 'Get him!', 'Drop dead!', 'Dickhead!', 'Get down!', 'Look at the big hero', 'Japan is at peace', 'Madman!'

Mishima was not about to be deviated from his purpose. He knew he had seen his wife and two young children for the last time, had made final visits to his family and friends. His preparations were meticulous, covering everything from how elements of the media should be briefed to the *fundoshi* (loincloth) he wore as the sole item of clothing beneath his uniform. That morning in the car on the way to the base, he envisioned the moment almost as the climax to one of his beloved yakuza movies and started singing the theme song of a hit yakuza movie series to keep his young accomplices at ease.

At the Ichigaya Assembly Hall close by were dozens of members of Mishima's Shield Society as well as two journalists who had been tipped off in advance by Mishima that something worth reporting might be happening at the base that day. And sure enough, at 11.22 a.m. an emergency call had been put through to the police who – after momentarily being under the illusion that a drunkard *pretending* to be Mishima was brandishing a sword in the commandant's room – dispatched 120 officers to the scene.[3]

Mishima had expected that his big speech would last for twenty minutes, but in fact it was over in only seven, and as he quit the balcony and came down the red-carpeted steps back into the office, he said to the general in a tone of resignation: 'I have no regrets. I have done this in order to return the SDF to the emperor.' He then took his watch off, handed it to one of his accomplices and immediately began preparations for his ritual suicide in traditional samurai fashion. He knelt on the floor, exposing his muscular stomach, brandished his short sword and with a grunt carefully inserted it into the left side of his intestines before inching it across the width of his torso. Masakatsu Morita, one of the four young acolytes who accompanied Mishima and who may have been his lover, had been chosen to play the role of *kaishaku-nin*, one who performs beheading of the person committing ritual suicide to shorten the pain. Morita stood over Mishima with the long sword and attempted to lop off his head with one clean blow once Mishima's own blade had finished the short, excruciating journey across his stomach.

Unfortunately, Morita made a hash of it. Instead of putting Mishima out of his misery, he brought his sword down on the novelist's shoulders, only partially taking off the head and exacerbating the agony. The other young men shouted for him to deliver the *coup de grâce*. Two more strikes also missed. As the general called for them to stop, one of the acolytes, Hiroyasu Koga, took control and struck again with the long sword, decapitating Mishima instantly. Now, as had been prearranged, Morita too dropped to his knees and attempted, much more tentatively than Mishima, to ritually disembowel himself. Koga then once more did the honours with the long sword. The remaining three acolytes then tidied up the dis-assembled bodies and heads, bowed to them and, releasing the general, allowed him to bow also.

By 12.20 p.m. it was all over. When the soldiers rushed in, the heads of Mishima and Morita were lying side by side on the carpet. A large picture of the two heads on the floor next to the scabbard of the sword used in the *kaishaku* would feature on the front page of that evening's edition of the *Asahi Shinbun*, alongside a picture of Mishima on the balcony, left hand on hip, other hand outstretched.

In Mishima's statement of protest explaining the reasons for his actions, despite referring to the SDF as 'a canary that has lost its voice' and 'a huge arsenal that has lost its spirit', he emphasized that he was not denigrating them. Rather he believed that the SDF was the only place in modern Japan where the true Japanese, the true warrior spirit, remained. It was in order to wake them up that members of the Shield Society had today opened their stomachs in the ancient way of warriors. Indeed the Shield Society believed this was the only way they could truly repay the debt owed to the SDF.

Neither the slow decays of nature, nor the tranquillizing effect of history, would get the better of the man who had reinvented himself not only as Japan's greatest modern writer (34 novels; over 70 plays; over 170 short stories), but also as an actor, bodybuilder, world traveller, kendo enthusiast and ultimately leader of his own private army.

Appropriately enough for a man obsessed throughout his life with death, who was enthralled with the aesthetics of death and believed that an eternal readiness to die and the acceptance of pain were the only means through which one could feel truly alive, the day of death really did mark a day of extraordinary transcendence. Death for Mishima was the true constant of nature, the true face of eternity, and the day of his death is the day on which his ultimate work of art – the life of Yukio Mishima – was completed and unveiled. The key to everything before the death seems in some way hinted at and curiously foreshadowed in the mysteries of that final day.

The Day of Death began the instant Mishima placed the final chapters of the fourth volume of his monumental masterpiece, *The Sea of Fertility*, in an envelope and left it on a table in his hallway. All his life Mishima, the consummate writing professional, was well known for having never missed a deadline, but this occasion, the day on which he concluded his extraordinarily prolific novelistic career, was also timed as being the day of his boldest drama. Mishima, who in his final years insisted on the complete separateness of his identities as writer on the one hand and man of action on the other, wanted to quit life's stage not as a contemplative slave to words but as a fearless, unflinching warrior.

There seem to be so many overlapping motivations concerning the events of the final day that any attempted portrait of the truth appears differently depending on the angle from which it is approached. Is the Mishima Incident (as it is generally known) really best considered at face value as a politically inspired protest? Was it not also the case that Mishima had fantasized erotically since being a young boy about pain and death, about the glorious deaths of soldiers? Was the Day of Death, then, a political mask that hid the orgasmic climax to a life of sadomasochistic fantasies?

And what of Mishima's well-known narcissism and determination never to suffer bodily decline? Surely vanity too was part of the nexus of motivations. Some offered yet another view: that it was Mishima's disappointment over his failure to secure Japan's first Nobel Prize in Literature in 1968 (the prize was given to Mishima's mentor Yasunari Kawabata instead) that set Mishima on his path to public self-evisceration.[4] Mishima was not prepared, it was argued, to wait until it was 'Japan's turn' once more. By then he would be too old and his sun would be setting; Mishima was determined to quit the stage while the sun was still at its zenith.

The public response to the Mishima Incident was intriguing. To start with it was shock, outrage and utter confusion as the frenzy of noontime news reportage assailed people in waves. First it was reported that Mishima was causing a disturbance at the army base; then there were images of him giving his speech on the balcony. Television news reported his suicide, then retracted it, then retracted the retraction. But as the news sank in, people huddled silently, mouths agape, around televisions in government buildings, in newspaper and magazine offices, in publishing houses and on film locations. In all these places, as well as at the police headquarters itself, Mishima was —

because of his political activities, family connections and high-level socializing – a man personally familiar to the most senior figures. The tentacles of his connections seemed to spread through every corner of society from young radicals to aged authors, from the prime minister to jobbing journalists, from super-rich businessmen to taxi drivers.

Those casually glancing at the blanket coverage on television, or dozing in the backs of cars and awakening to a commotion on the radio, could only presume that the long-anticipated award of his Nobel Prize was a reality at last. Yet now, across millions of households, phones erupted into a cacophony of noise as people raced to pass on the sensation: 'Have you heard the news? Turn on the TV!' Many thought they were being subjected to a bad joke; others were stupefied into silence.

Then came the indignation. When one commentator appeared on television to discuss the seemingly unbelievable event, the interviewer referred to Mishima with the standard polite 'Mishima-san', but the commentator kept on responding, insistently, with the bald word 'Mishima' without the '-san' honorific – a form of reference reserved for criminals and those not worthy of even the slightest social deference.[5] The government of Prime Minister Eisaku Sato, flummoxed by this weird thunderbolt from heaven, expressed 'regret'. That year, 1970, had after all brought the Osaka Expo, Japan's showcase to the world: 64 million visitors had flocked to witness for themselves the products of Japan's technological revolution and its phoenix-like rise from the ashes of the Second World War. The mood was confident: the 1960s had witnessed annual double-digit growth, the quadrupling of per capita income and the staging of the 1964 Olympics. As every home acquired a television set and a washing machine, the juggernaut of modernity and progress seemed unstoppable; Japan sailed past all the European economies in terms of GDP and many began to wonder how much further the nation's star might rise.

The age was referred to as being a second Genroku era (1688–1704), a period in Japanese history when peace and a surge in prosperity had led to an artistic flowering, though also a decline in military discipline and ardour. Mishima's favourite book was *Hagakure* (*Hidden by the Leaves*, *c.* 1716), a forceful reaction to the decadence of Genroku society that lamented how much young samurai were being mentally and physically enfeebled by the corruptions of the age. The author of *Hagakure*, Tsunetomo Yamamoto, had famously proclaimed that 'the way of the samurai lies in death' and that the samurai must be ready at all times to die. It was a sentiment that profoundly appealed to Mishima. He was deeply concerned that the 'death wish' of all Japanese citizens was not being satisfied by the country's government.

Yet to the general public, Mishima's eccentric stunt could only appear as a grotesque anachronism, an aping of the various attempts at coups by officers in the Japanese army that occurred during the 1930s, an expression of ultra-nationalist sentiment that Mishima adored but which the Japanese nation would frankly rather now forget. In a year in which the pressing news items were large-scale pollution problems, various aircraft hijackings by the Red Brigade and Arab terrorists, the death of President Gamal Abdel Nasser of Egypt and China's increasing international recognition, what exactly was the point of this throwback to the 1930s? After the initial shock and condemnation had subsided, however, a curious mixture of sympathy and respect began to manifest itself. Like a deep-impact time-delay bomb, the significance of the Mishima Incident has gradually burrowed its way into the national psychology and invites constant reconsideration. The Mishima Incident would become, for Japan's post-war generation, its never-to-be-forgotten JFK moment, when time appeared to be stopped in its tracks by jaw-dropping disbelief. And whereas at the time of the Incident, Mishima tended to be viewed as an anti-social fanatic who was assaulting Japan's cherished democracy, with the passage of time he has come to be seen more as a critic of the age in which he lived, and increasingly as a prophet now that Japan has begun to lose its 'economic superpower' status.

On the day itself, though, politicians were more concerned with distancing themselves quickly from Mishima's headlong assault on the post-war political order. Only a few months previously, Mishima's opinions on national defence had been expressly sought by the Japanese government and a lengthy diatribe recorded by him on tape had been typed up on cabinet paper and passed to the prime minister himself. Mishima had even been encouraged by high-ranking officials to stand for a seat in the Japanese upper house, with Prime Minister Sato offering to fund Mishima's private army.[6] Now everyone wished to cover their tracks quickly.

In September 1970, two months before the Incident, Sato – Japan's longest-serving post-war prime minister (1964–72) – had addressed the United Nations, remarking:

> The Japanese People, because of that grave historical experience [of losing the war], will always defend freedom and be devoted to peace and furthering the entire world's prosperity and peace, for we firmly believe that this is the means to preserve our own country's peace and prosperity.[7]

This was the message he recalled at the beginning of the important general-policy speech he delivered at 1 p.m. on 25 November, the very day of the Incident. At 9.30 a.m. Sato had opened the Cabinet meeting at his official residence before attending, at 11 a.m., the opening of the National Diet (parliament), with the emperor himself in attendance. Sato returned to the Prime Minister's residence at Nagata-cho at 12.10 p.m., and after being briefed about the Incident, found himself besieged by journalists:

'Something terrible has occurred, hasn't it?'

'What action will the government take?'

'What do you see as the background to the Incident?'

Sato responded: 'Genius and madness are two sides of the same coin, but I can only think of it as madness. It's completely off the rails. As for the reason for it I don't yet know.' But on his way back to his room at the parliament building he added: 'We've lost someone precious.'[8]

The Mishima Incident utterly obliterated the prime minister's speech on all channels that night and not only dominated the nation's newspapers, but produced the biggest-ever sales of their evening editions. The following day, as autopsies were being carried out on Mishima's and Morita's remains, the media produced a vast array of speculative analysis: Mishima had gone mad; reached a literary impasse; died for aesthetic reasons; had a love suicide with Morita; died as a statement of protest; had attempted a *coup d'état*; had reached an economic impasse. In the two months following the Incident, volume one of *The Sea of Fertility* sold 348,000 copies; volume two, 252,000 copies; and volume three, 228,000 copies. Magazines rushed out special editions. 'A Yukio Mishima Reader' sold 210,000 copies; a 'Yukio Mishima Special Edition' 500,000 copies.

Yasuhiro Nakasone, the future prime minister (1982–7) and then head of the Defence Agency, who had enjoyed warm relations with Mishima and allowed his Shield Society members to train with the SDF, was, however, openly critical:

> It's a completely regrettable incident. For a famous writer like Mishima to wreak havoc, injure and kill people is deranged behaviour and a destruction of the democratic order which

the nation has painfully created. We must thoroughly clamp down on it.[9]

The right wing in Japan were incensed and not only subsequently petitioned for his resignation but bombarded him with threats, requiring him to greatly increase the number of his bodyguards.

Whatever one might think of the Mishima Incident in terms of a symbolic act of daring and protest, on the purely political level, the purported aspirations for his country which Mishima proclaimed in the last years of his life were overwhelmingly obnoxious. Those, including some distinguished literary critics, who think that the politics of Mishima's final years were nothing more than a reaction to the anodyne state of Japan's culture and a reverence for Japanese traditions would do well to consider the details of the militaristic state that Mishima actually called for in *taidan* (conversations with other commentators) printed in such works as *For Young Samurai*, published a year previously in July 1969, which soon became a best-seller.

Envision if you will a 'Japan that Never Was', a projection of what might have happened had the SDF actually mustered some sympathy for Mishima's call for a revolution in 1970. Picture Japan ten years later as a fully militarized nation again, with a million men under arms, with concrete bunkers installed throughout Tokyo in readiness for any missile strike and a network of motorways across the country built for the sole purpose of transporting tanks.[10] In this Japan, history lessons consist of 'national mythology' classes and the country has now long since abandoned its alliance with the USA. All of these things are items of national policy specifically suggested by Mishima.

How easily we take it for granted that there should exist on the eastern edge of the world a nation as prosperous, endlessly inventive and internationally influential as Japan. But this nightmare Japan of Mishima's fantasies was actually more like how the nation might have ended up had there not been for Japan an earthquake in historical time in 1945. Had the Japan of the 1930s and early 1940s been allowed to continue unabated, this is how the Japan of the 1980s might well have looked. From 1925, when Mishima was born, Japan was dominated for twenty years by an increasingly repressive regime devoted to military expansion. The next twenty years saw a sociological about-face, with Japan renouncing war forever. Mishima's glittering literary career was played out against the background of a country coping with the trauma of wartime defeat and American occupation; one which had to learn quickly how to completely reinvent itself as a thriving capitalist powerhouse. Mishima flourished under the stream of Western influence in Japan, yet increasingly recognized suppressed parts of himself in aspects of Japanese culture that had seemingly been buried under the weight of Western influence. When he reached the age of 40 he had lived exactly half of his life under a militaristic state and half in an economy-first democracy, and had reached a tipping point in which the desire to return to Japan's martial traditions became an obsession.

Numbers and timing are a crucial part of the Mishima story. In Japan, twenty is the age at which you officially become an adult, in which you cross the border from childhood. For Mishima, this happened in 1945, the year in which history underwent a convulsion, when an entire political and social system collapsed and was declared bankrupt and corrupt. Mishima entered adulthood in a world reduced to ashes, in a country suddenly importing wholesale much of the belief system, as well as the commercial and cultural products, of the United States. On one level, this would prove tremendously liberating to Mishima and the new generation of writers suddenly released from the onerous restrictions of the previous militaristic regime. But eventually – after another twenty years had passed – a growing sense of dislocation, of being brutally cut off from the natural flow of historical time, began to manifest itself.

Mishima, in his yearnings to break through to the dislocated half of existence – the Japan that had existed in the first twenty years of his life – was flying in the face of historical reality, denying everything that had happened in the intervening twenty years. How could he transcend the forces of history itself? Yet this was indeed what Mishima attempted to achieve. If necessary, history itself would have to be deposed and the emperor restored in its place. For Mishima, the emperor was not so much a person as a spiritual embodiment of the Japanese nation. The emperor was the central presence in Japanese history, culture and traditions, representing the continuity and unity of its people; a head of state in a national structure (*kokutai*) superseding changes of government or political organization. This was the foundation of the Japanese state's very existence and so now and into the future must be defended. According to Mishima, the army's role in defending the emperor must be constitutionally decreed. Indeed it was specifically to defend the emperor that his Shield Society was formed.

In *For Young Samurai*, Mishima insisted that myths and illogicality are what should be taught at school and referred to the veneration of the emperor as a kind of esoteric Buddhism that should be prized.[11] For him, emperor worship stood in contrast to the rampant egotism of modern Japan. The emperor was important as an 'anti-force' – pitted against the psychology of modern people and the morals that they held. The emperor was the central balancing force in society, the last redoubt against Western decadence and decay. Mishima argued that the emperor prevented the sacred nation of Japan from being turned into nothing more than a Western-style state of legal structures and spiritless administrators and should be defended to the last, to the death.

Mishima claimed that he was all for urbanization, modernization and industrialization, but that people had a sense of frustration in a world devoted to the modern and that this is where the emperor came in. The emperor had to be the manifestation of a timeless ritual representing anti-egotism, anti-industrialization and anti-modernization. For this reason, he fiercely resented and openly criticized any action of the present emperor that betrayed a modern personality, such as the interest of Emperor Hirohito in marine biology or the appearance of gossipy articles about the imperial family in weekly magazines.[12]

Mishima declared that the defence of Japan relied on the resolve of each person to strike the enemy with a sword,[13] a sentiment that was a curious leftover from the mindset of the Japanese military government during the Second World War, some of whom wanted to keep on fighting even after the dropping of two atomic bombs. If every single Japanese person was prepared to have the same resolve as a kamikaze pilot and offer themselves up in death, then Japan would never be defeated, they argued.

The main conclusions of these conversations were that Japan had lost its samurai spirit and must resolve to defend itself; that it was being indirectly attacked by left-wingers and communists; that the nation had become cowardly and West-worshipping in a world where 'victims always triumph'.[14] A *coup d'état* might be required, they argued, in order to overturn the Peace Constitution and return to the previous constitution.[15]

Mishima had given up hope in politicians, bewailing their self-interest and jockeying for power, and now constantly warned of the insidious invasion of communism. It was hardly likely that Mishima believed that Article 9 of the Constitution would actually be changed. For one thing, such constitutional revision required the support of over two-thirds of all congressmen and even then it was subject to ratification by national plebiscite. So, instead, Mishima placed his faith in the long-inert tradition of revolts by corps of military officers.

Late polemical pieces such as *For Young Samurai* and *Introductions to the Philosophy of Action* have to be read in the context of the time in which they were written. In 1968, student riots had caused turmoil throughout the world and had been particularly intense at Tokyo University – the nation's leading university, from which Mishima himself had graduated. The professors had been variously abused, attacked and occasionally imprisoned within the university itself, while disturbances had spilled out on to the streets of Tokyo, where mass protests again turned violent. Things were expected to get worse in the build-up to 1970, when the security treaty with the United States – allowing the stationing of large American bases throughout Japan – was again up for renewal.

Mishima appeared to view these riots as virtually the end of civilization itself and repeatedly became involved in talks and debates with the students. He openly hated the student groups leading the protests and was mostly defensive of the professors, while chiding them for their timorousness towards the students.

In *For Young Samurai*, he refers in detail to the student disturbances at Tokyo University going on at the time and seemed frustrated that the SDF would not intervene. Tokyo University was supposed to be a self-governing body, so he declared that the whole university should be evacuated and turned into a zoo – like nearby Ueno Zoo. If the students were left entirely to their own devices, he argued, if the rule of law were completely removed, people would soon see that they would sink to brutality and savagery against one another. He was dismissive of people who said they wished to live their lives in the name of ideals for a better tomorrow; the only reality, he said, was the present and the existing cultural traditions that defined the nation. Only firm social order and a strong military, Mishima believed, would defend that culture and traditions.

Why did Mishima become so obsessive about the student riots? One reason is that he felt the riots and occupation of the campuses could yet escalate to an assault on the Japanese parliament itself and that at this moment the longed-for chance for constitutional reform would present itself. It was the job of the police to defend the political structure and of the army to defend the nation, but if the police proved incapable of controlling the riots, the opportunity would arise for the army to be mobilized and to restore its honour by showing everyone that they were the only ones capable of saving the nation. Then no one could argue a case against constitutional reform.

A key date was 21 October 1969, designated 'International Anti-War Day', with demonstrations taking place in 600 places across Japan ahead of Prime Minister Sato's forthcoming visit to America. Students and left-wing radicals protested about various issues: against the war in Vietnam; for the abolition of Japan's security treaty with the United States; and for the return of Okinawa, currently used as a huge American army base. Fearing disturbances, the authorities banned all public meetings, and from the morning onwards sporadic guerrilla insurgency broke out in the cities, with police boxes and military bases attacked. Yet the SDF were not mobilized and this day was to mark the collapse of left-wing opposition.

Mishima wrote in his 'Declaration of Protest':

This demonstration, occurring at the critical moment before the prime minister's trip to the United States, fizzled out under overwhelming police force. Seeing this in Shinjuku, I bitterly regretted that 'Now the constitution will not change.' What happened that day? The government saw the limits of the New Left's strength; they saw the general public's reaction to the martial-law-like clampdown of the police and gained the confidence to settle the situation without picking up the hot potato of constitutional reform.[16]

However disappointed he may have been that the riots did not escalate further, Mishima had already begun to live his life, following the prescription of his beloved *Hagakure*, in mental and physical preparation for some 'emergency', and in the student riots convinced himself that the 'emergency' had happened at last. Rather than seeing Mishima's outlandish politics as a realistic and viable alternative for Japan, however, it is more interesting to consider them as a projection of his own psyche and an attempt to mask some of his own unresolved inner contradictions.

The endless anticipation of an 'emergency' that overwhelmed Mishima from the age of 40 onwards was both an increasing obsession with the imminence of bodily decline and a constant playing out in his own mind of the event that dominated his youth – Japan's calamitous defeat in the Second World War and, importantly, his failure to have any part in this real national 'emergency'. Only by exaggerating illness had Mishima, as a short, willowy youth in 1945, narrowly escaped conscription and almost-certain death in the last days of the Pacific War. Instead he was cast into a desolate, post-war Japanese environment where people were simply scraping together an existence as the country was rebuilt from the rubble.

Mishima's obsessive interest in Japan's defence was a projection of this disturbed psychology. In his late political writings, he ridicules those on the left who argue that Japan might not have any need of a military at all. They do not live in the real world, Mishima scoffs. What nation ever defended itself without a great army and a fighting spirit and resolve? Yet in all this constant talk of the imperatives of defence, it is never entirely clear against whom Japan was supposed to be defending itself. What nation was it that wanted to invade Japan? Before the Pacific War – itself instigated by Japanese imperialism across Asia – the only attempted invasion of Japan in the nation's history was by the Mongols in the thirteenth century. Yet Mishima seemed to convince himself that Japan needed a million men in uniform to defend itself from some unnamed chimera.

What makes Mishima such a fascinating subject is that he represented in his own person the intense psychological traumas of the whole sweep of modern Japanese history, its precipitate caesuras and volte-faces under intense external pressures that produced a deep sense of cultural schizophrenia. To unpick the deep-seated psychoses at work within Mishima you have to examine both the profound trauma and supreme cultural achievements intrinsic to the creation of Japan as a modern nation state. Foreign influence and the threat of insidious Western colonization were always vital.

In the Edo period (1603–1868), Japan had very consciously attempted to arrest the march of historical time and retreat inwards upon itself. But by the nineteenth century, the government had no viable strategy regarding how to defend the nation from the ever more worrying encroachment of Western colonial powers. Britain's humiliating defeat of China in the First Opium War (1839–42) was a seismic event in Asian history that shattered forever the illusion that China was the timeless 'Middle Kingdom' and the only major fount of culture and philosophical wisdom with which the Japanese need concern themselves. In 1853, the dreaded foreigners arrived from the United States in the form of Commodore Matthew Perry and his 'Black Ships', threatening Tokyo with bombardment if the nation did not open itself up to trade.

The convulsions of the following fifteen years represented a shattering spiritual crisis for the Japanese nation. All the structures of Edo Japan were shown to be built on sand. The samurai, who were supposed to be the defenders of Japan, ever ready to give up their lives when an emergency beckoned, were shown to be completely impotent in the face of superior Western technology. The shogun, the so-called 'barbarian conquering general', had to meekly submit to the demands of 'barbarians' and agree to trade concessions. Patriots were placed in the clutches of multiple profound paradoxes. They wished to expel the barbarians and restore the emperor's honour, but to do so, they soon realized that they needed to learn from the Westerners, study their languages and absorb their technology. Moreover, the entire philosophic underpinning of Edo Japan, the belief in a divine, neo-Confucian order with a rigid social structure to match, was shown to be a sham. History was not immobile and circular, but demanding of constant renewal and reconfiguration. The samurai, if they were to fulfil their function of defending Japan and honouring the emperor, needed paradoxically to urgently abolish the very social system that supported them.

By 1868, the shogunate was abolished and Japan was recast as a modern nation state. In the years that followed, painful reforms continued, as first the samurai class were banned from carrying swords and then had their status completely nullified. Step by step, Japan embraced wholesale Westernization. Driving the reforms was the overwhelming desire to be able to compete as equals with the Western powers and revise the 'unequal treaties' that Japan had been forced to sign. The whole nation appeared torn between the desire on the one hand to defend Japan's proud independence and traditions and on the other to embrace modernity as the only means of competing in the realities of the new international order. Deciding how great the concessions to Westernization and modernity should be was the defining question. Not only was a war fought between the samurai clans calling for an overthrow of the shogunate and those who stoutly fought to defend it, but further wars ensued between the victorious 'modernizers' themselves, some of whom – like Takamori Saigo – drew the line at revoking the samurai's privileges and believed instead that the samurai should demonstrate their value by immediately embarking on a war of conquest in Korea. Certain modernizers, such as Arinori Mori, went as far as suggesting that Japan should abandon the

Japanese language altogether and adopt English instead. He, along with several other Meiji leaders, was rewarded with assassination by discontented conservatives.

The Japan that emerged in the Meiji era (1868–1912), then, was like a precocious, pent-up child, unassailable in its ambition to make up for lost time and go into the world to assimilate every scrap of Western learning, whether it be industrial techniques or philosophy, art or literature. Yet hand in hand with this driving ambition was a profound sense of national neurosis, of dizzying change being forced through from the top down at breakneck speed, of there being no time for natural assimilation, leaving the national sense of identity in tatters.

This widespread sense of a schizophrenic toing and froing between a rush to modernity and a determination to keep pace with the West on the one hand and a retreat into the secluded comfort of Japanese traditions on the other manifested itself in just about every way, big and small, in the early decades of the twentieth century. Indeed these contradictions and national neuroses continue to this very day. The bifurcations of Mishima's own personality – his ability to enjoy Western food, wear Western clothes, live in an entirely Western house and desperately crave due recognition for his works in the West while at the same time proclaiming his total devotion to the emperor and samurai ideals – were not, therefore, just a quixotic aspect of one individual, but rather an acute representation of the implicit contradictions in the whole of modern Japanese culture.

When Mishima was born in 1925, he was released into a historical tide that already contained all the paradoxes and schizophrenic tendencies which would define his entire life. Far from being able to transcend history, it was almost as if the spiritual tumult of his life were preordained. Why, though, should the paradoxes, pain and schizophrenia of modern Japan have manifested themselves so violently in the person of Mishima above all others? One reason, as already noted, was the precise historical timing of his happening to be born in 1925 and reaching manhood in 1945. Mishima's own supremely artistic sensibility, his sensitivity to the world around him, his intelligence, ambition and poetic temperament, further marked him out as a person who would be most influenced by such historical paradoxes.

From the macrocosm of Japanese history, we turn to the microcosm of the family into which Mishima was born and three more factors which were to have a defining impact on the development of his psyche. First, his sickliness and his grandmother's obsessively protective cloistering of him as a small child. Second, his dawning realization of his attraction to sadomasochistic and homoerotic fantasies. And third, Mishima's struggle with his father over abandoning a projected bureaucratic career, to step out of the shadow of his once-illustrious grandfather and devote himself to literature. All of these aspects of Mishima's childhood and family background were pivotal to his adult personality and development as a writer. Properly understood, however, they should not be seen as haphazard familial circum-stances that impinged on Mishima in a way different to the overarching, more distant drums of Japanese history. Rather, as we shall see, Mishima's family history and circumstances were themselves direct products of the traumatic storm of Westernization and radical change which had swept over the nation from the mid-nineteenth century onwards. Not only was Mishima the child about to have his psyche contorted by the monsters of history, but the people around him, too, had been traumatized by the family's rapid social descent in the years preceding his birth.

Mishima's decision, then, in 1970 to violently rip off the mask of hypocrisy that he believed was covering the face of the Japanese nation was a long-delayed act of revenge by a man over whose own face the Japanese nation had itself fastened the first of many masks as soon as he had been born. Those masks meant that Mishima, like the Japanese nation as a whole, would struggle to find his true self, but always be exemplary at adopting new faces that were perfectly suited to the demands of the age. As a writer, Mishima would be the man before all others who would reveal that there was something disturbing and brutal lurking behind those masks of social conformity and apparent contentment.

The schizophrenic paradoxes of the nation-state became ingrained in Mishima's own person, but in the end Mishima was to return the compliment by transferring his own personal neuroses onto the stage of national politics. If he could not rip off the mask of deceit covering Japan, he could at least take off, in protest, his own head, the wearer of so many masks, and deposit it ceremoniously and with an explosion of blood on the whitewashed floor of modern Japanese history.

2

Macrocosm and Microcosm

He was born Kimitake Hiraoka (the name 'Yukio Mishima' would come later) in the Yotsuya district of Tokyo at 9 p.m. on 14 January 1925, a fragile baby of little more than 5 lb (2.2 kg). In *Confessions of a Mask*, Mishima describes the house in which he was born and where he lived for his first nine years:

> It was a somewhat jumbled, overbearing house with a showy iron gate and front garden and a big Western-style room as large as some suburban chapel. If you looked from the top of the hill, it was two-storeyed; from the bottom of the hill three-storeyed, and had a smoky, dark feeling. There were lots of dark rooms and six maids. Including my grandfather, grandmother, father and mother, altogether ten people lived in this house which creaked like an old cupboard.

The fact that Mishima was born into a home where his grandfather and grandmother lived was the crucial determining factor of his childhood; to understand how greatly affected Mishima was by his grandfather, we need to briefly move the scene backwards in time, to the wild frontier of the island of Sakhalin in 1908.

In 1905, the southern half (below the 50°N parallel) of this large, remote island was ceded to Japan as part of the spoils after victory in the Russo-Japanese War (1904–5). Three years later, Mishima's paternal grandfather, Sadataro Hiraoka, a man of exceptional ability and promise, was appointed governor of this new province of Karafuto in the burgeoning empire of Japan.

Sadataro's family hailed from the village of Shimata in the modern-day prefecture of Hyogo in central Japan. They had been small-scale farmers who had gradually increased their wealth by selling a variety of salted, preserved foods, and by the advent of the Meiji era, Sadataro's father – Mishima's great-grandfather – was sufficiently wealthy and ambitious to secure places at the Imperial University (then the only university in Japan) for both his sons. Sadataro quickly became recognized as an outstanding legal scholar and after entering the Interior Ministry, he quickly moved up the ranks: governor of Fukushima Prefecture at the age of 43, and governor of the entire province of Karafuto at age 45.

But the new governor faced two major problems. First, his province was meant to be mostly self-funded, yet had a population of only 20,000 people and no industry. Second, he owed his political advancement to the patronage of Takashi Hara, the leader of the Freedom Party, a man widely perceived as the people's champion, who would in 1918 become the first prime minister of Japan not to hail from an aristocratic pedigree. As a consequence, however, Hara desperately required of those men whom he promoted that they connive to fill the coffers of the Freedom Party by whatever means possible.

To solve his first problem, at drinking parties in Tokyo, Sadataro gained the ears of senior figures in the Mitsui trading group and persuaded them to buy forestry rights in Karafuto and set up the first pulp factory in Japan's colonies. Sadataro's reputation soon became that of a man who got things done, and in 1913, after five years as governor of Karafuto, the newspapers were awash with speculation that he was about to be promoted to one of the important official positions in the Japanese Empire: the head of the South Manchuria Railway and de facto governor of Manchuria. From there, a cabinet position beckoned.[1]

Then, the storm broke. In April 1914, Sadataro's political rivals returned to power, and the following month newspapers turned on the golden boy and whipped up a scandal. After discussions with Hara, and fearing that others would be drawn in, Sadataro was forced to resign and stood trial in April 1915 for two counts of corruption. In May 1916 he was eventually found innocent, but it was noted that he had illegally sold at a discount a considerable volume of government bonds. Feeling his honour to be impugned, Sadataro took it upon himself to raise a loan and repay the missing amount (worth at least $5 million in today's money). Worse, to compensate for the sudden end of his illustrious bureaucratic career, Sadataro threw himself into speculative business ventures, with disastrous results. When a zinc manufacturing plant he had invested in went bankrupt due to a collapse in demand at the end of the First World War, Sadataro was saddled with debts of 700,000 yen (approximately $25 million today), utterly ruining his family's hard-won wealth and reducing his wife Natsuko and son Azusa, Mishima's father, to a precarious, humbled existence.

Previously, while her distinguished husband journeyed back and forward between Tokyo and his various appointments in the provinces or overseas, Natsuko and Azusa always remained in Tokyo, enjoying all the culture and luxuries of the capital. Their comfortable home in Hongo, Tokyo, had been built by craftsmen brought in from Kyoto and the house boasted a stone gate, large cherry trees and a spacious lawn. But now, after Sadataro's family's land, shares and heirlooms had been sold off, they moved to a rented house and creditors stalked them, terrifying Sadataro's wife with demands for loan repayments that fretted her and pushed her towards hysteria. Sadataro responded by disappearing on mysterious trips – secret operations that were meant somehow to recoup all their losses, but invariably never did.

At first, Sadataro believed he would be out of office for two or three years and restored to a new post once Hara returned to power. In the meantime he briefly appeared as the director of a sugar company set up in Sumatra, but this venture also failed to prosper. It did not seem to matter, though, as in 1918 Hara was raised to the position of prime minister. Yet Hara now turned his attention to attempting to drive out his political rivals' appointments in Japan's colonies and for that he needed to channel funds covertly to his supporters overseas. He turned once again to Sadataro, but once more he was found out. On New Year's Eve 1919, Sadataro was caught in Manchuria attempting to smuggle 44 kg (97 lb) of opium worth 12,000 yen (approximately $420,000 in today's money) in an attempt to fund political activities abroad.[2]

Still Sadataro dreamed of making a comeback and after a great election victory for his backers in the Seiyukai party, in February 1920, he was made head of the Tokyo Bureau of Public Roads in October 1920, the first step in his political rehabilitation. But two weeks later a road collapsed during a festival due to cheap construction and it was soon revealed that a Seiyukai member in City Hall had been taking bribes. Sadataro was advised to resign. He had been in the post only three months and was now 58.

Worse, the rivalries between political factions in Japan had now spilled out into shifting alliances with rival warlords in northern China as competing Japanese financial combines jockeyed for lucrative trading concessions. On 20 February 1921 Sadataro prophetically warned Hara that he was in danger of assassination and on 4 November 1921 Hara was duly knifed to death on the platform of Tokyo Station.

Sadataro's chances of being returned to high political office were all but expunged. His name would be splashed across the newspapers only once more and for all the wrong reasons. On 9 May 1934 – when his grandson, the future Yukio Mishima, was aged nine and living in the same house as his grandfather – the newspapers revealed how Sadataro and some accomplices had attempted to peddle a piece of silk with a fraudulent inscription as being by the deceased Meiji emperor, when in fact it had been bought from a second-hand shop for a miserly half a yen. Although the charges were later quietly dropped, this was the ultimate humiliation for a once-great man.[3]

Sadataro was a monumental figure towering over his grandson's childhood, both because of his achievements and his tragically ruinous fall. A photograph taken in August 1930 neatly symbolizes how the family lived in the shadow of Sadataro's once sunlit past. For all his calamitous fall from political grace, Sadataro was still feted by those business leaders who had gone on to make fortunes by the establishment of pulp factories in Karafuto and Manchuria. As a mark of gratitude, they paid an astonishing 33,400 yen (approximately $1.2 million in today's money) for a giant statue of Sadataro, in frock coat and tie, to be erected at Karafuto Shrine.[4] In front of the statue, sculpted to commemorate the 25th anniversary of the establishment of Karafuto, sits Sadataro next to his five-year-old grandson.

The responsibility for recovering the family's name and fortune now fell on the next generation. Sadataro's only child, Azusa, following his father's lead, also graduated from the ultra-prestigious law department of Tokyo University and entered the Ministry of Agriculture and Commerce, but there was just one problem: Azusa lacked any of his father's talent. A cantankerous man with poor social skills, his reputation was rather that of an idle, skiving bureaucrat who would fritter away his time wandering the corridors, dependent on kickbacks from relatives for commercial favours bestowed. On one occasion he even leaked highly important proposed legislation to the press, causing it to be abandoned. Lacking any original ideas, Azusa was first assigned to the 'Silkworm Thread' division of his ministry with a staff of only twenty people, before being made head of the 'Grain Accounts' section in 1932.

Commemorative picture taken in 1930 at Toyohara Shrine in Karafuto (modern-day
Sakhalin) on the day of the unveiling of a statue to Mishima's grandfather.
The 5-year-old Mishima stands between his grandfather and grandmother.

Azusa was clearly incapable of restoring the family's wealth and reputation. The mantle of responsibility must fall then on *his* son, and even when he was still a child it seemed preordained what the future would hold: he would, like his father and grandfather, study law at Tokyo University and from there enter the ranks of the bureaucracy. This time round, though, after the pre-war centralization of bureaucratic power had laid the framework for Japan's spectacular post-war growth, it was the more powerful Ministry of Finance which beckoned if he was to rise up the ranks quickly.

For Mishima's father and grandfather, this is how historical time would be redeemed. Father and grandfather entrusted the child to the care of the women of the house, thinking it hardly mattered what the boy did until he was ready to act on the world's stage as an adult. Yet Mishima's mother and grandmother would fight, not over the future of continents, but rather with each other in starkly marked out micro-territories within the home. And their obsession with 'time' was not the grand unfurling of historical time, but rather the bitterly contested hours and minutes spent with their son and grandson. In their confined world, constantly watching the passage of minutes on the clock, the only escape was to be found in nurturing a rich interior life, sharing with the child a love of literature and a passion for a world of artistic imagination which was utterly unknown to their husbands.

By the time at which Mishima's father might have expected the boy to be ready to adopt his place in the world, it was already too late. The boy had been too much infected by the infusion of a rich artistic imagination. The struggle that was about to unfold in the psyche of the child between a masculine world of 'macro-time' and a feminine world of 'micro-time' was one which would obsess Mishima throughout his entire life and indeed only find resolution on the day of the Mishima Incident itself. And as for the towering imposition of his grandfather in his life, the young Mishima was to spurn that entirely. In a breathtaking act of banishment, apart from the very briefest mention in *Confessions of a Mask*, Sadataro would never be mentioned at all. Mishima's fatherings were to be quietly strangled; instead it was a world of motherings, artistry and 'micro-time' to which Mishima would lend his lifelong allegiance.

Mishima's father Azusa had married Shizue, the well-educated daughter of a middle school headmaster, in 1924, when he was 29 and she was nineteen, but it was to be Sadataro's wife Natsuko, Mishima's grandmother, who was to become the dominant, defining figure in Mishima's childhood. She was a scion of the very top ranks of the feudal order in Edo Japan, being the granddaughter of Yoritaka Matsudaira, lord of Shishido in Hitachi Province, a subsidiary clan to the lords of Mito and one of the very closest to the Tokugawa shoguns. Although Natsuko's mother was Yoritaka's illegitimate daughter, she managed to have Natsuko raised in the household of Prince Taruhito Arisugawa, at the very top of the social pile. He lived in magnificent splendour on an almost 12-acre estate in Tokyo in a fantastically opulent mansion.

As if that wasn't grand enough, Natsuko's paternal grandfather, Naoyuki Nagai, was also a lord's child by a concubine and became adopted by the Nagai family, direct vassals (*hatamoto*) of the powerful Tokugawa shoguns. Naoyuki was to serve in a wide variety of high government offices, became an adviser to the last shogun, Yoshinobu, and even drafted the document returning authority to the emperor in 1868. His adopted son – Natsuko's father – was a judge at the Supreme Court.

With such a distinguished pedigree there was no doubting that Natsuko had married beneath herself in taking on a man like Mishima's grandfather Sadataro, the descendant of mere peasants from a country district in distant Hyogo Prefecture, who had to go out in the world to make his fortune. But then Natsuko was of a stubborn, hysterical disposition and was thought difficult to marry off. Worse, she was the eldest of twelve children and so needed to be married quickly if her eleven younger siblings were not to be seen to 'jump the queue' in an unseemly fashion.

Besides, Sadataro represented the new order in Meiji Japan, where talent, not birth, was supposed to determine your ultimate social status. He was already aged 30 when he married the seventeen-year-old Natsuko. In *Confessions of a Mask*, however, there is no mention of his achievements, only of his calamitous fall:

> I was born two years after the Great Earthquake.
>
> Ten years earlier, in a scandal that occurred while he was governor of a province, my grandfather took upon himself the sins of his subordinates and after withdrawing from his position . . . my family, with such rapid speed you almost want to call it humming nonchalance, began sliding downwards. A huge loan; repossession; the sale of the family mansion; and then, with the compounding of financial difficulties, like a dark impulse, came an ever more blazing, morbid vanity.

Not restraining himself, Mishima continues in devastating fashion:

> Grandfather's commercial ambitions and grandmother's illness and extravagance were the cause of the household's suffering . . . My grandmother, who hailed from a family of ancient lineage, hated and despised my grandfather.

After his family moved to the rented house in which Mishima was born, Mishima's grandmother Natsuko seethed in indignation and soothed her wounded aristocratic pride by indulging in extravagances which the family could no longer afford: shopping expeditions, trips to the Kabuki theatre and fine restaurants. Her husband reacted to his mortifying social descent by passing his days in a back room of the house, keeping away from his harridan of a wife and playing *go* with his cronies. He still had something of the air of a dandy about him and loved to sing, drink and womanize.

But Natsuko didn't just hate and despise her husband because of their straitened circumstances and his perceived worthlessness. As if it was not bad enough that, having once lived in the home of a prince, she was now living with her son and his family in a rented house, she suffered intense pain from sciatic neuralgia, the result of venereal disease passed on by her errant husband, sometimes becoming so hysterical with pain that the entire household felt as if it was being assailed by a great typhoon.[5]

Japan's rush to modernity, then, had not been kind to Natsuko. She, of ancient samurai stock, had been yoked to a man of more humble birth who, versed in the ways of the West, had promised her glittering success in the new world order. Before the Meiji era, such a union would have been near impossible and yet, instead of finding success, Natsuko had been infected with a horrible debilitating disease (the product of Sadataro's indulgences in the pleasure quarters during his long absences), publicly humiliated and reduced to a decidedly middle-class existence. Even the fact that she had only one child while her siblings were blessed with countless children was a symbol of the near-sterility to which she was subjected by her promiscuous husband's disease. Mishima's family situation, then, even before Mishima was born, stood as a stark metaphor for the schizophrenic trauma to which Japan itself had been subjected. The samurai half of the family felt betrayed and disappointed with the Westernized half; indeed, the samurai side was physically infected and invalided by what they had married into. The schism at the heart of the Hiraoka family between a samurai heritage looking with pride to the past and a commoner pragmatism desperately attempting to find success in the modern world was the dynamic tension that was to set in train, like a fall of dominos, all the domestic traumas that would terrorize Mishima's psyche.

Meanwhile, the no-nonsense male, bureaucrat side of the family, now represented by Mishima's straitlaced and insensitive father, was to feel burdened by the unworldly extravagance of the haughty grandmother. Despite having fallen in the world, the family still employed six maids, four of whom were devoted to Natsuko, as well as a houseboy, all of whom they could ill afford. Mishima's mother Shizue was from a family of Confucian scholars and had been taught to hold her tongue and know her place. Included in her wedding dowry had been a dagger,[6] a symbol that she should never bring such a disgrace to her own family as separating from her husband and returning to them. Her powers of stoicism were about to be tested to their ultimate extent by the actions of both her mother-in-law and her husband.

Azusa and Shizue on their wedding day in 1924.

Natsuko was determined to cling on to the memory of her distinguished forebears and somehow recover her lost dreams and pride. She demanded of her son that her eldest grandson be handed over to be raised exclusively by her, so that she might pour all her love into him. When the child was seven days old he was named 'Kimitake' (Sadataro chose the names of both his son and grandson, Azusa and Kimitake, in recognition of sponsors who had aided him when he had first arrived in Tokyo), and six weeks later his crib was moved to his grandmother's sickroom on the ground floor, the ostensible reason being that it was too dangerous for the baby to be upstairs, where his parents lived. Once the invalided grandmother had control of the baby, she had no intention of letting him go. Having herself had only one child, Mishima's grandmother was highly protective of her solitary grandchild. When it was time for the baby to feed, Natsuko rang a bell letting Shizue know she should make herself ready, then hobbled upstairs with a maid, handed the baby over and waited as she timed the breastfeeding with a pocket watch, counting the minutes before whisking the child downstairs again. Shizue would relate how she would wait for feeding every four hours, breasts full, fearful that her son – a placid child who gulped down milk – was hungry.[7] The baby was not allowed outside at all unless the weather was fine; Shizue was only allowed out with him, without the maids, when he was five or six.

When Mishima was barely one, his grandmother was at the Kabuki theatre one day and he attempted to climb up the stairs on his own after his mother had gone to get something. He fell down the bottom steps and cut his head. He was taken to see a doctor and his grandmother called for at the theatre. When she returned home she was incandescent with rage, and from then on the child was banned from going upstairs at all without Natsuko's express permission, further removing him from any contact with his mother. For Shizue, it was a living hell on earth. Her husband banned her from making plain her dissatisfaction – though even he

Mishima, age 1.

sometimes argued with his mother about the way she was raising her grandson. Shizue in turn hated her feckless husband and dreamed of running away with Kimitake.

Mishima himself was sickly and weak, suffering from a condition commonly known in Japan as 'auto-intoxication' (in the West, this condition is little known and referred to as 'acetonemia': it describes a sickly child, particularly of nervous disposition, suffering from low blood sugar due to anxiety and/or poor nutrition, which in extreme cases can cause loss of consciousness or even death). Indeed, when Mishima was five, he vomited a red, coffee-like substance and briefly lapsed into a coma. Mishima subsequently suffered some kind of attack, severe or mild, once a month for a year. His grandmother insisted that he be kept out of the sunlight and be prevented from playing sport of any kind or mixing with other boys. Not wishing the metallic noise of guns and cars to be inflicted on him, she permitted him to play only with wooden blocks in his grandmother's room or with female cousins when they called.[8] She controlled every type of food he ate, limiting the varieties of fruit, fish and sweets that he was allowed.

As the family expanded, Mishima was kept apart even from his younger sister Mitsuko and younger brother Chiyuki. His mother was only permitted to take him for walks to the park or to his preparatory school. Shizue bitterly recalled her beautiful, angelic child being imprisoned like a caged animal at his grandmother's bedside in a gloomy sickroom. She believed her mother-in-law was jealous of her and taking out her frustrations on the poor infant, who in turn sensed that any complaint would lead to more trouble for his mother. She suspected that Natsuko revelled in watching her misery. 'In this environment', his mother reflected, 'he was unlikely to grow up as a normal person. Like clay being kneaded, he would become more deformed with every second. I couldn't bear to watch such horrors.'[9]

Indeed, Mishima's upbringing was distorted. Caught up in the middle of the fierce rivalry between his mother and grandmother for his love, and feeling strong affection for both of them, Mishima quickly learned to keep the peace by concealing his own feelings. He accepted all Natsuko's instructions without protest and never complained to his mother, though it is likely that his concern for his grandmother's feelings was just as keen as for his mother's.

From his very first years, then, Mishima was forced to reside in an interior world where he could not show his own face. Worse, he was occasionally terrorized by his obtuse and sadistic father, who, utterly insensitive to his son's painful situation, suddenly decided that his upbringing was too feminine and, after having two or three big arguments with Natsuko, attempted to instil in his son some 'Spartan' training. This consisted of forcefully taking him to Shinjuku Station, standing by the embankment and threatening to throw him in a ditch if he flinched when a train thundered by. Instead, Mishima showed his father a completely emotionless face, something which he would continue to do throughout his life.[10]

Yet behind that mask of indifference, Mishima found his own space. What Natsuko passed on to the child was her love of storytelling and interest in the theatre. She knew French and German, had a vivid imagination and loved to read. Trapped in her room, listening to his grandmother reminisce about favourite Kabuki plays and being introduced to a world of samurai, sword fighting and seppuku (ritual suicide), as well as the allure of elaborate costumes and dazzling make-up, Mishima's imagination took flight as he began to absorb himself in a world of fantasies, books and films. In an autobiographical short story of 1951, titled 'Chair', Mishima adopted the perspective of his mother and wrote:

> Shut up in his grandmother's gloomy eight-mat room from morning until night, the child sits properly, lost in drawing pictures. I am the young mother who must endure having to watch this.

Yet Mishima then rejects his mother's ideas:

> In my mother's transferral of her own feelings to me, there was a miscalculation. I was not sitting at a sick person's pillow, not making a sound, suppressing the desire to go out and muck around. I liked doing what I was doing. I was not at all dissatisfied with my grandmother's morbid, despairing, tenacious love.[11]

Mishima acquired his grandmother's way of speaking, manners, punctuality and fastidiousness (all of which had skipped over Azusa), but he also acquired a deep sense of empathy which was lacking in his grandmother.

Yet it was not just any fantasies to which the child was attracted. He began to sublimate his inner woundings into excitement at the depiction of real-life woundings. Imprisoned in a repressed, protected space, he fantasized about the gory deaths of others.

According to *Confessions of a Mask*, he was aroused by pictures in magazines of

> blood-soaked duels; of young samurai cutting open their stomachs; of soldiers being caught by bullets and gritting their teeth, with blood overflowing from between the hands that clutched their chests; of lean and firmly fleshed wrestlers.

He also fantasized about being killed. Mishima's retreat into sadomasochist fantasies was his defence system against both a schizophrenic world of being cruelly torn between his mother and grandmother and being divided from his siblings and restrained from the normal activities of a child: a means of transforming painful circumstances into secret personal pleasure.

In April 1931, at his grandmother's instigation, Mishima entered the preparatory school of the elite Peers' School (Gakushuin), an institution particularly associated with educating the children of the aristocracy. Mishima's great-uncle Yoriyasu, who had inherited the rank of viscount, was his aristocratic sponsor, inspiring much ridicule among Azusa's work colleagues, for although about a third of the school's students were commoners like Mishima, they tended to be from far wealthier families. There was a clear class divide at the school, with none of the aristocracy, unlike the commoners, having to pay for their education or be bothered with entrance exams or any subsequent exams. The teachers made notes on the social ranking of each pupil and adopted appropriately deferential types of speech. The aristocratic children in their turn assumed superior airs with both commoner pupils and teachers alike.

Mishima was at first a very average student, often absent due to illness and missing 50 of 223 school days in his first year. He frequently had a sore throat and so always wore a compress around his neck and had a ghostly white face, earning him such nicknames as 'Whitey' and 'Snake Belly'. Suffering from a chest complaint,

Mishima at around the time he entered the Peers' School.

he was not permitted to do any physical exercise, eat in the school cafeteria or, to his regret, go on any excursions until he was in Year Four; and while the other boys played soldiers, sumo and sword fights, he stayed in the classroom reading books. He was thin, sickly and shy: a lonely, girlish little boy. Teased and bullied by the other boys, he learned to compensate by helping those boys who were lagging behind in their studies.

His mother Shizue was, however, delighted to be able to take him to school in the morning and, although he was confined to the grandmother's room after school, was at least able to watch him study. His mother, brought up in a cultured environment, could not discuss matters such as literature with her bureaucrat husband and so she too invested her dreams in her son. She introduced him from an early age to writers like Verlaine and he began to write poems and stories inspired by them. He read the Brothers Grimm's *Fairy Tales* and was also taken by his grandmother to the cinema, for, somewhat surprisingly for this scion of the old world order, she was a keen fan of western films.

In 1933, when Mishima was eight, his family moved to two small houses on the same street. Now the division of households was formalized, with Mishima, his grandmother and grandfather living in one house and his mother, father, brother and sister living in the other. The nominal reason for the move was that

Mishima (right) in 1933, with his brother Chiyuki.

Azusa, having been promoted, needed somewhere to occasionally invite his work colleagues, but the real motivation was financial: three of the six maids were let go. Shizue continued to walk her son to and from school every day, but Natsuko was waiting for him with homemade food every day when he returned at 3 p.m. He would often, though not always, be allowed to visit his mother in her house, but was never allowed to stay for dinner. He saw little of his brother and sister, who had grown used to his living apart and who, intimidated by their grandmother, preferred to play at home.

The grandmother's room was now soaked in the rancour of sickness and premature old age. Natsuko's sciatica was worsening and she was suffering from stomach ulcers and kidney disease. Mishima was required to tend to her daily. She would only take her medicine from him and relied on his assistance to be taken to the toilet or to have her forehead dabbed or back rubbed. She would cry out in agony at night and more than once threatened to kill herself. The seeds of Mishima's revulsion for ageing and bodily decay, as well as his later obsession with physical beauty and vigour, were all sown in this room.

The year 1937, when Mishima was twelve and on the cusp of adolescence, was when everything changed. Natsuko, now very ill, was finally persuaded by Sadataro that it was time for their grandson to return to his parents. Shizue was thrilled and three weeks after hearing the news, the family moved away to a house in the Shibuya area of Tokyo, separating from Natsuko and Sadataro for good (the grandfather's presence was always barely recognized by Mishima, who perhaps nursed the same resentment as his grandmother for the illness inflicted upon her). In *Confessions of a Mask* he wrote:

> My grandmother constantly hugged my photo and cried. It was agreed I would come and stay once a week and if I failed to do

so, she would suddenly have an attack. My thirteen-year-old self had a besotted 60-year-old lover.

He was also required to telephone her every day when he returned home from school.

Mishima now had a room of his own, but this was by no means the end of Mishima's familial torments. Having been released from his tyrannical grandmother, he was to come to realize what an ogre his father could be and see up close all the unhappiness of his parents' union. Mishima was already a very bookish child (this, after all, had been his means of escape during his years of confinement), but now his father made it clear how much he disapproved of such dilettante literary interests. Perhaps Azusa blamed himself for being such a weakling when it came to standing up to his mother over the raising of his own son. Seeing what an un-masculine, dreamy child his son had become (Mishima liked to dress up in sheets as characters such as Cleopatra), his father vented his frustrations with bullying behaviour. Because Mishima had a liking for cats, another 'feminine' trait which his father despised, the cat was thrown out, only for Mishima to find a new one. Azusa promptly put iron in its food in order to kill it, though mercifully failed to do so. The new home regime under Azusa also meant that literary books were confiscated on sight and the boy was sent to his room if found reading one.

Fortunately for Mishima, his father was promoted to head of the Forestry Bureau and from October 1937 until 1941 sent to work on his own in Osaka, where the Bureau had its headquarters. There – like his father before him – he dissipated himself in the pleasure quarters of Kobe, Osaka and Kyoto on money supplied by his cousins, warehousing merchants who had benefited from government contracts arranged by Azusa, and returned to Tokyo for only a few nights a month. Mishima, meanwhile, began to spend much unobstructed time with his mother for the first time.

In the summer of 1937 his mother took her three children, reunited for the first time, for a month at the beach, wishing to make her son healthier and fitter. Mishima's white skin and frail body had never previously been exposed to sunlight like this and while he revelled in the time spent there with his mother, he was disturbed by this first confrontation with the ocean. At the cusp of adolescence and sexuality, the sea as a concept impinged on Mishima's consciousness like a terrifying magma of life force seemingly opening up to infinity, an idea that would feature time and again in Mishima's literary works.

Back in Tokyo, and with his father mostly absent, his grandmother still exerted a waning influence, refusing to allow him to spend a year boarding at the Peers' School as was usually required. Needing reasons to be with him now that they lived separately, she also finally took him to the Kabuki theatre. Mishima had already read her programmes and had wanted to go since early childhood, and his first play, in October 1938, was the classic *The Loyal Retainers* (*Chushingura*). Soon Mishima too was a Kabuki devotee, unfailingly attending once a month and reading the whole repertoire. His passion for Kabuki was such that he would become capable of imitating perfectly the speech patterns of the Kabuki classics and eventually wrote numerous plays for the Kabuki stage. Not to be outdone, Shizue's mother Tomiko, a devotee of Noh chanting, also took her grandson to watch Noh theatre.

His compositional skills, meanwhile, impressed his new Japanese teacher. At primary school, Mishima's composition teacher had been critical of his tendency to fantasize and demanded writing that was more grounded in reality, but now he was encouraged to submit material to the school's literary club journal. The literary club was not just any old school society, but one that could boast a major literary group, the White Birch Group (Shirakaba-ha), among their alumni. With a surge in confidence, Mishima's school results began to improve as he read many of the Japanese classics, such

as *The Tale of Genji* and the *Manyoshu*. In December 1937 some
of his poems appeared in the bi-annual journal, having impressed
the twenty-year-old senior-school editor, Toshitami Bojo. Bojo took
a personal interest in the much younger Mishima, who was only
twelve when he was sought out by Bojo in the crowd of a school
baseball match. Bojo, an earl's son and aspiring writer who took
pride in noting Mishima's talent, introduced the young boy to
the writing of Cocteau and Huysmans and invited him to his
aristocratic mansion. For the next four years the two exchanged
voluminous letters, starting with a critique of each other's
compositions before discussing their reading, home life, 'poetic
experiences', dreams and latest writings. Mishima would rush home
every day to see if a letter had arrived from Bojo, and they would
meet just to exchange letters. Crushingly, though, in 1939 Bojo
showed his works to the famous writer Naoya Shiga, who dismissed
them, and in the summer of 1941 Mishima too ridiculed one of his
short stories as utterly prosaic. When he and two others formed
a new magazine, *Red Pictures*, Bojo was not invited to participate.

From the age of twelve until the age of sixteen, Mishima poured
out poems in particular (500 Western-style poems, 200 haiku
and 45 tanka) and later wrote: 'I believed myself to be a poet.' He
particularly liked Romantic poets who were beautiful and died
young. The mood of Mishima's poems was melancholic, but they
exhibited skilful contrasts and subtle shifts in perspective and
close-ups, and suggested – in places – the influence of the modern
poet Sakutaro Hagiwara. At the beginning of his autobiographical
story 'The Boy who Wrote Poems' (1954), he recalled:

> I composed poems with complete ease, one after another.
> I soon used up the 30-page notebook with the name of the Peers'
> School on it. Other boys were incredulous that I could compose
> two or three poems a day like this.[12]

3

A Mask Facing Inwards

If 1937 marked the year that Mishima was finally released from the captivity imposed upon him because of his grandmother's constant fear of his dying in early childhood, it was also the year in which death began its remorseless march on Japanese youth as a whole with the eruption of the Sino-Japanese War. The previous year had seen an attempted *coup d'état* by young officers, the February 26 Incident, that would later prove influential for Mishima, and from 1937 until the shattering defeat of 1945, death began to squeeze its tightening noose on the Japanese nation. At first, the footfalls of death would be heard faintly on the plains and cities of China, but eventually the whole of Asia would be embroiled in the conflict and the whole of Tokyo would become a vast carnival of death, with every young man waiting to receive a – literally – blood-red conscription notice and every family braced for a storm of destruction from the skies. Mishima's early fantasy raptures about death, far from being normalized during adolescence into more 'healthy' interests, would find themselves in perfect accord with the exterior world around him.

The circumstances of Mishima's early life can be reasonably ascertained by a comparison of the early sections of *Confessions of a Mask* with, for example, the recollections of Mishima's own mother and father. However, from Mishima's adolescence onwards, everything Mishima wrote about himself has to be treated with considerable suspicion, as calculated distortions of the truth abound.

It's tempting to take at face value Mishima's famous account in *Confessions of a Mask* of his first orgasm, but as we shall see, that seemingly autobiographical novel was in fact a carefully researched fiction that never even purported to be anything more than aspects of truth. With regards to that first *ejaculatio* (as he put it), what can be confirmed is that in March 1937 Azusa travelled to Europe and brought back from Italy museum guides which he hid in a closet either for safekeeping or for fear that his young son might chance upon the pictures of nude women contained within them. If *Confessions of a Mask* is to be believed, however, the young Mishima had no sexual interest in women whatsoever, and his fantasies to date had actually centred on such young rugged heroes as the night-soil man who called to collect the household excrement, or the ticket clippers at the station, or the young men bearing the heavy *mikoshi* shrine on their manly shoulders during frenzied street festivals. At the age of four, he relates, he had been fascinated by a picture of Joan of Arc, but only because he thought it was a man, and felt bitterly betrayed when informed by a maid that it was a woman.

Sometime after Azusa moved to Osaka, Mishima was off school with signs of a cold and discovered the hidden books. Leafing through the pages of one, he chanced upon a captivating painting. In *Confessions of a Mask*, Mishima wrote:

> I turned the remaining pages. At that moment, from one corner, appeared an image that I could only think of as having been waiting for me.
>
> It was Guido Reni's *St Sebastian* from Genoa's Palazzo Rosso.
>
> Against a Titian-like, gloomy background of melancholic woods and evening sky, the trunk of a slightly inclined black tree was the instrument of torture. An extremely beautiful young man was tied naked to that trunk . . . In his left armpit and right flank two arrows were deeply embedded.

St Sebastian by
Guido Reni,
c. 1615–16.

In this picture, 'there was only youthfulness, only light, only
beauty, only pleasure':

> My blood surged, my organ overflowed with rage. This huge
> part of me, as if almost split apart, ferociously waited for me to
> put it to a use I had never done before, and, mocking my
> ignorance, breathed vexaciously . . . No sooner had I thought
> this, than, with a dizzying intoxication, it gushed forth.

Whether truthful account or inventive fiction, *St Sebastian* was
to become a defining image in Mishima's life – one which, in the
1960s, he repeatedly recreated in photoshoots with himself posed
as the Christian martyr transformed into sadomasochistic fantasy.

Mishima posed as St Sebastian, 1966.

Given that Mishima's sexual awakening happened in the same year that the Japanese Army embarked on a wholesale invasion of North China, overran Shanghai and went on a notorious rampage in Nanjing (inspiring the twelve-year-old Mishima to write about heroic Japanese soldiers marching through swamps and drinking muddy water in cruel heat), it is perhaps not surprising that sex and death would become so closely linked in his psyche. Indeed *St Sebastian* is described as being such a powerful, erotically stimulating image in *Confessions of a Mask* that it is easy to overlook how the entire background story of the third-century captain of the Praetorian Guard executed by Diocletian for his Christian faith was to prove profoundly suggestive to Mishima throughout his later works. Mishima relates the legend of how St Sebastian was a beautiful youth who mysteriously appeared from the sea. Despite being martyred at a young age, he was miraculously to rise from the dead before being slain once more. In this legend, then, is the theme of the sea as a mystical representation of the protean, unknowable nature of the universe that would reoccur time and again in Mishima's novels, together with the motif of a magical rebirth of youth that was central to his supreme masterpiece, *The Sea of Fertility*.

At around the same time, Mishima apparently discovered another arresting image in a bookshop:

> I was probably eleven or twelve and saw an Iwanami pocketbook edition of Wilde's *Salome*. Beardsley's illustrations intensely attracted me. Taking it home and reading it, I felt as though I had been struck by lightning . . . Evil had been unleashed; sensuality and beauty had been liberated; moralizing was nowhere to be seen.[1]

Mishima seemed split between his secret world of *St Sebastian* and *Salome* and his public world of poem writing. Under *Salome*'s influence, Mishima now wrote some Bible-inspired pieces depicting satanic figures regarding Jesus's birth not with joy but hatred. There was in these juvenilia a sense of weirdness, as if something the boy didn't fully understand was pressing in upon the compositions.

On 18 January 1939, his grandmother died from a haemorrhaged ulcer. To his father, Mishima appeared, as ever, emotionless, but quietly he now transferred all his affection to his mother, towards whom he exhibited a phenomenal pride and love for the rest of his life. Mishima also now shed the image of the beloved little boy argued over by his mother and grandmother, and assumed the air of a doomed poet. He was reading Rilke, Proust, Tanizaki and, above all, Radiguet, and apart from physics and those subjects requiring physical exertion (physical education, martial arts and military drill) gained top marks, rising to be second in his class. He was still a poor physical specimen and even worried that his anaemia was due to excessive masturbation. His military drill teacher mocked him because he had a big head and waddled, and nicknamed him 'Mother Duck'.[2]

The divide between Mishima's awkward, comical exterior persona and the intense violence of his inner fantasies was acute. In November 1939 he published a story called 'The Castle', in which a servant relates stories of his cruel master, a European prince and 'modern Nero'. 'I, with this hand holding a honed, sharp knife, would like to go up to someone and see my hand soaked with warm blood', his master says. The servant is himself tied to a pillar in front of his master's victims and realizes that he too will be killed. The servant is eventually saved, but a girl who is involved in a rebellion is stabbed to death. Mishima's violent fantasies seemed to be gushing out of him, though as yet he fumbled to control them or find the proper means of expression.

In a lecture delivered two years before his death, Mishima recalled his first steps in literature:

> I was very worried about myself. What might I become, this person myself? If left to run free, I would collapse into little pieces. If I didn't maintain myself in the world of ideas, I worried that I would fall to pieces.[3]

Through an introduction from a friend of his father, Mishima had become a disciple of a well-known, minor poet, Kawaji Ryuko (1888–1959), an unaffected man who kindly corrected his verses. After

In the 4th year of
middle school, 30
June 1940.

a year, though, Ryuko commented to another disciple that Mishima
was not precocious or a genius, only a pervert. And gradually
Mishima too began to realize his limitations as a poet: that this
was not the form through which he could truly express himself.

His poetry was a skilful manipulation of superficial images and
difficult words, but the youthful Mishima teemed with mysterious,
strong and violent impulses that were only hinted at in his poetry.
In 'The Boy Who Writes Poems' (1956) he wrote:

> The boy would go into raptures and always in front of him a
> metaphorical world appeared. Caterpillars changed cherry

leaves to lace; small stones were hurled and passed over an oak, on their way to see the sea. A crane upset the creased sheets of the sea on a cloudy day and searched for a drowned body below. Sunset was an ill omen, the colour of a tincture of iodine.

Mishima's faults as a poet were later to become the bulwarks of his prose, his poetic style lending his novels richness and texture, freshness of metaphor and stylistic and linguistic dexterity. At the age of sixteen, at the same time as the affair with poetry was petering out, he was fumbling to find his way with novels.

Raymond Radiguet (1903–1923) was a crucial influence. In *The Devil in the Flesh* (*Le Diable au corps*), Radiguet had written of the affair between a married woman and a boy, based on his own romantic experiences between the ages of sixteen and eighteen. He then penned a psychological portrait of a love triangle in *Count d' Orgel's Ball* (*Le Bal du Comte d'Orgel*), with high society as the stage. Shortly afterwards, aged twenty, Radiguet died of typhoid. Mishima wrote of this latter book: 'What attracted my boyish self to this was firstly the distinctive, dry elegance with which the translation abounded' and that 'when I first read it when I was fifteen, I was bewitched, without understanding the difficult parts or the meaning.'[4] He read it over and over again, envious not only of the young author's obvious genius, but that his genius had attained benediction with early death.

To Mishima, who feared he was in danger of falling to pieces, a writer like Radiguet, who had so brilliantly ordered his inner life, was someone to be emulated and he now aspired to produce works of a similar ilk, though many were unpublished. If Radiguet's novels described love triangles, Mishima tried to trump him by describing four-person love rectangles. They were usually technically proficient, but Mishima looked in danger of ending up in the same cul-de-sac he had arrived at with his poetry. His attention was all given to the structure, not the content. Unlike Radiguet, Mishima was not writing from any experience of romantic relationships and so was not 'controlling his instincts and excluding anything extraneous'[5] in order to coolly create his own world.

At this time, an important mentor appeared in the form of Fumio Shimizu, a teacher of Japanese and Composition at the Peers' School. He had joined the school in 1938 and taught Mishima from 1939 onwards, but it was only after 1941 that the two became close. Shimizu was born in 1906 and was a scholar of Heian period (794–1185) literature, editing an edition of the Izumi Shikibu Diary, a Heian classic. In July 1938, he and three other up-and-coming scholars of Japanese literature (Zenmei Hasuda, Riichi Kuriyama and Tsutomu Ikeda), all graduates of Hiroshima University, had founded a magazine, *Literary Culture* (*Bungei Bunka*), which bewailed that 'although the loud voice of the Japanese spirit has been passed down . . . the literary classics have been turned into a tool of utilitarianism, entrusted to outrageous amputations' and that 'the authority of ancient texts is completely in ruin'. They believed that 'tradition itself speaks with authority, and they would confess their trust in that, and listen to the spirit of ancient texts.'[6]

Literary Culture was itself an offshoot of the Japan Romantic School (Nihon Romanha), which represented in the mid-1930s the 'new wave' of contemporary Japanese literature under the weight of the utilitarian objectives of total war. This was an age of increasing government censorship, with Marxist thinkers and writers rounded up and forced to convert to nationalist ideologies, and any writings which were not conducive to the fascist government's war aims proscribed. The leader of the Romantic School, Yojuro Yasuda (1910–1981), had himself flirted with Marxism as a young man and another prominent figure, Fusao Hayashi (1903–1975), had been turned from a belief in communism to a strident nationalism during imprisonment in 1930–32.

The result of the new cultural and political mood was that all the 'big hitters' of Japanese literature in the 1930s – such as Nagai

Kafu, Junichiro Tanizaki and Naoya Shiga – increasingly fell silent as the war intensified. Even the publication of early parts of Tanizaki's epic familial saga *The Makioka Sisters* (*Sasameyuki*) was banned in the early 1940s, forcing the great author to continue writing in seclusion and effectively to withdraw from public life until the war was over. On the other hand, a literary movement like the Japan Romantic School, wallowing in the glorious tradition of the Japanese classics and persuading its readers that their beauty was a reflection of the emperor's divinity and a cause worth dying for, was exactly the type of 'anti-establishment' movement that the fascist establishment was happy to tolerate. In 1938, a year after the Sino-Japanese War started, Shimizu's classes at the Peers' School naturally reflected the position of greatly valuing the Japanese literary classics. 'What was the heart of learning?' Shimizu asked. 'It was the feeling, like the chest pulsating, when you read a work with an open mind.'[7] It sounded noble, but the reality was that the literary coterie that was about to take Mishima under its wing represented an extremely nationalistic narrowing of literary tastes.

It was Shimizu's teaching to 'learn from the past' that led Mishima to write his first mature work: 'A Forest in Full Bloom'. Shimizu was a warden at the dormitory of the Peers' School and Mishima often visited him, with Shimizu watching Mishima's thin body and white face weave through the zelkova trees towards him. He read Mishima's 'Full Bloom' story in one sitting while the students slept and later declared: 'As I read it, I had the intense feeling of something which had been sleeping inside me being woken up.'[8] The story was subsequently published, at Shimizu's recommendation, in *Literary Culture*, in four instalments between September and December 1941. This was a sensational honour for a sixteen-year-old schoolboy: not only was it the first time the magazine had asked a student to contribute, but it was the first time they had run fiction as opposed to critical essays.

It also marked the birth of 'Yukio Mishima'. A variety of anecdotes compete to explain how the name was derived, but the standard version is that Shimizu had brought the manuscript of Mishima's story to an editorial meeting of the magazine at a *ryokan* (traditional guesthouse) in Shuzenji in the summer and proposed that they use a pen name in order to protect the sixteen-year-old author from the public – and out of deference to the Hiraoka family, whose reaction to their son's sudden celebrity was hard to gauge. On the way to Shuzenji, Shimizu had passed through the town of Mishima and looked up to see snow (*yuki*) on Mount Fuji and so instinctively came up with 'Yukio Mishima'. (This poetic reverie was, however, ruined by Mishima's father, who offered a completely different testimony: that Mishima arrived at his pen name by randomly opening a telephone directory and choosing the first name on the top left of the page, which just happened to be 'Mishima'.[9])

Mishima now assumed a persona much greater than that of a boy caught up in a household or school. He was now a published writer in a well-respected magazine. Indeed, he had been welcomed in the magazine by one of the founders, Zenmei Hasuda, with these words:

> It is an inexpressible joy that young men like this are emerging in Japan. His appearance may come as a surprise for those who have no faith in our national literature, but there is no cause for surprise: he is a heaven-sent child of eternal Japan's history. Although he is much younger than us, here is the birth of someone already mature. And it is from amongst us that he has been born.[10]

To gain the full measure of the lifelong impact on Mishima of the *Literary Culture* group, and of Zenmei Hasuda in particular, it is worthwhile explaining who Hasuda was and how he died. The most right-wing and nationalistic member of the coterie, and now Mishima's most ardent fan, Hasuda had written numerous books of literary criticism connected to 'national learning' (*kokugaku*) on subjects ranging from the creation myths (the *Kojiki*) to analyses of the medieval writer Kamo no Chomei and the Meiji author Mori Ogai. The 'national learning' that Hasuda spouted was a school of thought originating with Motoori Norinaga (1730–1801) and his attempts to filter out of Japanese culture the pernicious influence of China and produce something purely Japanese. Hasuda had been a teacher at Ibaraki High School, but was conscripted to fight in China as a lieutenant from 1938 to 1940 before returning home wounded. He was recruited again from 1943 to 1945 and sent off to Indonesia. Four days after the end of the Second World War and less than 100 km north of Singapore, Hasuda became enraged by his regimental commander's farewell speech to the colours, which observed that from now on the emperor would be considered equal to other men. He shot and killed the commander and then himself, thinking it unforgiveable for a professional soldier to slander the emperor and the Imperial Army in this way. He was 41 years old.

Over twenty years later, in 1968, a series of articles about his death ran in a magazine and Mishima wrote to the author, Jiro Odakane, saying: 'I feel that, thanks to this, I've confirmed and strengthened the ties between Hasuda and me' and 'I cannot be anything but jealous of Hasuda's magnificent end.' Indeed, in March 1970, eight months before Mishima's suicide, when Odakane published a book, *Zenmei Hasuda and his Death*, Mishima wrote the foreword. In it he quoted Hasuda and reflected:

'I think that the people of such an age must all die young. I know that dying like that is my culture today.' These lines by Hasuda cling to my mind and will not let go. Dying is culture . . . As I approached the age at which Hasuda died, his death,

and what the manner of his death meant, illuminated with
sudden revelation my long-standing fumblings in the dark.[11]

The literary critic who welcomed a sixteen-year-old Mishima into
print would also become the nationalist fanatic who beckoned the
45-year-old novelist to join him beyond the grave.

On the eve of Japan's attack on Pearl Harbor, with 'Yukio
Mishima' as his new mask of identity, the fledgling writer was about
to make a considerable impact in the heavily author-depleted world
of Japanese letters. 'A Forest in Full Bloom' is a tale in which the
narrator recalls his own infancy, then some stories of his ancestors
and those connected to his ancestors, from the Heian period
onwards. The narrator is fictional: it is not Mishima, though it
is not made clear who it is. He says: 'until a year or two ago,
I thought that recollection was boring', but now thinks that
'recollection is the purest proof of the present', immediately
linking the story to the ideals of the *Literary Culture* set.

The story is Borgesian in its dense, complicated construction,
requiring multiple readings, and though, like Mishima's poetry of
the time, it is over-written and over-allusive, it is an extraordinary
tour de force. What is most fascinating is the central nexus of ideas
that Mishima had already developed by the age of sixteen. In the
first, semi-autobiographical piece, he connects the child's fear and
fantasies of 'sickness' to the waves of groans issuing from his
grandmother, and when she dies, he implies that the child's fear
of death may yet be transformed into a longing for death. All the
characters we discover are longing for something: yet the longing
is also associated with fear and, when fulfilled, the result is a form
of ecstasy, though that ecstasy also often leads to death. Life,
longing, fear, beauty and death are all linked in a circle.

In November 1942, and from March to October 1943, Mishima
published more love stories in the Radiguet mould in *Literary
Culture*, this time drawing inspiration from classic texts and setting

them in the Heian and Kamakura (1185–1333) periods. After the war, in March 1946, Mishima wrote to Yasunari Kawabata:

> Looking back now, I can clearly see how, during the war, I did everything I could to escape from the branch of 'national learning' which had given me baptism in the form of *Literary Culture*. The weird story 'Night Car' I put into the final issue (August 1944) of *Literary Culture* marked my final parting with 'national learning' and when I wrote that, it was as if some pressure on my chest suddenly fell away.[12]

He remarked that he perceived that the problem with the Japan Romantic School was that, with its motto of 'art for art's sake', it was overwhelmed by a desire to imitate past works exactly, and became an empty, artificial literature. The letter was perhaps partly affected by Mishima's desire to distance himself after the war from *Literary Culture* and gain the patronage of Kawabata instead, but still shows that as early as 1944 Mishima was already seeking to move away from being seen as one of the Romantic School, that its restrictive aesthetic standards were no longer his own.

In March 1942, he was second in his class at the Peers' School and proceeded to the upper school's German form (competence in the German language being seen as key to future success). In May of the same year he was chosen as head of the literary club, having in 1940 become the youngest member of its editorial board in the club's history. Also in this year, his father Azusa – having previously narrowly avoided being sacked as head of the Forestry Bureau before being made head of the Fisheries Bureau in 1941 – finally left what had become the Ministry of Agriculture and Forestry and was appointed chairman of a major charcoal company as part of the increasing governmental control of the economy. The return of his father to the Mishima home cannot have been welcome, particularly as the responsibility for ensuring that the Hiraokas redeemed their place in history now rested mainly with Mishima after the death in the summer of this year of Sadataro, at the age of 80. It was an event that was not remarked upon at all by Mishima, though he complained bitterly that his father now only talked about the Nazis. Even while still in Osaka, Azusa had sent letters to his son attempting to dissuade him from literature, indeed advising him to 'recant' (*tenko*), and pointed his son in the direction of physics, chemistry and engineering instead. He invoked the examples of Einstein and the Japanese bacteriologist Hideyo Noguchi, but seeing how that had failed, now applied terror tactics, storming into Mishima's room and destroying any manuscripts he found.

Many of Mishima's early works were completely lost in this way. Nevertheless he still managed to produce eight novellas, three long essays on classical literature and a small volume of poetry between 1942 and the end of 1944, while also attending monthly meetings at Shimizu's house. What sustained the young Mishima in his writing ambition was his mother's support: she would wait for her bullying husband to go to sleep and then sneak into her son's room with supplies. As well as writing paper, ink, padded jackets and blankets in cold weather, flasks of hot tea, cups, cakes and fruit, she also brought him candles, worried that if the light was turned on they would be discovered. Even on the nights when Azusa did destroy his manuscripts, Mishima would continue writing all night – head down, tearful, alone. Shizue hated her husband for this, but restrained herself from saying anything. Instead she stroked her son's head and wiped away his tears, then silently left him. Subsequently, although he became adept at hiding manuscripts, Mishima would always show all his works to his mother first – a habit which continued for the rest of his life, apart from the non-fiction 'writings of the sword' of his last two or three years and the final chapters of *The Sea of Fertility*.

Under his father's influence, Mishima read books on the 'Jewish problem', Japanism, the Bible, insects and animals and, with his maternal grandfather, classical Chinese texts. He regretted in his letters to his schoolfriends, though, that he was a sickly, pale and utterly withdrawn creature who cared about nothing but writing, forced to wear a 'mask of normality'. One of his two collaborators on the short-lived student journal *Red Pictures* was a pupil five years older, Takashi Azuma, the previous head of the literary club, who now took over from Bojo as Mishima's confidant. Due to tuberculosis, Azuma had been confined to his bed from 1939, unable, because of the infectious nature of his disease, to take visitors. Mishima met him only once, but wrote him over 200 long letters, pouring out his thoughts on everything, and was devastated when he heard of his death in 1943. Twenty-seven years later, as a final act before his own death, Mishima engineered the publication of a book of Azuma's writings, to which he contributed the foreword.

In January 1943 Mishima won the Peers' School essay prize for the piece 'A Short History of Heian Period Psychological Literature', and in August received a letter from Zenmei Hasuda saying that the young novelist and poet Masaharu Fuji (1913–1987) would try to find a publisher for Mishima's collected works. At first it was going to be a publisher in Kyoto, before being switched to a small publisher called Shichijo Shoin in Kanda, Tokyo. However, after the Battle of Midway in June 1942, the Pacific War turned against Japan and now Hasuda was conscripted again in October 1943 and sent south. More worryingly, from December 1943 they started conscripting students, as the draft age was lowered from twenty to nineteen. From this point on, Mishima found himself concurrently preparing the first book edition of his works and expecting any day to die.

In 1944, however, the plan for the book was delayed as publishing controls tightened. In March, Masaharu Fuji, already working at a factory, was also conscripted, but formal permission for the book edition of *A Forest in Full Bloom* was finally granted in April. In May, though, it was Mishima's turn to have a preliminary conscription medical. Mishima's father had arranged the medical in his father's family prefecture of Hyogo in central Japan, thinking that Mishima's weak and gaunt state would stand out in comparison to healthy country lads, rather than in war-devastated Tokyo where sickliness was now the norm. The whole experience was, however, to be a humiliating one. In this corner of Hyogo, the name 'Hiraoka' was well known on account of its most famous son, the erstwhile governor of Karafuto, and now the famous man's grandson was made to appear a complete laughing stock. The medical was not just about measuring height, weight and checking eyesight, but also required running, jumping and lifting 40-kg sandbags. The country boys could easily raise such bags above their heads ten times, but Mishima could not even lift one once to his chest. Nevertheless, Mishima passed the medical, albeit as a '2B', meaning a very poor specimen. Ordinarily such a young man would have escaped military service, but now it became a question of waiting until the military had run out of class '1' and '2A' conscripts.

Previously, Mishima had learned kendo (Japanese fencing) and horse-riding as part of his curriculum at school, getting up at 5 a.m. to do kendo practice, but towards the end of the war, the Peers' School military training intensified and Mishima was forced to train with a backpack and rifle all night at the base of Mount Fuji (a precursor to the training he would demand of himself and his Shield Society recruits over twenty years later). Despite being weak, his instructor complimented him on his perseverance while others collapsed. When he got home and took his shirt off, his shoulder was red from the weight of the gun.

In September, six months ahead of schedule, Mishima graduated top of the class from the Peers' School and at a ceremony at the

With his father
Azusa, 31 July
1944.

palace received a silver watch from the emperor himself, much
to his father Azusa's delight. The entire family was taken there
in the headmaster's car and afterwards went to the theatre and
a restaurant. Given the unfolding of Mishima's last years, it is
curious how this meeting between Mishima and Emperor Hirohito
in 1944 generally passes without notice. Certainly, at this stage in
his life, the personality of the emperor does not seem to have been
much of a presence in the budding young writer's psyche. Yet it is
fascinating what *did* burn itself into Mishima's memory of this day.
Mishima was never to describe what the emperor looked like or the
clothes he wore, only that he had been 'magnificent' because he
managed to sit completely unmoving for three hours. The emperor,

the transcendent symbol of the eternal and unchanging in the tumultuous unfolding of historical time, was able to hold a pose like a statue for hours as if time itself did not exist. Mishima's young existence was already formed not only in his father's and grandfather's onerous expectations of how historical time would be redeemed, but conversely in the precise management of 'micro-time', vigorously allocating his night hours to his furtive writing activities: time management was already an overwhelming Mishima obsession. Into the hands of such a youth was now placed a silver watch – a precise timekeeping instrument – by the emperor, the ultimate symbol of time transcendence.

This was no mere footnote in Mishima's youthful career, but rather a defining moment. For the rest of his life, the religious keeping of time was something about which Mishima was utterly devotional. Not only was he, famously, to observe every publishing deadline without fail, but also precise timekeeping was to rule his world in every conceivable way. No party was ever so entertaining that he would not promptly leave it to return to his desk for his habitual all-night writing sessions; if a friend or girlfriend failed to arrive punctually for a date, they were granted a maximum of fifteen minutes, after which Mishima was gone, leaving a sarcastic note behind him. Sloppiness about time was something that Mishima could never forgive. When a longstanding collaborator missed an agreed deadline, Mishima broke off the friendship. In his book *For Young Samurai*, invocations to be punctual featured more strongly than a call to martial prowess. Mishima would even later admit to loitering on the Ginza, coveting through the glass windows of shops fabulously expensive clocks and – emperor-like – he would bestow on those he most admired the latest precision watches as gifts. For Mishima, time itself was the emperor, the absolute to which he was utterly respectful, and it was Mishima's indivisible union with clocks, watches and a reverence with timekeeping that was to define his entire life. The ceremonial bestowing of a watch by the emperor was symbolically to mark the curtain raising on the life of 'Yukio Mishima' in just the same way as his taking off his watch on the day of the Mishima Incident – the very last thing he did before committing seppuku – marked his leave taking from life itself.

But Mishima, the obsessive devotee of micro-time, was soon to be pulled once more by the dictates of macro-time. In October 1944 he entered the Law Department of Tokyo University, where both his father and grandfather had studied – the first rung in his projected bureaucratic career. Everyone had naturally recommended that Mishima study literature, but Azusa was insistent that his subject be German law. It hardly seemed to matter, though, as almost immediately the entire class was mobilized and sent to work in a naval dockyard on the outskirts of Tokyo. At the same time his collection of works (also featuring two stories set in Heian Japan, one during the Meiji Restoration, and one in Germany) was published by Shichijo Shoin and on 10 November a publication party was held in a famous restaurant in Ueno, organized by his school mentor Fumio Shimizu, with Mishima attending in his

9 September 1944, the day Mishima received a silver watch from the emperor.

school uniform. The windows were blocked out because of the air raids so the room was gloomy, but the publishers had put on a fine spread, and for a brief time Mishima's family felt as though they were stepping into an enchanted, war-free world. Mishima's mother was happy, proud and excited. Azusa, still strongly disapproving of his son's literary activities, casually remarked: 'You'll soon be dead anyway.'

Mishima recalled the singular circumstances of this publication project:

> It was quite an achievement to bring out a useless and non-urgent collection of stories like *A Forest in Full Bloom* in Tokyo when the air raids had already started. First of all we had to secure the paper ration so on the application form I remember writing a big speech about 'defending and maintaining the literary traditions of the imperial nation'. Eventually we received permission for the paper ration and Shichijo Shoin used a really splendid, cotton-like yellow paper . . . it was an age when there were no other books so 4,000 copies sold out in a week. With that, I felt I was content to die whenever the time should come.[13]

This, however, was another example of Mishima reconstructing his own past and spinning his own mythology. Despite his claim that the print run of 4,000 copies had sold out in a week, there were reports of Mishima taking unsold copies to second-hand bookshops, and while Mishima portrayed the publication of his first book as a matter of good luck and artfully pulling the wool over the eyes of propagandists, what he carefully neglected to describe fully was the key element that made publication a reality – the securing of a precious paper ration. This was down to his furtively making use of his grandfather Sadataro's powerful contacts in the paper-making companies. Crestfallen that the initial plan for publication had fallen through, from February to April 1944 Mishima worked frantically behind the scenes, liaising directly with the publisher and the Japan Publishing Board and, most crucially of all, contacting Oji Paper, whose success was based on the pulp factory established in Sadataro's province a generation earlier. The chairman of Oji Paper, Ginjiro Fujiwara, was the man who in 1930 had ordered the large statue of Mishima's grandfather to be erected and upon Sadataro's death in 1942 had given the family a lavish funeral gift of 10,000 yen, equivalent to almost half Azusa's annual salary.[14] Now Fujiwara held very high government office as the overseer of all wartime production.

At this stage in the war, with acute shortages everywhere, a publisher would be only too happy to publish a book by a young writer able to summon up supplies of paper magically, particularly if they received the sanction of the ultimate government authority. As soon as he had received permission for publication, on 24 April 1944, Mishima immediately wrote to the prize-winning poet Shizuo Ito, a frequent contributor to *Literary Culture*, and begged him to write an introduction, but received a rejection within the week. On 17 May he went to the trouble of visiting Ito in Osaka at the school where he worked, but was again turned down. Still not giving up, after his humiliating recruitment physical he visited Ito again at home on the 22nd and was given dinner, only for Ito to refer to him in his diary as a 'mediocrity'. Even so, when a first draft of the book, without any introduction, appeared on 31 May, Mishima posted a copy to Ito, accompanied by a note gushing in admiration for him.

Meanwhile, with the fall of Saipan on 7 July, Japan was now within range of enemy B29s. Mishima's concerns about the progress of the war, though, centred on an anxiety that the publishing house might be burned down in air raids before the publication date of 15 October. He finished the proofs of the book on 7 August, but unlike some of his classmates failed to take officer-class exams at the end of the summer, much to his headmaster's surprise. Only one sample copy of the book was produced on 15 October and this contained mistakes, such as noting Mishima's year of birth as 1915 instead of 1925, nullifying his desire to be recognized as a nineteen-year-old genius, and corrections pushed publication back to 17 November, meaning that only six copies of the book – with small bits of paper covering the typos – were actually available at the publication party.

Mishima was now writing one work after another, thinking he might die at any time and that each work might be his last. He remarked that at the age of twenty he could fancy himself as anything he pleased:

> as a genius earmarked for early death; as the final flowering of Japan's aesthetic traditions; as a decadent among decadents; the Last Emperor of an age of decadence; even as beauty's suicide attack unit.[15]

And he recalled:

> it was a rarely seen age, a time when not only could one not forecast whether I as an individual would live or die, but also it was hard to forecast the fate of Japan tomorrow, a time when my personal sense of doom and the sense of doom of the age and society as a whole were completely fused.[16]

His stories continued to be published in various magazines as the bombing intensified.

In 1945, things were to get a lot more complicated. In January he was mobilized to work at an aircraft factory (manufacturing Zero planes for suicide missions) in Gunma Prefecture. Using his poor physique as an excuse, Mishima was given an office job that allowed him to spend all afternoon writing, but on 4 February, when on short leave, he received military mobilization papers and was immediately ordered back to Hyogo Prefecture for an enrolment medical. In *Confessions of a Mask* he wrote:

My mother wept with sadness and my father was more than a little depressed. When the order came, even I was unwilling, but on the other hand I expected a splendid death so assumed an attitude of resigning myself to fate. However a cold which I had caught at the factory started worsening on the train and by the time I arrived in an acquaintance's home in the village (where, since my grandfather's bankruptcy, we didn't own a square metre of land) I had a high fever and couldn't even stand up. However this family's great care, and in particular the large numbers of antifebrile tablets I took, had an effect so I set off in high spirits and was accompanied to the camp gates.

But the fever, which had been suppressed by the medicine, once again raised its head while we were hanging around, completely naked like animals, and I kept sneezing during the enrolment medical. A greenhorn doctor mistook my bronchial wheezing for 'rhonchus'. Moreover this misdiagnosis was confirmed by my fanciful report of illness so my blood sedimentation rate was measured. Because of my high fever, the sedimentation rate was high. On the grounds of infiltration of the lung, I was ordered home the same day.

According to Azusa, who accompanied his son to the medical, none of his family expected to see him again: his mother had been sick in bed but still got up and came to the door to see him off. They could not believe that Mishima had been relieved from service, and indeed when he was re-examined in Tokyo, he was found to be suffering from nothing more than 'severe bronchitis'. In a supreme irony, Mishima, who always fantasized about death, had lied to save his life, while all the others who only dreamed of living were sent off to slaughter: the entire unit was later massacred in the Philippines.[17]

When he had received his call-up papers, Mishima had left 'final words' directed to his father, mother and all those from whom he had received instruction at the Peers' School and at Tokyo University, starting with Fumio Shimizu. He wished a glorious future to his schoolmates and thanked them for their friendship; he wished that his younger brother, too, should become a warrior of the Imperial Army as quickly as possible and ended, as he would 25 years later, with thanks to the emperor and the words '*Tenno heika banzai!*' (Long live the emperor!).

Yet how different was the reaction now that the draft had been so narrowly dodged. Mishima's father recalled:

> As we stepped outside [the military barracks] the sky seemed so high and so bright it was dizzying. The minute we were past the gate I took Kimitake's hand and broke into a run. How we ran! I don't remember how far but it must have been quite a distance. And the whole way I kept looking back, for all I knew a soldier would come after us shouting 'It was all a mistake, Congratulations on qualifying!' and that possibility had me scared to death . . . When we got home we went into the living room and had some green tea and I remember how delicious it tasted. My wife had with her the will and the nail clippings [a traditional memento] Kimitake had placed in her room secretly before he left. As we gradually relaxed everyone began to feel exhilarated.[18]

In *Confessions of a Mask*, Mishima wrote:

> I knew my life did not soar up in front of me as something so wonderful as to want to flee from a military death, so the

origin of that force which had made me flee from the camp
gates mystified me. Was it that I wanted to live after all?

The obvious answer was that, yes, while Mishima may have
fantasized about death in abstract form, as a moment of individual
apotheosis bestowing upon him eternal youth and confirming him
as a heaven-sent and heaven-snatched prodigy, the kind of death
the Imperial Army was offering was something entirely different:
the undifferentiated death of mass slaughter.

Far from mass death, Mishima was ruthlessly striving for
individual glory, shamelessly using the wartime situation and
his grandfather's influence to his own advantage. Through an
introduction by Riichi Kuriyama of the *Literary Culture* group,
he gave his story 'Circus' to Utaro Noda, a poet, critic and editor
of the magazine *Bungei* (*Literary Arts*), asking him if there was
a publisher who could bring out another book collection of his
works. Noda was surprised because he had hardly finished writing
them, but Mishima told him that he could supply the paper
because his father was the director of a paper company. Noda
was still reluctant, so Mishima asked him if he needed paper for
his magazine. Again Noda refused, but gained the impression of
Mishima being a young man in a hurry.

The situation in Tokyo was deteriorating by the day. Azusa had
reported to his son on 27 January that an air raid had left 1,000
people dead in Ginza, with corpses strewn around Hibiya Park,
and the following month all dogs were ordered to be killed lest
they eat the bodies. By April, Mishima had left the aircraft factory
after Tokyo Imperial University withdrew its students in protest at
the militia's brutal treatment of workers. Lectures recommenced,
but abruptly stopped again in May owing to a lack of professors.
Mishima's university class was transferred to working at a navy
arsenal in Koza, Kanagawa Prefecture, 48 km (30 miles) southwest
of Tokyo, and once more a daily apprehension of death combined

with voluminous reading and frantic writing. Mishima heard rumours that any day now the American army would be landing nearby and that all of his class would be sent out to meet them on the beaches and die fighting to the last man. In the meantime, however, while the rest of the class worked as a maintenance crew, he had once more wangled his way into an ideal position – this time looking after the notional, unused 'library' at the base. This meant that, while not dreaming of his imminent death, he had all day long to read ancient creation myths, eleventh-century court diaries, fourteenth-century novels and the modern stylist Kyoka Izumi or to translate a Yeats play. He remarked that in the midst of a world in total collapse and carnage, he would observe from a distance the beauty of the capital in flames and retreat into his own private world. He later recalled that this was the only time he did not feel himself to be a burden on anyone, and with no worries about employment or exams and little food, he felt happy. The air-raid shelter there was a good place to write and Mishima brought home lots of manuscripts.

As an extraordinary youth placed in extraordinary circumstances, Mishima was also struggling with all the usual, run-of-the-mill angsts of young men and attempting to have his first romantic relationship. After aping the novels of Radiguet and the love stories described in the Japanese classics, it seemed only natural that Mishima himself should taste such a relationship before he died. So he courted Kuniko, the younger sister of his classmate Makoto at the Peers' School (the girl's father, Takanobu Mitani, was the Japanese ambassador to Vichy France, and after the war the grand chamberlain), and later to be portrayed as Sonoko in *Confessions of a Mask*.

Unlike Mishima, Makoto had volunteered to be an officer and Mishima had noticed his attractive, seventeen-year-old sister playing the piano while visiting their expansive home. After Makoto was mobilized in October 1944, he sent postcards to him every

Saturday while also becoming acquainted with his sister. On 9 March, Mishima went with the Mitani family, including Kuniko, to Maebashi, around 100 km (60 miles) northwest of Tokyo, so that they could visit Makoto at his officer school for a Sunday picnic the following day. That night 89,000 people were killed and a million people made homeless when 300 tonnes of incendiaries were dropped on Tokyo. On their way back to the capital, the family were overwhelmed by the sight of the streaming columns of refugees and Mishima put his arm around Kuniko and felt pangs of infatuation.

Another massive air raid struck Tokyo on 24 May and Mishima walked back to the family home in Shibuya along smouldering sleepers of private railway line, now out of use. The whole area around the house had been burned, but the immediate vicinity of the house remained intact. The reunited family celebrated by eating tinned *yokan* cake and Mishima's sister teased him about having a sweetheart. Meanwhile, the female members of the Mitani family – grandmother, mother and three sisters (their father was abroad) – evacuated to the mountains of Karuizawa, from where frequent invitations to visit arrived at Mishima's door. When Mishima visited in mid-June, Kuniko greeted him like a lover, and in a world far removed from the war turmoil of Tokyo, Mishima experienced his first kiss. One month later, Makoto wrote to him, saying that his whole family was thinking about arrangements for the engagement and wedding ceremony, but how did Mishima feel? Mishima made excuses: that his father could be difficult to live with and his household old-fashioned for a modern girl like Kuniko. Mishima was not yet in a position to set up his own household and did not want to be under pressure to do so. At the age of twenty, his concerns were reasonable. Plus there was the small matter of his feeling that death might be imminent. But then the war suddenly ended. Mishima did not feel tearful. 'Tears were distant from my state of mind at the time', he later wrote. 'Thinking of the adventure of a new, unknown, sentient world, my heart was in a fluster.'[19]

In August, suffering from a high fever and headaches, Mishima had been taken home by his father from the navy arsenal and returned to the house in Gotokuji, in the suburbs of Tokyo, where his family had evacuated. It was there, while he was struggling to recover, that he heard the emperor's message announcing the end of the war. The story goes that, in profound relief at his family surviving the war, even Azusa now briefly relented and informed his son that, as this marked the beginning of a new age of culture, if he really wanted to be a writer, then he could do so. However, he soon changed his mind again.

For Mishima, surviving the war meant he would no longer have to write every work as if it was potentially his last. That was a relief, but it also meant that, now and forever, he had lost his chance to die a glorious youth in the universal theatre of death. The incessant tide of death that had lapped ever closer and closer from 1937 onwards, and had by 1945 almost submerged him, now suddenly pulled back again, and Mishima was left alive on what looked like a depressingly desolate and empty beach.

4

Sentenced to Live

With the end of the war and the beginning of the American occupation, everything changed overnight: entire cultural and social edifices collapsed. The American GHQ immediately arrested all the wartime leaders and set about putting them on trial, as well as abolishing the secret police, the propaganda ministry and the Board of Censors. Political prisoners were released and left-wing writers, who had been imprisoned or in hiding, now flooded back to Tokyo and not only resumed writing with a vengeance, but were actively courted by the Americans, who asked them to point the finger at all those writers (now designated 'literary war criminals') suspected of conniving with the fascists. Mishima temporarily lost his way. He had done well with youthful enthusiasm fuelled by the adrenaline of war. But when forced to reassess everything, he at first floundered and only when he rejected Romanticism in favour of confessional and shocking autobiography did he find his literary voice and the beginnings of fame.

At the top of the list of writers to be purged were those of the Japan Romantic School. Blacklisted into silence were its central figure, Yojuro Yasuda, whom Mishima had visited in 1943, and the poet and novelist Haruo Sato, whom Mishima had been considering as a potential patron. Other writers very quickly had to reinvent themselves as 'misunderstood liberals'. For Mishima, who had prospered in the cultural desert of wartime Japan, it was a disaster. Previously he had been able to play the trump card of magically summoning up paper rations, but now even the paper company, Oji Paper, whose executives were well disposed towards Sadataro's grandson, was broken up in the post-war *zaibatsu* (financial combines) dissolutions. Similarly, Mishima's obsessive death aesthetic, introspection and referencing of Japanese literary history had once been perfectly in tune with the age, but now all of that was washed away. Suddenly, in a world in which everything had been destroyed, people yearned to read outward-looking works with social vision about how things could be rebuilt. They wanted to hear from those voices which had been silenced during the long fascist nightmare. Not only did the big beasts of Japanese literature – Tanizaki, Shiga, Kafu and Masamune Hakucho – now all make a return, but new magazines flooded onto the market in prodigious numbers, with 60 new titles appearing by the end of 1946.

There was a yearning too for the great writers, now dead, of the previous generation. The novels of Natsume Soseki (1867–1916) once more became best-sellers as people looked for the solidity and certainties of an age before Japan had been caught up in a vortex of repression, war and disaster.[1] For quite a time, it was the old voices and the old certainties that people wished to read and the works of long-established writers, not new talents, with which the magazines were desperate to fill their pages. And when a new literary school – the post-war school – did emerge, it was made up of men who had narrowly survived the trauma of fighting with the Imperial Army, determined to assert that death was not remotely glorious and that it was life which should be prized as something precious.

Japan's humiliation was stark: the emperor was demoted to the ranks of ordinary men and photographed together with General MacArthur. Japanese cities were flooded with GIs and government-sponsored brothels appeared, with urgent appeals for girls to fill them to slake the foreigners' sexual thirst and save the rest of the female population from rape.[2] In cities that were naught but charred remains as far as the eye could see, makeshift nightclubs began to appear, welcoming American servicemen and their Japanese girlfriends and with doormen addressing all comers in English. In the two years after the war, 800,000 ex-soldiers of the Imperial Army returned home, and for many of them, physically or emotionally maimed, there was no life and no jobs waiting for them. Some became beggars on the streets, others members of thriving black-market gangs. Inflation soared and newspapers bewailed the plight of those people who literally starved to death because they refused to buy food on the black market. Thousands more, left homeless, lived in the parks and froze to death in the harsh winters of 1946 and 1947. Families sold off their every possession just to survive.

To many, the end of the war was a huge shock, but the effect on Mishima was complex, its full impact not felt until many years later. At the time a much more serious blow was the death of his younger sister, Mitsuko, to typhoid in a squalid, run-down hospital on 23 October 1945. Clearing the burned-out remains of a school, she had drunk water from a nearby well: five or six of her classmates also contracted typhoid, but she was the only one to die. She was three years younger than Mishima and only seventeen when she died, and Mishima had kept vigil over her, shooing away flies. When told of her death, he let out a howl of grief.

A month later, his first female love interest, Kuniko, became engaged to someone else, and when he heard the news, his mother recalled that for the one and only time in his life, Mishima drank himself into an oblivion. Mishima later remembered his reaction to these two heavy blows:

> Japan losing the war was not to me a matter of grief. Much more painful was the sudden death of my sister a few months later . . .

After the war, there was another personal incident.

A girl whom I had courted during the war and who should have become my betrothed, because of my last minute hesitation, shortly afterwards became the wife of someone else.

My sister's death and this girl's marriage, I think it was these two things that became the force driving my subsequent literary fervour. For a variety of reasons, I washed my hands of life. Even now when I recall the desolate sense of emptiness in my life for years afterwards, I cannot but shudder. The years from 1946 to 1948, when I was at an age when I should have been most bounding in life, was when I was closest to death. I had no hopes for the future and my recollections of the past were all ugly.[3]

These traumas in his personal life at first seemed to overshadow the trauma that the defeated nation was enduring. Yet, as the years passed, Mishima's reaction to the defeat itself began to shift. Having once written that 'losing the war was not a matter of grief', he moved to a more ambiguous position when, in 1961, he recalled: 'My twenty-year-old self greeted the end of the war in a drowsy state, neither indignant nor dancing with joy.'[4] By November 1970, his account of the same incident had completely shifted, when he remarked in his last *taidan* (conversation): 'It was a lie to write that "my younger sister's death was much more painful than losing the war": losing the war was an enormous shock.'[5]

Losing both his sister and a potential bride increased Mishima's sense of despair and emptiness, and now he had no choice but to confront the problems in his personal life: impotence and nihilism became linked in his mind. Mishima wrote: 'I thought I must somehow or other completely affirm myself and my life.'[6] Yet, with the end of the war, he felt a spiritual death. Where should he look for continuity in a life torn apart by defeat? This was the intellectual problem that Mishima wrestled with for the rest of his life and which ultimately led him to the 'emperor as a cultural concept' and the desire to demonstrate through seppuku 'the existence of values greater than respect for life'.

'I discovered that at the age of twenty I had already become an anachronism', Mishima wrote. He continued:

> My beloved Radiguet, and Wilde, and Yeats, and the Japanese classics – everything I had valued – was now suddenly offensive to the tastes of the age. The boy who had carried on like a genius within a small group during the war was now a helpless student taken seriously by no one.[7]

Mishima continued hawking to publishers some stories he had started during the war, such as 'The Middle Ages', set in the Muromachi period (1336–1573) with the doomed young shogun, Yoshihisa Ashikaga, as its protagonist. In 'A Tale at the Cape', featuring a theme reminiscent of 'A Forest in Full Bloom', a boy who loves to fantasize is once more entranced by the sea. He is both conscious of the sea calling to him and aware that answering that call would be both beautiful and terrifying. He is invited to walk along a cliff by some young lovers who commit suicide together, answering the call of the sea, while he has his eyes shut playing what he thinks is a game of hide-and-seek. The dreamy mood of these works was somehow at odds with his newfound reality.

After the war, Mishima looked for a publisher and sent these stories, together with six others including 'Cigarette' and 'Circus', to the editor of a new magazine by the publishers Chikuma Shobo, which had merged with Shichijo Shoin, the publisher of 'A Forest in Full Bloom'. The editor was tempted to run 'The Middle Ages', but passed the stories on to his adviser Mitsuo Nakamura, a literary critic, translator of Flaubert and later to become one of Mishima's closest friends, though at the time

Nakamura had never met Mishima, nor had Mishima ever heard of him. Famously, Nakamura scored the eight stories he read 'minus 120 points' – something Mishima did not learn until much later – and sent them back to the author.

Mishima needed to quickly realign himself in the new literary world. He dropped his association with many of the writers of the Romantic School and began looking around for an established figure who could further his interests. It was a tricky business. Those writers who had suffered repression under the fascists and were now experiencing a boom were hardly likely to look kindly on him. What was needed was someone who was both established and yet sympathetic to his unfashionable aesthetics. The perfect candidate was Yasunari Kawabata, an older writer who in November 1945 had already declared his unwillingness to live in the post-war age, stating that all his future works would be concerned solely with Japanese concepts of beauty, 'the mountains and rivers of the past'. Mishima's brother was to describe him as the Hand of God, who suddenly reached down from Heaven and took Mishima into his palm.[8]

In January 1946, having been introduced by Utaro Noda, Mishima took to Kawabata's home in Kamakura some of his stories, including 'Cigarette', a short story with homoerotic undertones set in an aristocratic school like the Peers' School, and 'A Tale at the Cape'. In a typically subtle distortion of the truth, Mishima recalled that:

> He [Kawabata] was at the time renting the house of Ariake Kanbara [a minor poet] and lived with the owner. There were no buses at the time so you had to walk from the station, but when I got there the reception room was full of guests . . . for me, who until that time knew only the monotony of my school life and home, this was the first time I came into contact with the seething vitality of the post-war literary world . . .

Like bamboo shoots after the rain, publishers emerged and fell over themselves begging to reprint his [Kawabata's] old works . . . I, who was distant from the literary world, watched Kawabata sit silently in the middle – calmly, impassively, unsmiling.[9]

Yet in reality there were no other guests present when Mishima called after 11 a.m. – in fact Kawabata was not even up. After Mishima was kept waiting, seated in the *kotatsu*, Kawabata eventually emerged and engaged in stiff conversation, remarking that there would probably soon be a war between the u.s. and the ussr, while taking in Mishima's penetrating gaze.[10]

Kawabata was a director of Kamakura Bunko, a newly formed publisher which in 1946, at Kawabata's instigation, had started a magazine called *Man* (*Ningen*), and Kawabata passed to the editor of the magazine, Tokuzo Kimura, Mishima's stories. Kimura was unimpressed by the artificiality of 'A Tale at the Cape' but agreed to run 'Cigarette', and Mishima was thrilled:

I flew down to Kamakura to express my thanks [to Kawabata] and even now have not forgotten how happy I was at the time. It would be the first time my work was published in the post-war, that is to say the orthodox, literary world.

Also I think it was then he told me they would also soon publish 'The Middle Ages' and my joy only increased.[11]

From then on, Mishima began visiting Kawabata frequently, and was soon introduced to Kimura as well, though was forced to wait as, month after month, his story failed to appear in *Man*, shunted to the next issue because of manuscripts arriving from major established writers. Kimura recalled Mishima in his university uniform, a nervous-looking, long-faced and pallid youth.

In June they finally ran Mishima's story, though it passed unnoticed. From then on, Kimura offered Mishima technical advice for his stories, going through them sentence by sentence with Mishima revising them straightaway. Mishima recalled these as 'joint efforts' aimed at tightening construction and removing any florid writing or long-windedness. In April 1947 he published the story 'Prince Karu and Princess Sotoori', about the earliest love suicide in Japan's recorded history, and, in August, a novella, 'Preparations for the Evening', set in Japanese high society in the last days of the war. In the novella 'Haruko', published in December, he offered a portrait of a lesbian. Still, no one apart from Kawabata and a few others were impressed. In November a small publisher brought out his second volume of short stories, *A Tale at the Cape*, but it failed to attract any reviews.

Mishima, meanwhile, was continuing to lead an entirely schizophrenic existence. By day, he was plain Kimitake Hiraoka, law student at Tokyo University, who kept himself to himself and who tried to develop the ability to listen to a law lecture as if it was literature. He came home to his family's modest house in Shibuya, which had survived the war unscathed, ate his dinner and then began writing in his room. There, he was transformed in the early hours of the night to his alter ego, Yukio Mishima. He restricted socializing to Saturday nights, when he went out with wealthy young aristocratic friends he knew from the Peers' School, seeking out black-market liquor and American music in the barracks dance halls that mainly catered for GIs. Mishima was not much of a drinker and at this stage was quite prim and proper. However, he apparently loved to dance, and in 1946 even took dancing lessons, despite having little talent for it. Sometimes his crowd also threw parties in the mountain resort of Karuizawa, though in the summer of 1947 Mishima broke with this set completely, declaring that he needed to retire from the world for a while in preparation for taking his civil service exams.

In uniform while a student at Tokyo Imperial University.

Mishima's concerns about his sexual orientation and impotence were still very much to the fore. A friend who later became a dramatist, Seiichi Yashiro, recalled a defining event in January 1947 when he took Mishima to a cheap brothel. This is described in *Confessions of a Mask* as follows:

> The prostitute opened her big mouth of gold teeth, fringed with lipstick, and thrust out like a pole a brawny tongue. I imitated her and thrust out my tongue. The ends of our tongues touched ... Other people won't understand. Insensitivity resembles a sharp pain. I felt that my whole body spasmed with an intense

pain, the pain of not being able to feel anything. I dropped my head to the pillow. After ten minutes, I had confirmed that it was impossible. Shame made my knees tremble.

Yashiro claimed that this description had considerable novelistic embellishment, but there is no doubt that Mishima was fearful of his relations with women and that they ended without consummation was something of deep concern to him.

Yashiro was also responsible for setting up one of the most famous encounters in Japanese literary history when he dragged Mishima along to his sole meeting with the hugely famous novelist Osamu Dazai (1909–1948). Mishima would later recall this as happening in the autumn of 1947, but this appears to be just another of the many distortions in Mishima's autobiographical essays. (Mishima probably shifted the date to after Dazai's novel *The Setting Sun* had finished its serialization in the magazine *Shincho* [*New Tide*] so that he could claim that Dazai's clumsy use of aristocratic speech was one reason why he did not critically rate him.) However, the encounter actually occurred on 14 December 1946. At the time, Mishima was known for little more than the stories that had appeared in *Man* magazine. On the other hand, there was an unmistakable Dazai mania going on among young men at the time. Nevertheless, Mishima professed an obstinate dislike of Dazai and for that reason, Yashiro, a devotee of Dazai, wanted all the more to introduce them.

Dazai was the tenth child of a member of the House of Peers (the upper house in the Japanese parliament) from the far north of Japan. Utterly disillusioned both with the decadence of his privileged background and the political and cultural directions that Japan took in the 1930s, and supportive of the communists, his life was a spectacular trail of disfunctionality, self-harm and rebellion. He attempted suicide on multiple occasions, including, in the mid-1930s, an attempted double suicide with a Tokyo bar girl that left only her dead. He was variously addicted to drugs, became an alcoholic and suffered from tuberculosis. He was twice married, though also fathered a child out of wedlock. Mixed in with this pathologically self-destructive lifestyle were frequent bursts of outstanding literary achievement. The brutal honesty of his chronicling of self-despair, together with his ability to combine mordant wit with profound tragedy, makes him one of the most enduringly popular and iconic Japanese writers of the twentieth century.

Explaining years later why he personally could not appreciate Dazai, Mishima wrote:

> I had previously, at a second-hand book shop, looked for *Fictive Wanderings* and I read those three volumes and *Das Gemeine* etc., but this was perhaps for me the worst choice to have made in starting to read Dazai's works. Their self-caricatures were the thing I innately hated the most, and the consciousness of the literary world and the small-town ambition of the satchel-carrying boy arriving in the capital which is scattered throughout the works was something I couldn't stomach.
>
> Of course I recognize his [Dazai's] rare talent and the fact that, unusually for me, I felt a physiological repugnance like this from the beginning was perhaps because, according to the laws of love and hate, he was the type of writer who deliberately exposed the parts of me I most wanted to hide.[12]

Revealing that Dazai's works 'exposed the parts of me I most wanted to hide' conveyed a very powerful truth. For ultimately, despite Mishima's vehement protestations of how much he hated him, Dazai would be the writer who, above all others, made Mishima's fictive universe possible. Dazai's unflinching exposure of his own inner sense of nihilism and the tragic decadence of the world around him was exactly the literary formula that Mishima required to smash through to his own subterranean vaults of inner futility, impotence and violent sexual desires. Far more than the influence of the second- and third-rate talents of the *Literary Culture* school, it was exposure to Dazai's fiction that allowed Mishima to find his voice.

In Japan, the meeting between Dazai and Mishima has an iconic status as a kind of James-Dean-meets-Marlon-Brando collision of two literary superstars – one on the way up, the other about to quit the stage – and both with gargantuan egos to match. But it is actually deeply revealing about both men. Mishima's ideological relationship to Dazai is similar to that of Nietzsche to Schopenhauer. The two men's world view – their perception of the ultimate futility of existence and the fakeness of cultural and social institutions – was extremely similar. The difference was that Dazai exhibited an unremitting Schopenhauerian pessimism towards the world, with death as the only escape from the pointlessness of life. But Mishima, having been trained from his first conscious years to sublimate inner torture into thrilling fantasies of pain and death, was able to both adopt Dazai's penetrating analyses and transform them into a Nietzschean lust for life and death. Indeed he believed that death itself was ultimately what gave life its meaning.

Mishima had begun his first full-length novel, *The Thieves*, in January 1946 and finished a draft by June, before slowly revising it. It was published in parts in various magazines from December 1947 onwards before coming out as a book in November 1948, with an enthusiastic preface by Kawabata. The story is about a man jilted by a woman meeting in turn a woman jilted by a man and their marrying according to a secret agreement. They then commit suicide on the day of their union without having consummated it. Some critics have speculated that, as Mishima was denied sex through his impotence, he here sublimated this into a story of protagonists who deliberately rejected sex as a rebellion against their fate. The title *The Thieves* refers to the fact that the couple who kill themselves have stolen the 'true beauty and everlasting youth' of their erstwhile partners by refusing to let themselves age like them. *The Thieves* was not, however, a successful work and given that its subtitle was 'An Episode in the World of the Upper Classes in the 1930s', it was hardly likely to appeal to the devastated Japan of 1948 when the aristocracy had just been legislated out of existence by the post-war reforms.

Mishima was in an extreme state of angst. On 28 November 1947 he graduated from the law department of Tokyo University and on 13 December passed the higher civil service exams (of 167 successful candidates, he was position 138). Just graduating from the law department guaranteed him a comfortable bureaucratic career, but to be fast-tracked to the higher echelons, to be earmarked as a future minister, meant passing these exams, and his father had demanded that he take them. Mishima meekly agreed. Azusa was keen for him to enter the all-powerful Ministry of Finance, the most difficult ministry to enter, which he himself had failed to enter at the beginning of his bureaucratic career. Azusa had always been impressed by the power of the bureau chiefs of the Ministry of Finance vis-à-vis their peers in other ministries, who were effectively their underlings and had their budgets controlled by them. He was thus delighted when, at Christmas 1947, Mishima received an appointment in the Banking Bureau of the Ministry of Finance.

Now Mishima agonized over whether he should remain as a civil servant or whether he could make writing his career. Even Azusa visited *Man*'s editor Tokuzo Kimura and asked him whether his son could become a first-class writer and make a decent living from it. This was not just concern about Mishima's future, but reflected a sudden change in Azusa's own circumstances. As boss of the Japanese Charcoal for Gas Company, Azusa had received a salary roughly the same as that of the governor of Tokyo. But the company had lost its function with the end of the war and after changing its name in 1946 was closed down in January 1948. The role of being chief support for the whole family now passed onto Mishima's shoulders, yet even Azusa could see that his son was not suited to the life of a bureaucrat.

Meanwhile, Mishima kept determinedly writing every night until three in the morning, despite having to be at his desk at the ministry at 8.30 a.m. He was reprimanded for sleepy carelessness, yet also came across as a promising young bureaucrat. His literary skills were put to some use in helping to edit the Ministry of Finance's journal, but when he drafted a speech, he found it returned covered with red ink because of its over-elaborate style. Meanwhile, he managed to publish twelve stories, some in major magazines, during the nine months he was at the ministry, and in December 1948 his third volume of short stories, *Preparations for the Evening*, was published by Kawabata's publishing house, Kamakura Library.

There is a wonderful anecdote about how Mishima's career as a bureaucrat came to an end. The story goes that one rainy morning at the beginning of September 1948, an exhausted Mishima was wearing wellington boots and standing on the platform at Shibuya station waiting for his morning train when he slipped off the platform and had to be helped up by someone. Returning home and relating this to his father – who must have feared that having nearly lost his son in the war and having lost his daughter shortly thereafter, he was in danger of courting tragedy again – led to Azusa finally relenting and saying: 'Then quit your job and become a novelist, but make sure you become the best novelist in Japan!', to which a humble Mishima replied: 'Yes, I will.' The story then continues that Mishima handed in his resignation, remarking to a colleague that he hoped, like many French novelists, to find a job in which he could also find time to write, but that the Ministry of Finance position was just too demanding.

In 1948, while publishing *The Thieves*.

The train story, whether truthful or invented by Mishima to fool his father, is classically Mishima-esque. There is the brush with death, providing a benediction for what is to follow, and a declaration of vaunting ambition and fearlessness in the face of the unknown. Unfortunately, it does not sit with the more prosaic reality, related by the editor Kazuki Sakamoto (father of the composer Ryuichi Sakamoto), of what actually happened in the late summer of 1948.[13] On 28 August, Sakamoto, together with another colleague from the publishing house Kawade Shobo, visited Mishima at the makeshift Ministry of Finance building in front of Yotsuya station and over a hamburger lunch formally requested that he write a full-length novel as part of a series of novels by up-and-coming authors that they had already started publishing. (The first book in the series had been published in June; Mishima was the fifth and final writer asked to contribute.) Mishima was delighted, recognizing that this commission represented the 'big break' he had always been looking for, and vowed in front of Sakamoto to resign and stake his fate as a writer on this. On 2 September, he handed in his resignation and devoted himself to making preparations for this major book. (Mishima deliberately distorted this sequence of events in his memoir, 'My Wandering Years', and claimed that it was only in October that he received the request from Kawade Shobo and that this was a 'lifeline' thrown to him after he had bravely resigned his position at the ministry, not knowing what the future would hold.)

On 2 November, Mishima wrote to the publishers saying that he planned to start writing on 25 November and that the book would be called *Confessions of a Mask*. It was to be his first 'I-novel'. The 'I-novel', in which the author revealed the details of his own personal history and current circumstances, had been a particularly popular genre in Japan since the Meiji era – in fact is claimed by some critics to be the default mode of all Japanese fiction. In Japan, where, since ancient times, people have been required to hide their real emotions (*honjo*) in the name of 'duty' (*giri*), the 'I-novel' was felt to be a particularly liberating genre that allowed the author to reveal his or her true self. Many of these I-novels were anodyne and artless, but at their best (Soseki's *Grass on the Wayside*, 1915, for example) they were capable of penetrating psychological insight into both their authors and the world around them. Dazai had given the genre a new twist in his landmark *No Longer Human* (1948), published only one year before *Confessions of a Mask*, by showing that the gap between the pleasant face shown to the world and the despairing bleakness of the protagonist's inner life was vast. This was the literary current in which Mishima now chose to swim. He explained to the publishers:

> Of course it won't be a literati novel. The sharp knife of psychological analysis I have so far applied to fictional characters I will turn upon myself. It will be an attempt to perform upon myself a vivisection. I vow to make it as scientifically precise as possible, making myself, in Baudelaire's words, both 'executioner and executed'.[14]

His original plan had been to spend three months in preparation and three months writing, but in the end he started the book in December and finished it on 27 April 1949, two months behind schedule. In fact, Mishima's notes show that he had already been planning on writing a big autobiographical novel called *The Passing of a Crowd of Demons* that was going to take him a full ten years. (Two years later, a completely different short story appeared with this title, about a 40-year-old man as a symbol of post-war degeneracy.) *Confessions of a Mask* was not, however, going to be any ordinary 'I-novel'. Rather, it was very carefully conceived as an exploration of Mishima's sadomasochistic fantasies and nihilism narrated from a very particular perspective: that of someone coming to terms with his own homosexuality.

The enormous influence of Dazai did not stop simply with the format of 'shocking confessions'. Dazai had committed suicide (by jumping into a canal with a mistress) on 13 June 1948, and from June to August his final masterpiece *No Longer Human* had been serialized and became a sensational best-seller. Dazai had taken to the limit the autobiographical presentation of nihilistic sexual relationships, consumed by a voracious readership for whom all aspects of sexuality in literature had been proscribed during the war. Mishima now carefully noted the new mood and attempted to explore another sexual taboo, long suppressed in Japanese letters: the inner life of the homosexual. The months of 'preparation' that Mishima required before he started writing the novel was time needed both to organize his material and conduct research on psychological theories about homosexuality which he found in the works of Cocteau, Havelock Ellis and the German 'sexologist' Magnus Hirschfeld (1868–1935). Once he had marshalled his material, Mishima began to reconstruct his past according to the new mask he had donned – that of a homosexual.

This was significant because in all the source material that Mishima used – such as his notes recording an accidental re-meeting with Kuniko or his youthful essay on *St Sebastian* – homosexuality had not featured. But now it was systematically linked to one episode after another. In July 1949, Mishima explained the novel to the psychologist and critic Ryuzaburo Shikiba in the following way:

What is written in *Confessions of a Mask*, apart from adjusting some of the characters modelled on real people and conflating two characters into one etc., is all a faithful rendition of facts taken from my own personal experience. I think that both in this country and abroad, candid, confessional descriptions of 'sexual inversion' are rare. There are a few things like Gide's *A Grain of Wheat*, but there the psycho-historical side is emphasized. I looked at a little-known book, Jean Cocteau's *Livre blanc*, but this too is just a short piece. At the beginning of summer last year I read *Sexual Inversion in Man* [sic] and *Love and Pain* [sic] by the sexologist Ellis, and while it's an extremely comical thing to say, both took great pride and gained the bravery to confess from the fact that all the examples listed there come from intellectuals. At the time,

I suffered much more because of my physical inability to proceed in a normal direction rather than because of my innate sexual orientation and so thought that confession would be the most effective means of psychotherapy.[15]

After starting to write, he at first proceeded at an incredible rate, but from the end of January 1949 gradually started to slow down. Having been too enthusiastic, his stamina could not keep up and he went on a trip to the island of Oshima to recuperate. At the beginning of March he handed over the first 250 pages of handwritten manuscript to Sakamoto. In the final stages of writing, pressure from the publishers was intense and Mishima was staying up all night one night after another. After finally finishing the manuscript, bleary-eyed, he handed over the remaining pages on 24 April 1949 at a coffee shop in Kanda called Ranbo, frequented as a writers' haunt. Mishima, concerned about whether he could make a living as a writer, had consoled himself that 'at least I'm OK for now.' He did not know if he would be managing about five or six years hence, but concluded that 'to still be OK five or six years from now, I will have to devote all my energies to some works that will firmly establish me.'[16]

Yet, at first at least, *Confessions of a Mask* did not sell. Mishima begged Kimura to publish a review in *Man* and Kimura entrusted it to a Kiyoshi Jinzai, a novelist and scholar of Russian literature, whose two-page spread appeared in the October issue. Kimura highlighted the novel's unusual erotic passages, but noted the difference between the first and second halves of the book, the former concerning Mishima's childhood and the latter his relationship with the girl Sonoko. Still, for six months after publication nothing happened and bookshops started to return copies. Then the novel unexpectedly appeared in the *Yomiuri* newspaper's list of the best literature of the year, with six out of nine distinguished writers putting it down as one of their best three books of the year. The reason for this was an article analysing the novel in the January edition (released in early December) of *Bungei* called 'The Face of St Sebastian', in which the writer Kiyoteru Hanada startlingly declared that 'with this novel, Japan's twentieth century begins'. He also noted that, while Dazai and Mishima both exhibited interior masks, Dazai felt shame while Mishima was unflinching. On the back of this publicity, there was another print run of the novel and it suddenly began to sell.

A chief difficulty with *Confessions of a Mask* lies in knowing to what extent Mishima's 'confession' of homosexual impulses from childhood was real and how much was systematically fabricated for sensational effect. The conclusion of the novel concerns the protagonist's remeeting with his former love interest, Sonoko, after she has married and his realization that no relationship was possible because of his innate homosexuality. The description of events was similar to what actually happened to Mishima. His first love, Kuniko, had married in May 1946 and he had remet her on 16 September, when she had called out to him on the street, prompting him to visit the Mitani family home a few days later. She asked him why they had not married – did he dislike her? He answered that he had never said that they could not marry, just that he was not ready. In November, however, Kuniko's husband was arrested and sent to Hong Kong, pending investigations into atrocities against prisoners of war, and after being pronounced innocent finally returned to Japan at the end of 1947. Yet it was the return of her husband – not Mishima 'coming out' – which brought to a conclusion Mishima's relationship with Kuniko, and it is interesting to speculate what might have happened had her husband been found guilty and imprisoned abroad or indeed executed: 920 of the 5,700 Japanese arrested for war crimes *were* executed. This, after all, was the woman over whom Mishima had drunk himself into oblivion upon hearing of her engagement.

Given this background, some critics have speculated about whether many of the 'confessions' in the first half of *Confessions of a Mask* were fabricated to make sense of the plot line in the second half of the novel. While it might seem obvious that Mishima did have strong homosexual and sadomasochist impulses, it is also curious that, despite writing a novel 'confessing' to this, his parents and many others dismissed it all as an outlandish pose – especially as, at the same time as temporarily reviving his meetings with Kuniko, Mishima was also stepping out on dates with a girl called Teiko Sassa, a former schoolfriend of Mishima's sister, before she rebuffed his attempt to kiss her.

Mishima seems to have been particularly influenced by Mamoru Mochizuki's best-selling book *Sex and Life*, which was not published until March 1949 but had been serialized in magazines over the previous two years. This book distinguished between 'true' homosexuality and 'fake' homosexuality. The latter form of homosexuality, the theory ran, was really just a product of narcissism. The male narcissist wanted to make himself more beautiful, muscular and sexually attractive, and if he recognized that which he desired in others, he felt desire for them. Mochizuki noted that many people when very young have narcissistic sexual desires, relieved by masturbation, but that they did not usually continue into adulthood. But in rare cases, if the child was introverted and did not play with other children and wished to stay indoors, this tendency would gradually strengthen, with the child just wanting to sexually satisfy him or herself. However, if approached by others, and particularly people of the same sex, sexual desire could be triggered within the narcissist. Mochizuki noted that, while it was difficult for such narcissists to approach the opposite sex, if they were approached by the opposite sex, a 'normal' life was possible. Mishima, who had visited Mochizuki in person, must have felt that this theory described him to a T and used this theory of the 'fake homosexual' as the backbone for his *Confessions* book.

Mishima also discovered material in *Sexualpathologie* (1917) by Magnus Hirschfeld, which he had borrowed from Mochizuki and read in German and which he must have felt represented his own psychology and physical needs. Hirschfeld had founded the Institute for Sexual Science in Berlin in 1919 and quoted in his book letters from a young law student to his father, a high-ranking government official. The son had been involved in a homosexual incident and wished his father to understand his true nature. Referring to the 'mask' which he must show the world, he talked about his first experiences of homosexual love.

If Mishima had now adopted the mask of the homosexual, he cryptically noted: 'You can only confess masks that have bitten into your own flesh, that are a continuum of flesh. The reality is that "confession is impossible".'[17] In his afterword to a collected works in 1953 he explained:

> By writing a kind of confessional novel, I feared methodological contradiction and so thought I must scrupulously expunge the 'writer' from the work. Because if I, as a 'writer', was to appear in the work, there would have to be a writer writing the writer, and without the integrity of the representation being assured, the format of a confessional novel would collapse.[18]

Confessions of a Mask was therefore a careful transformation of the reality of Mishima's life in two significant regards. First, it systematized all Mishima's experiences into a pattern of revealing homosexual tendencies – transferring, for example, his desire to kiss Kuniko into Sonoko's desire to kiss the narrator while concealing the deep wounding he actually felt about his relationship with Kuniko.

Second, *Confessions* carefully excluded Mishima's existence as a writer. The 'I-novel' traditionally relied on a system of trust existing between author and reader about the confession, but Mishima deliberately undermined this, realizing that it was impossible to represent the totality of any life and that all narratives are ultimately 'fictions', focusing on some material and editing out other distracting material, employing a selective system to make the confession appear convincing.

Many people were mystified when they read the novel, but gradually public acknowledgement of the exceptional talent of its writer and interest about its contents increased and it became a best-seller, selling 20,000 copies in hardback and being much discussed in newspapers and literary journals. The critic Tsuneari Fukuda appraised it in 1950, remarking that '*Confessions of a Mask* does not just stand at the pinnacle of the works written by Yukio Mishima, but will also, I think, be one of the greatest and long-lasting achievements of post-war literature.'[19] Even Mitsuo Nakamura revised his opinion and acknowledged Mishima's achievement, while Kawabata penned an article in December 1949 entitled 'Mishima: The Hope of 1950'.

Mishima's shift to an 'I-novel' had been inspirational on two levels. First, while his death aesthetic had not appealed as fiction to the traumatized post-war age, turning it inwards and showing a young man's nihilism as a product of what Japan had lived through in the last twenty years was perfectly in tune with the mood of the time. Second, it finally allowed Mishima to reveal aspects of his true self, with all his unalloyed lusts and impulses. In an age that rejoiced in being free from oppressive wartime censorship, it was satisfyingly shocking and frank. With this, Mishima overcame his spiritual crisis of the post-war years and, having firmly established himself, began a busy career as a young writer universally recognized as brimming with talent.

5

Mishima à la Mode

Having finally had his big break with *Confessions of a Mask*, Mishima was determined to grab success with both hands and show himself to be infinitely adaptable. Whereas his works before *Confessions of a Mask* sometimes seemed solipsistic and out of touch, now almost overnight Mishima utilized his new-found fame to transform himself into an enormously popular writer who was utterly integral to the zeitgeist. He did this by three methods: first, by radically attuning the level of difficulty of his works to the commissions he received; second, by basing his novels on actual contemporary happenings which he infused with his own distinctive psychological analysis; and third, by deliberately seeking out what was new and distinctive about the age.

From 1950 onwards, the terrible hardship and trauma of the immediate post-war years receded, and something new began to filter into the air. The first big change, of course, had come the previous year when, after the communist takeover in China, the occupation government abruptly decided to undermine the labour unions and socialists that it had previously encouraged. While laying out plans to relaunch the Japanese economy as a low-cost, high-volume exporter, it introduced stringent economic measures that generated mass layoffs and bankruptcies. When 100,000 employees of Japanese National Railways were laid off, a series of terrorist incidents on the railways followed and the prime minister blamed the communists and moved to mass arrests of union members, even though behind the scenes the police were busy fabricating evidence. The occupation government then moved to purge supposed communist sympathizers from all educational institutes, discharging 1,700 schoolteachers in September 1949, before moving on to a purge of the media, as well as forcing out 10,000 civil servants.[1]

The outbreak of the Korean War in June 1950, however, provided a boon for the Japanese economy as well as the first explicit contradiction of the 'Peace Constitution', as General MacArthur ordered the creation of a Japanese militia euphemistically named 'Police Reserve Force', which by 1952 had changed its name to the 'Security Force' and finally become the 'Self-defence Force' in July 1954. In September 1951, Prime Minister Yoshida also signed the San Francisco Peace Treaty with 48 nations, as well as the mutual security treaty with the USA. With the advent of the Cold War and the beginning of the Korean War, Japan was no longer the enemy and pariah of a few years earlier: suddenly Japan was an important Western ally, undergoing a mini economic boom.

Mishima started 1950 with the serialization of a novel called *The Immaculate Night* (*Junpaku no yoru*), a tale of a beautiful young woman's adultery and subsequent disillusionment, in a popular women's magazine. The novel was to be the first of Mishima's so-called 'entertainments': deliberately 'non-literary' works, stripped of philosophical musings and poetical expression and designed as highly lucrative 'easy reads' for the mass market. Mishima found such novels extremely easy to churn out and would carry on writing them for the rest of his life, spending up to a third of his creative life working on them. The obvious reason for writing them was financial, but even when Mishima's 'literary' works became huge best-sellers, Mishima still kept going with his potboilers. His writing pattern was to be at his desk by 11 p.m. every night, when he would warm up for a few hours on the 'entertainments' before hunkering down to the slow diamond-polishing of the sentences in his 'literary' works. Mishima was keen to demonstrate mastery of all literary genres and was rewarded with *The Immaculate Night* becoming a hit and being turned into a film in August 1951.

Mishima also published *The Blue Period* in 1950, serialized between July and December, the true-life story of an outstanding graduate of Tokyo University's prestigious law school who had set up an investment loan company and briefly enjoyed spectacular success before being arrested and committing suicide. Having kept eight mistresses and left behind a sarcastic death note, the press latched on to him as a symbol of modern degeneracy and Tokuzo Kimura asked Mishima if he would not like to write up the story with the protagonist as a modern-day *The Red and the Black*-style Julien Sorel. Mishima came back to him, informing him that – amazingly – the leading publisher Shinchosha had approached him with the same idea and would be providing a special editor to help with his research. In the space of just four years, Mishima had gone from a youth loitering around the office of *Man* magazine waiting to see if his story would ever be published, to a literary star who could now turn down a well-known magazine in favour of more lucrative deals.

His major literary novel of 1950, *Thirst for Love*, also commissioned by Shinchosha, was published in June. It is a superb piece, wonderfully evocative of what life was like in the central Kansai region in 1950, still coming to terms with the devastation of the war, the years of rationing and disease, and the post-war reforms. Mishima got the idea for the story from his mother's younger sister, who worked at a garden in the Osaka region. It is the tale of Etsuko, a widow whose husband has died of typhoid, who is living with her dead husband's family and has become the mistress of her father-in-law. She becomes obsessed with the young boy Saburo, who is working as a gardener on her father-in-law's estate, and is tormented with jealousy when he starts to have a relationship with a maid. She too leads the life of a 'mask', keeping a false diary that contains nothing but inverted meanings that fool her prying father-in-law. Like the narrator of *Confessions of a Mask*, lusting after his classmate Omi, she longs for the strong, unintellectual form of Saburo and seeks to slake her sexual desire through violent impulses.

It is an incredibly assured work from an author who was only 25 years old. Etsuko is a magnificent creation, at once convincing in her characterization, and yet also someone whom Mishima is said to have thought of as being a 'man'. Mishima describes the process by which a person whose interior has been eaten out by nihilism seeks respite against the world, and as a novel exemplifying the seething desires and trauma of the post-war generation, it won high praise. Mishima had now become a fashionable novelist and *Thirst for Love* sold 70,000 copies, making Mishima 1.4 million yen. With it, he bought his first home (three times the land area of their previous home) – at Midorigaoka in southwest Shibuya – and moved his whole family there. Mishima was now the main breadwinner and his father, despite being disconcerted by the contents of *Confessions of a Mask* (which he dismissed as 'preposterous nonsense'), was at last reconciled to his son's career, even presuming to act as his agent and helper, and was to be seen at the front of the house most days burning his son's discarded manuscripts. Tensions between Mishima's parents, which had at one stage looked like ending in divorce, now resolved themselves, and Mishima set to work on his next major work, the two volumes of *Forbidden Colours*.

In *Confessions of a Mask*, the narrator had revealed himself as someone suffering from solitary 'perversions' caused by suppressed homosexuality, but looking around Tokyo, Mishima spied a whole new world of openly gay bars springing up in the metropolis. This was an entirely new phenomenon (such bars had simply not existed before the war), and their emergence seemed to owe their origin to the large foreign homosexual community, including soldiers stationed in Japan. Mishima soon started frequenting them. His favourite gay café was the Brunswick on the Ginza, replete with a tropical aquarium, a bullfighting poster and sombreros on the walls, doughnuts and a fabulous array of Western drinks. The café had very attractive young boy waiters, who also doubled as performers in the evening floor shows upstairs, before making out with the paying customers on the dance floor while others watched from spectator seats along the sides. Mishima was soon swooning over them. 'At the moment, whether sleeping or awake, I constantly sigh, as if I had just started puberty again, unable to forget the image of that boy at the Brunswick',[2] he wrote to Tokuzo Kimura. Some of the young waiters at the Brunswick would go on to become stars in the films of his works, including Akihiro Maruyama, later a transvestite singing celebrity known as Akihiro Miwa, who was to star as the 'actress' in the stage and screen versions of Mishima's dramatization of Edogawa Ranpo's novel *Black Lizard*. He recalled Mishima in those days as looking deathly pale, with clothes hanging off his body, and having a keen eye for beauty that was repulsed by the sight of himself.

For many years after Mishima's death, it was unclear whether he was actively homosexual as far back as the late 1940s and early 1950s, although Tokuzo Kimura and Seiichi Yashiro could remember him being in the company of a handsome boy from the Peers' School and there were rumours of his having been dropped by a young Kabuki actor. Yet thanks to the memoirs of his former lover Jiro Fukushima, published in 1998 (before being suppressed by Mishima's children), we have a first-hand account of one of Mishima's serious gay relationships. Fukushima, a young student up from the provinces and an avid reader of *Forbidden Colours*, had the chutzpah to call at the Mishima home and enquire of the famous young writer if he would show him where the gay bar that featured in his novel really was. After being kept waiting by a maid,

Fukushima was thrilled to see Mishima not only appear in a kimono, but whisk him off to a friend's house and then hand him a card with the time of their next meeting in a gay bar written on it. Soon he not only became Mishima's lover, but was kept on hand to do odd jobs at the Mishima house. Mishima even took him to the hotel on the Izu peninsula where he went to write, and Fukushima marvelled at how, after enjoying sex and alcoholic drinks, Mishima would calmly sit down to write throughout the night. Fukushima also revealed how unsatisfactory he found love-making with Mishima, and after he candidly confessed this to Mishima – surely devastating to Mishima given his concerns about impotence with women – the relationship quickly fizzled out, though it would be revived again ten years later in the spring of 1962. Fukushima also discovered that, at the time he and Mishima began their affair, Mishima was nurturing a broken heart after having been dropped by one of the boys at the Brunswick. In short, we now know that Mishima was already a very active participant in the Tokyo gay bar world.

Developing hand-in-hand with 'Mishima the homosexual', however, was an entirely different Mishima who stepped out with an array of attractive and very well-heeled young ladies. An important link to this other Mishima was Ryoko Itaya, a former classmate of his sister at Miwada High School. She had first called at the Mishima home on the fifth anniversary of Mitsuko's death and then became a regular visitor, chatting with both Mishima and his parents until late at night. She was recently married, but her husband returned home late most nights and so Mishima's father would ask his son to escort her home, providing opportunity for furtive romance. One night the husband caught them walking arm-in-arm and after dropping Mishima home, screamed at his wife: 'What the hell are you doing arm-in-arm with a tuppenny ha'penny scribbler?' Having been brought up in a home with dozens of servants, Ryoko was not the submissive type and, after responding in kind, matters escalated to the point where her husband frogmarched her to the Hiraoka house, demanding to know what was going on. As Mishima was not in, a bewildered Azusa declared there was nothing in it, though immediately afterwards Mishima suggested she join him at a hotel on the island of Oshima. 'What's this? Elopement?', she asked, wavering, but came to her senses when Mishima equivocated with: 'If you want to turn back, now's the time.'

Meanwhile, in an echo of his grandmother's desires, Mishima revelled in high society. At school he had been forced to go horse riding, but had hated it and once fell off. Now, though, he started attending a horse-riding club and went up to stay at the Green Hotel in the mountains of exclusive Karuizawa while he worked on a manuscript and was observed riding on the road by the Tokyo literati summering there. Literary men like 60-year-old playwright Kunio Kishida and 42-year-old Kenichi Yoshida, son of the prime minister, lived in north Karuizawa and invited other important writers and critics to come up to their homes. In this way, Mishima began associating with Kishida's daughter, Kyoko, the model for the heroine in the novel *Natsuko's Adventures*, which he was writing at the time (shortly after being published, this novel would be turned into Japan's second colour film). Later she would also appear in Mishima's plays, as well as star in the film *Woman of the Dunes* (1964).

Mishima was soon spoiled for choice when it came to the availability of alluring and talented, not to say extremely rich, young women, as illustrated by the confluence of attendees at a noteworthy party towards the end of the 1951 summer season in Karuizawa. While her husband was away in Europe, Ryoko Itaya had been staying at the country house of a high-school friend called Kaoru Kanetaka, the hostess of the party. Ryoko invited Mishima, knowing it was his last night in the resort, and came to pick him up in a taxi only to discover, to mutual surprise, that

Mishima had also invited another girl, the aforementioned Kyoko Kishida. Arriving at the party, Kyoko thought Kaoru, a girl of mixed Indian and Japanese parentage, stunningly beautiful; indeed, with the stage name 'Rose', she would later go on to host one of the longest-running and most popular TV programmes in Japan. As if this array of rich and attractive female company was not enough, earlier that day, Kaoru had strolled up to the magnificent villa of Morinosuke Kajima, president of the country's largest general contractor, and invited his nineteen-year-old daughter Mieko to the party that evening.

At a time of austerity and shortages, the bright young things at the party enjoyed an array of wines, cheeses, fruits and meats and danced cheek-to-cheek. When Kyoko grew tired and was led upstairs by Kaoru, they opened a bedroom door and discovered Mishima canoodling with Ryoko, and when Kyoko burst into tears he comforted her with: 'It's all right, I'm going to be spending all night writing.' In fact, he spent all night shuttling between Ryoko and Kyoko while also working on his novel *Natsuko's Adventures*. He continued with it on the train back to Tokyo that he took the next day with Kyoko before handing over the manuscript to an editor waiting at the station.

Still, it was neither Ryoko nor Kyoko who became the focus of Mishima's heterosexual interest from that night onwards – rather it was Mieko, the daughter of one of Japan's richest men, that Mishima now set out to woo, taking her out on fantasy dates. With money no object, he could request that she dress up in a kimono for evenings at the Kabuki or in black evening dress for French comedies. Or, when they tired of that, they could pretend that they were poor and dress down in casuals, with Mieko meeting Mishima outside the gate of Tokyo University, where he would take her to a Greek class and then out to eat cheap curry rice at a student café. Perhaps most revealingly, Mishima even asked her to dress up as a man, and, wearing her brother's jacket and a Stetson she was taken to Ketel, a famous restaurant set up by a former German POW, and from there on to the Brunswick, where the couple were surrounded by gay boys who all ignored her while pampering Mishima.

Mishima also began socializing with Ryoko's elder sister Atsuko, another married woman, who was later to become the inspiration for the character Kyoko in his 1958 novel *Kyoko's House*. Tall and attractive, she became an even more frequent visitor to the Mishima home than her sister – so much so that, hearing that Mishima desired a fridge, she procured one for him through her Japanese-American husband, who was attached to the occupation headquarters.

In this busy whirl of relationships, Mishima seems to have also been interested in forging a marital union with Kawabata's family, but as Kawabata's birth-daughter was still at school, he turned his attention to the adopted daughter. He brought her cakes and, at a funeral in June 1952, casually raised the subject of marrying her – only for the idea to be immediately dismissed by Kawabata's wife.

The first volume of *Forbidden Colours* was published in the magazine *Gunzo* (*The Group*) from January to October 1951 and was to be groundbreaking in its description both of the lascivious world of post-war Japan and the new homosexual demi-monde that had sprung up. Critics, having no knowledge themselves of what went on in gay bars, were perplexed as to how to assess it. The plot is that the aged novelist Shunsuke Hinoki, having had three failed marriages and many miserable relationships, hates women and takes revenge on them by using a beautiful young man, Yuichi (described as a statuesque Apollo), as a tool. Shunsuke encourages the hesitant Yuichi to marry a nineteen-year-old girl, forcing her to taste the unhappiness of being married to a homosexual, and subsequently enjoys manipulating Yuichi's affairs with both men and women.

One of the most interesting aspects of the book is that, whereas in *Confessions of a Mask* we have Mishima as the narrator of a supposed 'I-novel', tortured by his sexuality but whose life as an author is entirely absent, in *Forbidden Colours* there is a duality created between the controlling novelist and the beautiful, young gay man. At first it seems as though the novelist can control and manipulate the sexuality of the young man, but eventually Shunsuke himself, who has not previously been homosexual, starts to fall in love with Yuichi. Having taken the narrative that far, Mishima fretted over how to resolve the tension. He considered various endings, unsure about whether Yuichi should accept or decline Shunsuke's approaches, before deciding to proceed with him rejecting Shunsuke. Mishima even considered having Shunsuke commit suicide because he could not bear the thought of a beautiful young man being in love with such an ugly man as himself.

The shift in power between the ugly, old novelist (Mishima referred to himself as an 'odd, grinning 25-year-old old man'[3]) and the beautiful though utterly unintellectual Adonis is reflected in the revolution in Mishima's own life between the first part of *Forbidden Colours* in 1951 and the second part, which was serialized in the journal *Bungakkai* (*Literary World*) between August 1952 and August 1953. In the interval, Mishima had headed off for six months on a life-changing round-the-world trip. Despite his tremendous success during the two years since the publication of *Confessions of a Mask*, Mishima would later recall that his emotional life was still full of ups and downs and he was constantly assailed by loneliness. Up until this point in his career, Mishima had been desperately concerned to be recognized as a legitimate member of the literati, fulfilling the childhood ambition nurtured by his mother. But now a counter-impulse, derived from his father and grandfather, increasingly came to manifest itself. Both Sadataro and Azusa had hated with a passion the posturings of 'literary men', whom they believed to be useless, hypocritical spivs.

Now Mishima too began gradually to create a persona that would distance him, both in dress and action, from that of 'literary men'. But first he sought out going abroad and re-examining himself, away from intrusive eyes.

Unfortunately, leaving Japan in 1951, at the height of the Korean War, was virtually impossible. This was an age when there were still no passports and leaving the country required a permit signed by MacArthur himself (strict controls were not lifted until April 1964). Mishima fantasized about hopping on a whaling ship and disappearing to the South Seas and went round his newspaper friends asking if any of them knew a means by which he could get a posting abroad. Luckily, his potboiler for 1951, *Natsuko's Adventures*, had been published by Asahi Shuppan, the book division of the *Asahi* newspaper, and his father was old friends with the editor-in-chief of the publishing wing, through whom he was able to acquire an appointment as the *Asahi*'s 'special overseas correspondent'. At Christmastime in 1951, he set sail on the ss *President Wilson*, a premier luxury liner, from a drizzling Yokohama wharf. He was seen off by his family, the sisters Ryoko and Atsuko, Mitsuo Nakamura, the critic who had previously marked his works 'minus 120', and some close editor friends. Mishima wore sunglasses to hide his tears, but when his eyes met with one of his friends he comically mimed weeping. A few days earlier, his mentor Kawabata and his wife had called at Mishima's home to wish him bon voyage.

Mishima intended the epic voyage that lay ahead to be a journey not only of self-recovery, but of self-discovery and self-improvement. It would be a communion with the sun that would have as its ultimate destination the glories of ancient Greece. In 1963 he wrote:

As we approached Hawaii, the sunlight became stronger each day and I started sun-bathing on the deck. This is when my habit, which I have pursued these last twelve years, of sunbathing

Christmas 1951, on the ss *Woodrow Wilson*.

began. I felt like I had come out of a dark cave and discovered the sun for the first time . . .

Then, while bathing in the sun all day long, I started to think about remodelling myself.

What was superfluous in me and what was missing?

If I had to say what I had too much of, then clearly it was sensitivity; if I was to say what was missing, it was a certain corporeal sense of existence . . . To have that, it was no use being cooped up in a cave-like study or research room: I needed the mediation of the sun . . .

Luckily, my travel itinerary included sunny lands like South America, Italy and Greece.[4]

Mishima was bursting with a desire for bacchanals, to be devoured and reborn. In America, he passed a day each in San Francisco and Los Angeles before spending ten days in New York. There he was chaperoned by a fast-talking 37-year-old New Yorker called Mrs Kluger, of the 'American Committee for Cultural Freedom', who showed him the Empire State Building and Radio City Music Hall. According to *Apollo's Cup*, published in October 1952, he saw the opera *Salome* in New York, together with *South Pacific* and some other shows, went to the cinema to see *Rashomon* and *A Streetcar Named Desire* and visited the Museum of Modern Art. He said he thought that New York looked like Tokyo 500 years in the future. The translator Meredith Weatherby, then at Harvard, called round to Mishima's hotel with his translation of *Confessions of a Mask* and the two spent the day combing through the manuscript. Weatherby also introduced Mishima to the Japanese film critic Donald Richie, then at Columbia University, who fulfilled Mishima's request to be taken to a gay bar, though the one they visited in Greenwich Village, Mary's, was apparently dull. Another night Mishima found his way to Harlem, where he watched, with fascination, black lesbians necking.

After America he called at Puerto Rico and got drunk on the light of the tropics. Then, on 27 January, he arrived in Rio, where he waited for Carnival, the ultimate bacchanal, to begin at the end of February. He was shown round by a correspondent of the *Asahi Shinbun* called Mogi, who remembered Mishima – as everyone did at the time – as being pale and frail, polite and free-spending. Even while abroad, Mishima kept up his usual practice of being at his desk at 11 p.m. and writing through the night, then sleeping until lunchtime. According to Mogi, Mishima also gorged himself on boys, teenagers hanging around in parks, whom he took back to his hotel room every afternoon. Until the memoirs of Fukushima were published, it was even speculated that Brazil must have offered Mishima his first real taste of gay sex. Yet ironically it is now known that, far from it, Mishima would complain in a letter to a friend of the *lack* of gay life in Brazil, while casually mentioning two '*aventures*' fitted into his short stay in the USA.[5]

Mishima then went to São Paulo and from there to Lins, 16 km (10 miles) outside the city, where he was entertained by a grandson of Emperor Meiji called Toshihiko Tarama, the owner of a coffee farm whom Mishima had known from his schooldays and whom he would later sketch unflatteringly in his play *The Termite Mound*. Then, on 23 February, Carnival began. Mishima was, throughout his life, entranced with the half-naked dancing and frenzy of the *mikoshi* (portable shrine)-pulling celebrations of festival days in Japan, but Carnival was this on an altogether epic scale: three days and nights of giving oneself up to the life force, the swirling waves of humanity in which every year great numbers of babies were said to be conceived. After three nights of dancing in clubs, on the final night Mishima pulled off his shirt and joined the crowds on the streets. Exposing his sunbaked torso, he threw himself into that sea and was never happier.

On 3 March he flew via Geneva to Paris, intending to stay a week before continuing his dance with Dionysus in Greece. But the gods had other ideas. Staying at the Hôtel Grand, he went onto the Champs-Elysées and met a man offering to change his u.s.-dollar traveller's cheques for 40 per cent better than the official rate of 350 francs. The inevitable happened. Mishima was taken to a back room, whereupon a whistle sounded, the man warned that it was unsafe, snatched the cheques and ran out. Mishima followed, but when he emerged outside, there was no one there. After reporting the matter to the Japanese Legation (there still being no Japanese Embassy at this time), a stop was put on the cheques, but it took a month before Mishima was reimbursed. Furious at the Legation for fobbing him off with diplomatic language and offering no real help, Mishima worried whether he would now be able to go to Greece after all. Effectively penniless, he moved to a boarding house called Botanya opposite the Opéra on Avenue Mozart, the only place prepared to take him on credit. The experience naturally coloured Mishima's experience of Paris and he spent much of his time indoors writing the play *Sunflowers at Night*, watching old people and children on the street outside and concluding that Paris must be a place where you go directly from childhood to old age. He recalled in an essay, 'Not Falling in Love with Paris', that he found Paris expensive and Parisians haughty; he had little success with the boys there, either. The only other lodger at the Botanya was the Japanese film director Keisuke Kinoshita, who introduced Mishima to the composer Toshiro Mayuzumi, then resident in Paris. Mishima – now darkly tanned and described by Mayuzumi as 'odd-looking' in his diary – immediately asked to be taken to a gay bar and was escorted to La Reine Blanche in Saint Germain. Once they got there, though, Mishima discovered that the boys were only interested in the French-speaking Mayuzumi (Mishima could speak English and German, but not French), much to Mishima's vexation.

On 18 April he flew to London and visited all the usual sights, as well as seeing productions of *Much Ado about Nothing* and *Billy*

Budd, before on 24 April finally arriving in the land he had always dreamed of: Greece. He stayed for a week in Athens, spending two hours on the marble seats of the Theatre of Dionysus and looking at the columns of the Temple of Zeus in the afternoon, and took a two-day trip to Delphi. He wrote: 'In my beloved Greece, I felt as if all day long I was drunk . . . Greece healed my self-hatred and loneliness and beckoned a Nietzschean-style "Will to Health".'[6] Mishima's embrace of Greek classicism had been an important development in his intellectual life even before the trip and was to have a lasting liberating influence. He recalled:

> In ancient Greece, there was no such thing as 'conscience', just the balance of body and intellect. The 'conscience' was a horrendous invention of Christianity . . .
>
> I found the conclusion of my leanings towards Classicism here. That's to say, making a beautiful work and making yourself into something beautiful are discoveries of the same ethical principles.[7]

Moving on to Italy, there was time to look at Guido Reni's pictures of *St Sebastian* in Rome's Palazzo dei Conservatori and to be moved by a sculpture of Hadrian's boy lover Antinous, the so-called 'Last Flower of Greece', at the Vatican Museum, before flying home on 10 May.

Returning to Tokyo, Mishima developed in a complex cluster of new directions. He resumed his association with Tokyo's gay community, but also now became obsessed with the idea of self-transformation, of turning himself by sheer willpower into the man he wished to be. This consisted of not only transforming himself physically, but also changing his style of writing.

First came the physical transformation. Mishima did not want to be a prematurely old, frail and pale author living in a cave; he wished to be a beautiful Antinous, and for this he needed a physique

In his study in the family house in Midorigaoka, 1953.

of which he could be proud. Having as an infant been completely shielded from the sun, the adult Mishima now made sunbathing part of his daily routine. Similarly, his first attempt to acquire an athlete's physique took the form of taking up swimming, an act of considerable symbolism given his childhood fear of the sea. Sadly this was an activity for which he seemed to have no natural talent (friends commented that he sank like a stone when he first went into a pool). It was only in September 1955 that he finally latched onto the perfect vehicle for his physical transformation. Having discovered bodybuilding by seeing pictures of Waseda University's Barbell Club in a weekly magazine, he visited the captain of the club and invited him to his house to help him train. The sessions continued three times a week for the next three years. Progress seems to have been agonizingly slow, but finally Mishima summoned the courage to train in public gyms and, after reading an article called 'What is Bodybuilding?' in the magazine *Only for Men* (*Dansei Senka*), started training at the gym. Finally, in the 1960s, he became a devotee of Tokyo's Korakuen gym, showing up there mid-afternoon, strutting and posing in his weightlifter's garb and delighting in being considered one of the boys. Mishima became so preoccupied with bodybuilding that the first thing he would do when arriving in a foreign city was find out where the gym was. He was utterly thrilled when asked in 1963 to pose for a photograph to be included under the entry 'Bodybuilding' for a new encyclopaedia and said it was the proudest day of his life (though he fretted that his legs would look weedy compared to his torso). Famously, on one occasion he even sent an editor instead of going himself to meet his friend, the influential translator and critic Donald Keene, at the airport in order to have time for a gym session instead.

Meanwhile, Mishima was attempting to transform his writing with an infusion of Greek classicism. *Forbidden Colours* had seen the ultimate defeat of the misanthropic old novelist and the

Working out at the Korakuen gym, May 1958.

triumph of the beautiful young man, whom Mishima was both enthralled by and desirous to turn himself into. But if Mishima could transform himself physically, then why not also his fictive universe? In his novel of 1954, *The Sound of Waves*, all the usual trademarks of grotesqueness, violence and perverted desires were banished. Instead we are in a fairy-tale world of young boy-meets-girl love on a Japanese island off the Mie coast. The story is exclusively heterosexual and has a happy ending, its most risqué moment being when the two young lovers strip off in front of one another by a fire in a cave, but vow, after exchanging a first kiss, that they will stay chaste until their wedding night. Mishima based the story on the second-century romance of Daphnis and Chloe, transforming the shepherd and shepherdess of Greece, raised together but feeling a naive love for one another, to a young fisherman and diving girl, on the island where her father is the richest man.

This was Mishima's attempt to reinvent himself by creating a Greek fairy tale on Japanese soil, imbued with optimism, normality and healthiness. Mishima conceived the idea for the novel early in 1953, when he enrolled for Greek classes at Tokyo University and said he saw Greece wherever he looked, but struggled to find a Greek idyll, an equivalent to the island of Lesbos, in a Japanese setting. His father, however, used his influence as a former director of the Fisheries Bureau and, after a number of expensive long-distance phone calls, ministry officials obligingly teed up a choice of two islands, one north and one south. Mishima plumped for the southern option, the island of Kamijima ('Deity Island'), 20 km (13 miles) off the Shima Peninsula in Mie Prefecture. Mishima first visited in March, throwing himself into the fishermen's daily routine, and received a huge welcome from the islanders, although as there were no hotels on the island he was forced to stay in a stinking house with a tin bath. Wishing to witness a storm on the island, in August he visited again, having been tipped off that a typhoon was on its way.

By autumn he had started writing and he completed the novel in April 1954. The book was published by Shinchosha in June and immediately broke all post-war records, going through 70 editions in the first three months. There was a scramble among three production companies – Shochiku, Toho and Daiei – for the film rights, to the extent that when one company heard that Mishima was shopping in a department store in Ginza, they paged him on the store announcement system. Both Shochiku and Daiei had already produced films of Mishima's novels, but Mishima left the decision with the Shinchosha president, who decided on Toho; by July they had rented the whole island of Kamijima for a three-week shoot. On 8 August Mishima boarded a night train from the resort of Atami, where he was writing, in order to see some filming on location. He was joined on the train by Toshiro Mayuzumi (his friend from Paris), who was writing the score, and eight journalists from all the major newspapers, who together all crossed to the island. The film was released in October, with a cast including the famous Toshiro Mifune as captain of a fishing boat, and was a great success. Indeed the novel has subsequently been filmed no less than four times. In January 1955 the novel won Mishima the inaugural Shinchosha Prize.

Notwithstanding the novel's massive popularity, *The Sound of Waves* seems irremediably bland and sanitized and leaves you longing for the return of Mishima's blood lust. Mishima himself was horrified at just how successful it was, later referring to it as 'that joke on the public', and remarked in 1963 that 'its popular success . . . threw icy water on my Greek fever'.[8] Attempting to create a fictive world that was the opposite – heterosexual, healthy, free of violent desires – of the world of his own experience was one thing; but Mishima soon felt a reaction against that, too, as if it risked turning him into an anodyne writer of popular romances.

Yet an important and easily missed aspect of *The Sound of Waves* was a subtle symbolism concerning the nation of Japan

On location for the filming of *The Sound of Waves*, August 1954.

itself. Following the end of the American occupation and the signing of the San Francisco Peace Treaty, the future course of a 'newly born Japan' was a subject of much topical interest. The young lovers of Mishima's novel bore, respectively, the characters for 'new' (*shin* in Shinji) and 'first' (*hatsu* in Hatsue) and seemed to represent a Japan that was attempting to find its place in the world by pulling out of the shadow of American dominance and reconnecting to traditional values. Mishima said that he chose the island because it was so lagging behind the modern world that it did not have a single bar or *pachinko* (Japanese pinball) parlour, but the island was also profoundly connected to the nearby Ise shrine in Mie, the most revered Shinto shrine in the country and an important link between the Japanese creation myths and the mystique of the imperial line. There was, then, a first hint here of Mishima's turning towards the sanctity of the imperial line as a means of reasserting Japanese values away from the overwhelming cultural and political influence of America. Indeed, at the climax of the novel, the young man, Shinji, proves his valour when his boat is assailed by a storm off Okinawa, a point laden with symbolism given that Japan was struggling at the time to wrestle back control of Okinawa, retained under American administration in the San Francisco Peace Treaty.[9]

Meanwhile, having started his physical transformation and experimented with a radically different style of novel, Mishima was attempting the trickiest task of all: asserting control of his sexual orientation. If it was the case that Mishima could turn himself through sheer will into his opposite, a being like the beautiful gay man Yuichi in *Forbidden Colours*, could he go one stage further and turn himself if he wanted into Shinji, a beautiful straight young man?

Mishima confessed to friends that he liked courting women – it was just the thought of sex with them he could not bear. His relationship with Mieko had remained platonic and when she called at the Mishima home she had noted the strong attachment between mother and son, with Shizue even sometimes accompanying them on their dates. Mishima, though, soon had an intriguing new female companion. In July 1954, he met – in the dressing room of the Kabuki actor Utaemon Nakamura at the Kabuki-za theatre – Sadako Toyoda, the nineteen-year-old daughter of the owners of a *ryotei* (exclusive, top-class restaurant) in the Akasaka government district of Tokyo. She had white skin, frail arms and a long, thin nose, and when Mishima met her the following week on the Ginza, he invited her to the Victoria coffee shop. He was to date her until May 1957. They went together to see Utaemon's Kabuki performances, to new films, French restaurants on the Ginza and Japanese restaurants in Shinbashi, before Mishima succeeded in bringing her to a *ryokan* near Shibuya. At first they tended to have dinner together and then went to a *ryokan* for love-making before inverting the pattern, presumably to fit in with Mishima's late-night writing habit, by first making love and then having dinner before proceeding to a nightclub. Descriptions of the trysts as they had happened in the afternoon, including detailed descriptions of Sadako's elegant kimonos, often found their way into that evening's manuscripts.

In a new twist to his relations with the opposite sex, however, whereas previously it had always been *his* impotence which had been the stumbling block, now Mishima discovered it was his new companion who was frigid. This appears to have entirely fascinated Mishima, and by January 1955 he had published a novel, *Sunken Waterfall*, where the subject of a woman's frigidity takes centre stage.

In this novel, the protagonist Noboru is the grandson of the founder of an electrical company for which he works as an engineer. He is popular with women but has never slept with a woman more than once. The first night he sleeps with Akiko he realizes that she is frigid. He and Akiko start dating, but Noboru is away over the winter working on the construction of a dam (the sexual symbolism of 'dams' and 'sunken waterfalls' was all too obvious) and Akiko is in Tokyo, so they communicate by letter and telephone. After the winter, they date for a year and Akiko's frigidity is overcome. However, what Noboru loved was the frigid Akiko: learning this, Akiko despairs and commits suicide.

While Mishima managed simultaneously to maintain the life of both a gay man and a straight man, he was also conducting yet more diversifications in his writing career, establishing himself as a first-rate dramatist in an extraordinary variety of genres. He would always refer to drama as his 'mistress' (he claimed to need to write one full-length play a year) while novel writing was always the stay-at-home wife, and his dramas were often written at dizzying speed in three-day marathon sessions in a room at the Imperial Hotel. Mishima had been attempting to write pieces for the stage since his early days at the Peers' School and some had been published in literary journals, but the first one that was actually performed was *Burning House*, based on a parable in the Lotus Sutra, in November 1948. This was performed at Tokyo's Mainichi Hall for a week from 24 February 1949 and was (yet again) due to an introduction from his friend Seiichi Yashiro. The result was a failure. In the programme, Mishima said that it was a drama depicting a family whose relationships were falling apart, intended as a microcosm of post-war society. But in the actual performance, there was no uniformity in the characters' words and actions and as a result the audience's attention was soon dissipated. Undaunted, in February 1950 Mishima himself directed his play *The Lighthouse*, though his direction was judged uninspired.

What provided a turning point was a production of Jean Anouilh's *Antigone* in Tokyo from 27–30 June 1949. This modern retelling of a Greek tragedy attracted much attention and as well as piquing Mishima's interest in Greek classicism, prompted him to attempt modern adaptations of classic Japanese theatre. Mishima was already a devotee of both Kabuki and Noh, having gone to the theatre 100 times between January 1942 and November 1947 alone, and he now utilized this rich depth of knowledge. His first adaptation of a Noh play was published in October 1950 and performed in December by the Bungaku-za, one of the five major repertory companies specializing in modern drama, which also produced his four-act play *Sunflowers at Night* in June 1953. His first masterpiece of modern Noh drama, though, was *Komachi at the Stupa* (*Sotoba Komachi*), published in January 1952 and performed the following month, while Mishima was away in Brazil.

Meanwhile, Mishima became friends with many of the younger members of the Bungaku-za troupe, including Hiroshi Akutagawa – an aspiring actor and theatre director and son of the famous Taisho-period writer Ryunosuke Akutagawa – and Takeo Matsuura, who was later to direct many of Mishima's plays. At the same time as writing modern Noh plays, through his friendship with Utaemon Nakamura, Mishima also started writing modern Kabuki plays. Utaemon was an *onnagata* (female impersonator) upon whom Mishima had first lavished praise in an article of February 1949, and in November 1951 he visited him in his green room while he was performing *The Loyal Retainers* (*Chushingura*). Mishima's first Kabuki play was commissioned by the theatre company Shochiku; it was an adaptation of the famous short story 'Hell Screen' by Ryunosuke Akutagawa and was first performed, with the same title, in December 1953.

His second Kabuki play, *The Sardine Seller's Love Net*, was Mishima's idea and also starred Utaemon. This was the comic story of a sardine seller who falls in love at first sight with a courtesan, who is in fact a princess who ten years earlier fled her castle after being attracted to the sardine seller's voice. It was based on a fairy tale, and despite being a new play, it took the format of traditional Kabuki seriously and has often been performed since Mishima's

With Utaemon Nakamura, 1956.

death. At the end of the play, the couple get married on a colourful, crowded stage, showing that, in contrast to the stark solitude of his Noh plays, Mishima could also achieve spectacle. Subsequently, at Utaemon's request, Mishima wrote a *buyo* (Japanese dance) drama called *Yayu*, performed in February 1955, and *Dew on the Hibiscus: A True Account of the Ouchi Family*, an adaptation of Racine's *Phèdre*, which was performed at the Kabuki-za in November 1955 and directed by Mishima. In May 1957 he recalled:

> I wrote *Hell Screen* half on a whim, and then with *The Sardine Seller's Love Net*, I got quite into it, but *A True Account of the Ouchi Family* I put absolutely everything into, and with that realized my limits. After that I got sick of it.[10]

In the early 1950s Mishima wrote another Kabuki play for Utaemon and in 1959 edited a photo collection of him, but subsequently their association petered out and Mishima turned to writing more modern, Western plays.

In the early 1950s, Mishima's ever-expanding social circles also gained him access to an exclusive literary clique when he was welcomed into the Potted Tree Group. This group counted the novelist (and son of the former prime minister) Kenichi Yoshida, the novelist Shohei Ooka, the translator, critic and director Tsuneari (also known as Kozon) Fukuda and the art historian Itsuji Yoshikawa, together with Mishima's friend Mitsuo Nakamura, among its members. It met once a month at one of the members' houses to discuss literature and would later publish the magazine *Voice* (*Koe,* October 1958 to January 1961). Mishima, however, appears always to have been an awkward, peripheral member of the group, for apart from his reluctance ever to get drunk, he also found it difficult to engage in light banter about literature.

By the mid-1950s, even before his 30th birthday, Mishima was a well-established celebrity with a considerable back catalogue of works. At the age of 28, he had become the youngest writer ever to have his *Collected Works* (in six volumes) published and was already

A meeting of the Potted Tree Group, January 1955. Right to left: Mishima, Kenichi Yoshida, Mitsuo Nakamura, Shohei Ooka, Itsuji Yoshikawa, Tsuneari Fukuda.

musing on the stages of his psychological development, publishing memoirs such as 'The Boy Who Wrote Poems' (August 1954) about earlier stages in his writing career, or pieces such as 'Radiguet's Death' (October 1953), which was both a description of Radiguet's death and a nod to his younger self, who had worshipped Radiguet. A play, *Young People, Resurrect Yourselves* (June 1954), describing the existential crises suffered by a group of law students at an aircraft factory in the days immediately before and after the end of the Second World War, allowed Mishima to reflect on his own experiences.

Yet how far away that must have seemed now! For Mishima was now a man of the new age. He looked like one of those fashionable young men racing around Rome on a Vespa in a Federico Fellini film. Sporting a crew cut and hiding behind dark glasses, he wore sports shirts open halfway to the waist, with a medallion or necklace on his hairy chest, and pointed black shoes on his feet. When a thief broke into his house and stole twelve of his suits, all the major newspapers covered the story. The media sometimes mocked him, but also begrudgingly recognized his genius.

Mishima had achieved so much in so many different genres by the age of 30, had already lived through two vastly different ages and had in his own person undergone major transformations. It seemed now, in the high noon of 1950s optimism, that anything was possible. If Japan itself could go from one type of society to another in the blink of an eye, then why not the individual, too? You could, it seemed, transform yourself into your complete opposite if you put your mind to it. Where once Mishima had laughed with a whimper, now it was replaced with a heroic roar of mirth that impressed all who heard it. In his serialized 'diary' of June 1955, Mishima even noted that Dazai would surely have been saved had he regularized his life through physical therapy and workouts.

But just as Mishima recoiled from the alternative fictional universe he had created in *The Sound of Waves*, so too inner voices

Mishima in 1955.

would remind him that all the transformations were in fact nothing but fake masks. The sickly, haunted, impotent Mishima still lived on beneath the brash exterior. For years, Mishima had been suffering from stomach cramps, and at the end of 1955 Toshiro Mayuzumi recalls that when staying with Mishima in a hotel in Atami, he suddenly heard agonized groans coming from the room next door. When he entered, Mishima was writhing on the bed pointing to a hypodermic needle, which Mayuzumi passed to him so he could inject himself with painkillers. The fear of sickness lurking beneath the muscles, the homosexuality beneath the heterosexuality, the perception of inner ugliness behind the facade of beauty, the longing for death in a land of peace, was not going to go away.

6

Nihil

By 1956, Mishima was untouchable, successful every time he put pen to paper and feted by critics and the public alike. Mishima could produce a stream of masterpieces in the space of two years that might take another writer a lifetime. He was the man of the moment, expertly surfing the currents of macro-time, making sure he kept in step with the age. And when the mood of the age changed, Mishima was quick to change with it. A classic example was provided in July 1955 when the future governor of Tokyo, Shintaro Ishihara, published a novel called *Season of the Sun*, which, with its descriptions of casual sex and violence, soon became a best-seller and won the prestigious Akutagawa prize. Ishihara was a mere 22 years old, eight years younger than Mishima, and in the vanguard of 'angry young men' literature. If Mishima wanted to keep his literary crown, it seemed he needed to move quickly with the times and come up with some 'angry young men' literature that was all his own.

Mishima's response was his literary novel of 1956, *The Temple of the Golden Pavilion*, serialized in the magazine *Shincho* from January to October and then immediately brought out as a book. A defining work of Japanese post-war literature, it was translated into a diversity of languages and is claimed by some critics as the very apogee of Mishima's art. As with several previous novels, Mishima took as his base material a real-life event: an arson attack on the Golden Pavilion in Kyoto some six years earlier,

With Shintaro
Ishihara, 1956.

on 2 July 1950. The Golden Pavilion, built by the shogun
Yoshimitsu (1358–1408), is an iconic piece of Japanese architecture:
sumptuous, painstakingly ornate and delicate. Mishima's model
for his angry young man was the perpetrator of the attack: a
stuttering, introvert monk at the temple called Hayashi. After
lugging a futon, clothing and a mosquito net from his room
and setting them alight inside the pavilion shortly before dawn,
Hayashi took fright and fled to the mountain behind the temple.
There he attempted suicide by stabbing himself in the chest with
a short sword and swallowing 100 sedative pills. However, he
was discovered by the police, survived and on 28 December 1950
was sentenced to seven years in jail. In prison, he periodically
suffered from paranoid delusions, refusing to eat and hearing
voices, and was put for spells into solitary confinement. In 1955
he was released but immediately transferred to a hospital, where,

racked with schizophrenia, anorexia and tuberculosis, he died on 7 March 1956.

Asked about his motives for the arson attack at his trial, Hayashi made many contradictory statements but noted:

> Seeing the crowds of visitors coming every day in search of the Golden Pavilion's beauty, I started to feel a strong resentment both against beauty and that social class. I felt that what the world thought beautiful was ugly, and yet I was unable to suppress a sense of jealousy towards that beauty . . . In the end, to find a resolution for my suffering self, I decided that I should move to actual action in the name of social revolution.[1]

His remarks fascinated the critic Hideo Kobayashi, who wrote an essay about the incident, seeing it as symbolic of an age where new freedoms had driven many Japanese to act in a wanton, unrestrained manner.

Mishima had read the essay and now minutely researched the details of Hayashi's upbringing and his statements at the court case, using them as background material for his novel. It describes the protagonist, now called Mizoguchi, from childhood until the day of the attack. Stung by criticism that some of his descriptions in *Sunken Waterfall* were inaccurate – even though he had gone to the trouble of visiting remote dam sites – Mishima did considerable fieldwork, flying to Osaka in November 1955 and taking a taxi to Kyoto to visit the temple where the Golden Pavilion had now been rebuilt. The temple refused to cooperate in any way but, undaunted, Mishima stayed at a *ryokan* near the Nanzenji temple before spending a night at another temple to observe the daily life of the monks. He also visited the town of Maizuru and desolate Cape Nario northeast of it where Hayashi had grown up. However, Mishima in no way felt obliged to be constrained by the factual details and he spread his creative wings, transforming his material into a convincing psychological portrait of how a monk could become so saturated in nihilism as to wish to destroy the Golden Pavilion.

For some critics, *The Temple of the Golden Pavilion* is a classic of twentieth-century fiction because it utilizes a contemporaneous social event to project a unique world view. If *Madame Bovary* is the classic analysis of post-Revolution French society, they argue, showing how romantic dreams and imagination have been crushed by reality and employing a naturalistic writing style to do so, here was the Japanese equivalent, embodying all the disturbing memories of war and guilt that still lurked in the post-war era.

First and foremost, though, this was intended as a novel about art itself. Discussing the novel with Hideo Kobayashi in November 1956, Mishima said:

Discussing *The Temple of the Golden Pavilion* with Hideo Kobayashi.

I wrote it with the intention of having a man obsessed by the
concept of beauty as a symbol for the artist. Some critics have
said that it's curious to have a novel about art where the
protagonist is a monk but that's just what I had in mind.[2]

Mishima invested in Mizoguchi many of his own characteristics,
including a vivid interior world of imagination. Where Mishima's
imagination had been fostered by being physically cut off from the
outside world as a child, for Mizoguchi it is his speech impediment
that distances him from the exterior world and causes him instead
to focus on the world inside his mind. But Mizoguchi doesn't just
wallow in imagery; his imagination assumes an ordered structure,
with the beauty of the unseen, fabulous Golden Pavilion, which
even in his country village he has heard about from his father, at
its apex.

When the power of the imagination is too strong, though,
it becomes impossible to live like a normal human being. For
Mizoguchi, the image of the Golden Pavilion reduces him to
impotence – an addition of Mishima's that had nothing to do
with the real perpetrator Hayashi, but everything to do with the
author himself. The novel is key to understanding Mishima at that
period, who was beginning to feel that his own fecund imagination
and addiction to words was itself cutting him off from life. The
more outpourings there were from the Mishima pen, the more
acute the problem was getting, and in later works such as *Sun and
Steel* (1968) he would argue that he found his life as a writer, the life
of words, an insufficient means to verify his sense of existence. He
needed something antithetical to words and the life of the mind,
a physical reality, to gain a true sense of self, and this was what he
sought to derive from such activities as bodybuilding.

Mishima's dislocation from life was most obviously manifested
in his impotence, but in 1956 his thoughts on this subject underwent
a revolution. Previously, in *Confessions of a Mask*, the narrator's

impotence with women was ascribed to latent homosexuality. But now, in *The Temple of the Golden Pavilion*, it is artistic imagination itself which is at the heart of impotence. Furthermore, as we have seen, Mishima had already set himself upon a course of achieving – by sheer strength of will – the life of a straight man who could normalize his relations with women. Briefly, in 1956, it appeared that this longed-for breakthrough had been achieved.

Mishima spent New Year's Day with his girlfriend Sadako and in March 1956 they went together to Kyoto and stayed at an exclusive *ryokan* in the Gion district, while he conducted yet more research for *The Temple of the Golden Pavilion*. They had now been dating for a year and a half, but it was only in the late spring that Sadako's frigidity appears to have finally been overcome. On 3 June, at past two o'clock in the morning, the phone rang at the home of the literary critic Takeo Okuno. An excited Mishima was on the line. Okuno recalls that 'he was quite drunk and gloating, repeating that he had been able to sexually satisfy a woman'.[3] This was hugely significant to Mishima, for it meant there was now no need to be crushed by the fear of impotence that had always assailed him. He had succeeded in becoming an 'ordinary' adult man at last. This might seem like a blessing, but soon the flip side of this development must have begun to dawn on him. If it was the case that a heaven-sent gift for art, an over-vivid imagination, was at the root of his ongoing crisis of identity and led to his suffering from nihilism and impotence, was it not also true that if the impotence was taken away he might risk losing his imaginative powers?

Mishima might feel bitterness towards his imagination for cutting him off from life, but that did not mean he was prepared to sacrifice his artistry for the sake of a normal life, any more than he was prepared to abandon his dark probing of the human psyche in favour of more 'healthy' romances like *The Sound of Waves*. As Mishima had already hinted in *Sunken Waterfall*, it was Sadako's very frigidity, her nihilistic core, which attracted him in the first place. Now that the frigidity was gone, after a brief period of euphoria, it must have sunk in that a 'normal' sexual relationship with a woman could be disastrous to him as an artist. In mid-August 1956 he wrote the final chapter of *The Temple of the Golden Pavilion* in the Atami Hotel where he was staying and then summoned Sadako. From a nearby tempura restaurant on a hill overlooking the sea they witnessed the eerie sight of brightly lit boats carrying out a Buddhist ritual to the spirits of the dead. Mishima immediately turned this experience into a short story, 'The Remembrance Boat' (*Segakibune*, October 1956), which illustrates his state of mind at the time. It is a dialogue between a father and child at a *ryokan* in Atami. The father is a famous author and, remembering the child's mother, who died six months after giving birth, speaks of their life together: 'It was such a happy life you can't imagine . . . Little by little I became infected, compromised with all human things and accepted all the world's conventions.' Yet, recognizing that such compromises are poison to an author, the story then closes with: 'It's a difficult thing to say, but it was a blessing to me that your mother died.'

Mishima must have already been turning over in his mind the idea that he might need to rub out the existence of the woman who had brought him happiness and forcefully tear off the mask – which had now started to become part of his true face – of the man who loved a woman. This was not just rejecting Sadako, but rejecting a part of himself, reverting to the face of an artist whose reason for existing lies in being aloof from ordinary happiness. Perhaps Mishima felt himself on the edge of drawing back from life once more, so that same month he sought out a means to forcibly assert his sense of existence and fulfilled a lifelong ambition when he joined the melee of local merchants carrying a huge *mikoshi* shrine on a festival day. The sight of this swirling tangle of half-naked bodies, which engulfed the individualism of each participant into the seemingly drunken swaying of the shrine, was something which had fascinated Mishima since childhood. Now, sporting his incipient muscularity (though he still looked thin in the photos) and decked out in loincloth, pristine white trousers, waistband, festival jacket and headband, he abandoned himself to the ecstasy of dissolution in the heaving crowd.

The following month, believing that the wall between him and physical sports had collapsed, he took up the most demanding sport of all: boxing. Yet despite employing the services of a well-known trainer, he proved hopeless and repeatedly took a beating. Mishima gave up the sport after a year, but nevertheless remained a boxing aficionado for the rest of his life.

Pulling the *mikoshi* at the Kumano shrine summer festival, 19 August 1956.

Mishima had probably already decided on a break from Sadako when he wrote 'The Remembrance Boat', but the day they actually broke up was 15 May 1957, when they went to see a dramatized version of *The Temple of the Golden Pavilion* at the Shinbashi Theatre in Tokyo. Mishima's family had always been staunchly opposed to his union with the daughter of a mere *ryotei* owner and by now Sadako too had various concerns about sharing a future with Mishima and so ended the relationship, though this was surely what Mishima was secretly hoping for.

Meanwhile, Mishima was producing quality work of extraordinary diversity at an incredible rate. In complete contrast to the high seriousness of *The Temple of the Golden Pavilion*, Mishima's light fiction offering for 1956 was *The Overlong Spring*, serialized in *Women's Club* between January and December 1956, concurrent with his literary novel. It satirically depicted a couple trying to see out their engagement without resorting to physical relations and was released as a film in May 1957. In April 1956, his *Modern Noh Plays* was published by Shinchosha and then at the end of November came the opening of his critically acclaimed play *The Hall of the Crying Deer* (*Rokumeikan*), a smash hit that initially toured for two years and has subsequently been performed by many dramatic groups, been turned into a film, had three television adaptations and even recently been turned into an opera.

The year 1957 saw Mishima still operating at full throttle. *The Temple of The Golden Pavilion* had sold even better than *The Sound of Waves*, shifting 155,000 copies in two months, and in January won the Yomiuri Prize, with Hideo Kobayashi lauding Mishima: 'Your talent is extremely excessive!' Meanwhile, *The Overlong Spring* nearly matched this success, selling 150,000 copies adorned with a cover over which Mishima himself had taken great care. From April to June Mishima published his light fiction, offering *The Wavering Virtue*, which dealt with a young wife's infidelity with a still-younger bachelor. When it was published as a book in June it became an

Mishima does a cameo in his own adaptation of Racine's *Britannicus*, 1957.

instant best-seller, selling 300,000 copies by the end of the year, and 'wavering' became a word of the moment as a euphemism for adultery – there was even gossip as to whether Mishima himself was having an adulterous affair. In October, a film of the book was released. Somehow or other in the dizzying explosion of creative energy that marked 1956–7, Mishima also found time to direct his own dance drama, *Orphée*, based on Cocteau's film; carry out a 'rhetorical rewrite' of Racine's *Britannicus* for a production in March 1957; write a stream of brilliant short stories and essays; be the judge for a new writing competition set up by *Chuo Koron* (*Central Review*); and direct one of his modern Noh plays. Mishima's own success seemed matched with the optimism in Japan itself as, in July 1956, an economic white paper declared that the age was no longer 'post-war' now that there was no more fear of starvation, the Korean War was over and the balance of trade was looking up.

Meanwhile, Mishima's fame spread abroad. In September 1956, an English translation of *The Sound of Waves* by Meredith Weatherby was published by Knopf in America. Despite being Mishima's least representative novel, it won wide acclaim, sold 10,000 copies and for a week hit the *New York Times* best-seller list. In July 1957, Knopf followed it up by publishing Donald Keene's translation of Mishima's *Modern Noh Plays*. In 1957 Mishima was aged only 32 and yet universally recognized as a major author. From November of that year until July 1959 Shinchosha published his *Selected Works* in nineteen volumes. Mishima took special interest and remarked:

> It is not an ordinary *Selected Works*: I wanted to make it an interesting edition. Not just a collection of works by me but one where you could gauge the background in the literary world and society in general at the time, so I have arranged the works in chronological order and tried to insert as much discussion and criticism of the works as possible, whether positive or negative.[4]

This was the type of thing an aged author might write looking back over the span of a long career.

After the break with Sadako, Mishima looked for a change of scene, and as Knopf were publishing the English translation of his *Modern Noh Plays* he was urged by Knopf's editor Harold Strauss to come over to America and promote it. Having brushed up his English with language tapes, Mishima set off on 9 July 1957, and after a few days in Waikiki and California (where he was taken to a Hollywood film set by Christopher Isherwood), gave a lecture on 'The Present State of the Japanese Literary Establishment' at Michigan University, before arriving in New York and staying at the top-class Gladstone Hotel on the east side of Park Avenue. Here, in the world's metropolis, Mishima's seemingly boundless success seemed to reach its zenith. There was a large launch party for *Five*

Modern Noh Plays and Mishima did the rounds of promotional interviews with Donald Keene. The book was favourably reviewed in the *New York Times Book Review*, and several producers contacted Keene about putting the plays on stage. Mishima, meanwhile, was feted with invitations, including yachting and cocktails in Connecticut with the rich young poet James Merrill; an evening at the publisher Alfred Knopf's estate in Purchase, New York; and being introduced to Tennessee Williams and the Rockefellers. He also frequented a gym on Times Square, saw eight Broadway shows and made several visits to the New York City Ballet.

Yes, Mishima might complain that a journalist at the *New York Times*, not quite knowing who he was, had enquired whether he was a dramatist or a novelist, and grumbled, 'What do you have to do to become famous in this city?'[5] But he was consoled by Keene that even if Faulkner and Hemingway walked arm-in-arm through Times Square, no one would recognize them. The grumblings and ego-soothings alone showed just how infinite was his ambition: it was surely only a matter of time before Mishima conquered Broadway in the same way as *The Hall of the Crying Deer* had run to rave reviews back home.

As for staging his Noh plays, Mishima was taken with a proposal for a long run at a small off-Broadway theatre from Keith Botsford, a man of diverse, eclectic interests. The wealthy scion of Italian aristocrats and the lifelong friend of Saul Bellow, he at the time worked for CBS Television with his colleague Charles ('Cheese') Schultz, a former football star at Princeton who also became a producer. Botsford was full of confidence that the show would open before Christmas. Mishima left them to it and in late August 1957 went travelling to Cuba, Puerto Rico, Haiti, the Dominican Republic, Mexico, New Mexico and Louisiana, looking forward to a period of relaxation and renewal. His travels were eventful: he went searching for voodoo in Haiti, came down with diarrhoea and fever, and absorbed Maya ruins and Mexican Independence Day celebrations. But in his absence things began to unravel in New York. As summer turned to autumn, the unstoppable steam train of success was suddenly derailed, leading to a chain of events that had significant consequences for the unfolding of the second half of Mishima's professional writing career.

When Mishima returned to New York on 2 October 1957 he expected that preparations for the play's opening would already be underway, but discovered instead that everything had stalled: Keene had nothing to report and there was stony silence from Botsford. Americans in the 1950s might be interested in Japan's traditional arts, but Noh was difficult even in Mishima's modernized renderings and finance for the production was not forthcoming. No main actors were cast and many female stars turned it down: Dolores del Río, the celebrated Mexican actress and former consort of Orson Welles, pulled out in mid-November. With Mishima back in town, some progress was made: a director, manager, stage designer and costume designer were hired and auditions started, with over a hundred young actors applying. Mishima was thrilled by all the beautiful girls and James Dean-like boys, but made his producers furious when he insisted on coming along to the auditions and offering advice.

Meanwhile, having expected to be back in Japan in October, Mishima started to run out of money and was forced to move to a cheap hotel, the Van Rensselaer in Greenwich Village (where he paid $4 a night compared to the $16 he had been paying at the Gladstone), and further economized by learning how to use the subway. He put his coat in for cleaning and stopped going out, staying cooped up in his cheap hotel room. Feeling betrayed, his relations with Botsford turned sour and in stark contrast to his intention for the trip – which was supposed to offer a relaxing change of scene – he dropped instead into a state of fretfulness and loneliness. He visited the expensive apartment of his former 'girlfriend' Mieko, whose husband was working for the Japanese foreign office at the UN. One of Japan's most eligible young women, she had married Wataru, the son of right-wing historian Kiyoshi Hiraizumi, who held that the emperor was the defining element in Japanese history. Now Mishima became good friends with Wataru and sat in their flat making preparations for his next novel, word-sketching New York.

Suddenly, everything seemed to be going wrong. Mishima had already talked up the forthcoming production of his plays, telling the *Tokyo Shinbun* that it would open in January and run for a month, so the lack of notices became a subject of gossip among the Japanese in the city. At a Japan Society party on 14 December he was repeatedly asked: 'When's the opening night?' Worse, at the party he ran into Kuniko, his first girlfriend, who had accompanied her husband and two small children to New York the previous summer. In a state of shock, Mishima frantically sought over the next few days to make sense of what he was doing in New York, questioning the producers about progress, but was told instead that negotiations with two actresses had fallen through and that sufficient backers for the production had still not yet been found.

On 21 December Mishima spent the day with Mitsuru Yoshida, the most senior surviving officer on the former Japanese flagship *Yamato*, sunk during its suicidal mission to defend Okinawa in 1945, as described in Yoshida's book *Requiem for the Battleship Yamato*. Yoshida was then working for the Bank of Japan and personally witnessed Mishima, after receiving news of the further postponement of his play, change all his flights for an immediate return to Japan. In the afternoon they visited Washington Irving's old home, Sunnyside, before Mishima took him in the evening to Mary's gay bar in Greenwich Village. That day Mishima told Yoshida three things: that he had a novel in mind he wished to start as soon as he got home; that he would soon build a house; and that he would be married in the next year.

On Christmas Day Mishima wrote to Tennessee Williams, expressing his regret that his play would not be produced in New York, and left on 31 December without saying a word to either Kuniko or Mieko. He went home via Madrid and Rome, spending a few days in each city, before arriving back on 10 January 1958. Lest he forget just what a success he was, he had upgraded all his flights to first class, stayed in the best hotels and indulged in retail therapy on Rome's Via Condotti. He arrived home just in time to see the final night of the triumphant second Tokyo run of *The Hall of the Crying Deer*. In Japan at least he was still a star.

Back in Japan, Mishima first wrote a three-act comedy play, *The Rose and the Pirate*, which he had promised to the Bungaku-za, before starting a major work, *Kyoko's House*, in March. In contrast to many of his previous works, this was not serialized in magazines but only released in book form, at the end of 1959. Mishima intended it as a monumental work that would garner even greater success and critical recognition than *The Temple of the Golden Pavilion*. He took his time over the piece, devoting himself to it until its completion on 29 June 1959 and recording in a serialized 'diary' both the discipline required to keep going with it and the exhilaration he felt when the writing was going well. Mishima's ambition was now not just to be a successful writer, someone who could move with the age, but rather to be a great writer, one who could transcend time and be its master rather than its slave. He had spoken of the constant strain of keeping up with the demands of Japanese journalism and how he would like to work in the fashion of a Western author, producing a major novel once every two or three years. Yet what he failed to compute sufficiently was that, with his previous novels, the process of serialization had enabled him to gauge the critical response early on. Now he took a considerable gamble by writing such a long novel and not releasing it until it was finished. Hubris got the better of him and the result was a major disappointment that would cast a considerable shadow.

Kyoko's House is set between April 1954 and April 1956, the end of the immediate 'post-war' era. The Korean War had finished in 1953 and, due to the end of special procurements, Japan suffered an immediate recession, but by 1955 things picked up and by the following year the economy was growing again. Yet Mishima's heroine, Kyoko, feels only nostalgia for the burned-out ashes of the post-war period, booting her husband and his dogs out of their home and opening it as a salon where young people can gather. These include a promising salaryman, a prize-winning modern painter, a handsome actor and a graduate who has become a professional boxer. Each seems successful in his own field but feels alienation from the age, and in the second part of the novel each one experiences an existential crisis. The central character of Kyoko (the name means 'mirror child' as she was meant to be the mirror of the age) was based on Atsuko Yuasa, one of the two sisters who had become so close to the Mishima family, and she did indeed have her own salon of admirers who gathered at her mansion in Shinagawa, taking advantage of an understanding second husband who did not interfere in his wife's socializing.

Mishima said that *Kyoko's House* was his 'nihilism research'. As with the undermining of life by artistic imagination in *The Temple of the Golden Pavilion*, the existential crisis of the artist Natsuo in *Kyoko's House* takes its starting point from the fact that, when a scene is being painted within Natsuo's mind, there is a swift process of dismantlement of the real world as he plunges into the infinite freedom of artistic transformation. But, as a consequence, the real world collapses around him, a result presented by Mishima as an intrinsic problem of art. In a newspaper interview of October 1959, Mishima said:

The subject [of the novel] is, in a word, 'nihilism'. I treated this to a certain extent in *The Temple of the Golden Pavilion*, but there it was concentrated in one person. This time I wanted to universalize it and describe an age. I had been thinking for a while that the spiritual situation of Europe at the beginning of the twentieth century is defined in this one word, *nihil*. Whether eating or smoking a cigarette on the street, their condition was ruled by nihilism . . . In Japan there wasn't such a big *nihil*, but I think that in the period described in the novel, from the end of the Korean War, the same thing happened.[6]

In other words, Mishima was attempting to fuse the existential crises of his characters with the spiritual situation of Europe at the beginning of the twentieth century and link it to Japan's situation after the end of the Korean War. Mishima's intention was that, whereas previously he had drawn individuals in his work, now he was 'drawing an all-encompassing mural of society'. As well as utilizing his experiences in New York, he also undertook considerable research for each of his characters, for example basing the boxer on Koji Ishihashi, who had in August 1957 become Japanese bantamweight champion, and employing his knowledge of the Japanese theatre scene in his depiction of the actor Osamu. But the result of all this careful effort was a critical fiasco and a work that would be appraised as Mishima's first big 'failure'.

The main problem, which Mishima would surely have detected if he had serialized the novel, was that his readership were simply not consumed with nihilism in the same way that he was, and depicting a central character who feels nostalgia for post-war ruins was not remotely in tune with the age. Only three years earlier, when he had published *The Temple of the Golden Pavilion*, people were still haunted by memories of the war and uneasy with the facile post-war revival, though even then the popularity of that novel was not because of Mishima's metaphorical delving into artistic angst but rather because readers were gripped by the psychological depiction of a real-life event. By 1959, Japan was in the midst of boom times and high-speed growth and readers were unable to see the link with an existential crisis in Europe at the beginning of the twentieth century.

What Mishima failed to clearly elucidate at the time, and which has only gradually come to light, is the sophistication of Mishima's symbolism and his historical analysis. As already seen, *The Sound of Waves* contains a subtle symbolism about the birth of a 'new Japan', and in *The Temple of the Golden Pavilion*, too, the Golden Pavilion can be read as a symbol of Japan itself – something which transcends historical time and for that very reason infuriates Hayashi for its failure to suffer the same miserable fate as the rest of the nation at the end of the war. At the climax of that novel, in the midst of arson, Mizoguchi attempts to gain access to the small, exquisitely decorated apex room known as the Kyukyokucho, but finds it locked (in reality, the actual arsonist Hayashi had been unable to gain access even to the first floor). In other words, Mishima seemed to be hinting that there was something 'untouchable' at the heart of Japanese culture, later clearly defined as the transcendent presence of the emperor.

In *Kyoko's House*, too, the arena of nihilism is created and then closed by the departure and subsequent return of a missing patriarch, Kyoko's husband. Opinions vary as to the precise meaning of this – the critic (and recent governor of Tokyo) Naoki Inose, for example, interprets the return of the patriarch as an allusion to the return to power in 1957 of Prime Minister Nobusuke Kishi, who had previously been arrested by the occupation regime as a Class A war criminal and was representative of the pre-occupation political elite. But more persuasive perhaps is the idea that Mishima intended the 'missing patriarch' to be a symbol of the absence of the 'emperor as deity' – the concept that was at the heart of all nationalist creeds before 1945. If Europe had been overwhelmed by a sense of nihilism in the late nineteenth century after Nietzsche proclaimed the 'Death of God', then Japan too,

Mishima seemed to be saying, was caught up in an existential vortex after the 'death' of its own god in 1946 following the emperor's public declaration of his humanity. According to Mishima, in Europe the nihilism engendered by the collapse in belief opened the door both to exhaustive Freudian self-analysis and to absolutist politics such as fascism, and he imagined similar gropings towards compensating creeds, whether those proclaiming the redeeming power of art or a lurch to extreme politics, in Japan. Mishima's message was that the immediate post-war period had offered freedom – a release from the oppressions of the previous order in the infinity of ruins. But with the end of 'post-war', suddenly a new socio-political order had taken shape, so the young protagonists of *Kyoko's House* all find themselves up against a 'wall' (one of the first images of the novel), a new order that was not only soulless but also, in its panderings to the impositions of the American occupation, hypocritical and fake.

Given the way in which *Kyoko's House* is saturated in nihilism, one can only conclude that something quite terrifying must have happened to Mishima in 1958. Indeed it had: he got married. Why, after breaking with Sadako in 1957, fearing that his imaginative powers were in peril, did he suddenly get married? One reason must have been that, having pulled out of that relationship, he experienced acute loneliness after six months of isolation in America that reached a peak with the accidental meeting with Kuniko. This persuaded him to put out feelers for an introduction to a suitable partner among his alumni at the Peers' School as soon as he returned to Japan. His father had been very ill while Mishima was away, and his mother was exhausted looking after him and now had a swollen thyroid gland that needed further tests. For his mother's sake, Mishima decided that a traditional arranged marriage (*omiai*) would be the best means of meeting a suitable girl and was soon inundated with applications, but he and his father rejected most of the candidates on the basis of their photos or CVs alone. He attracted love and hate in equal measure. There were countless young girls who were ardent fans of his books, but Mishima discounted them on the grounds that he did not want a woman interested in his work. On the other hand there were plenty of women who found him – with his now bulked-up, top-heavy torso, shaved head and domineering presence – physically repulsive.

Mishima was told about a girl at the University of the Sacred Heart called Michiko Shoda, the daughter of the president of Nisshin Seifun, a major food-manufacturing company. She was an excellent student, learning English, and also liked tennis, and Mishima met her casually at the Kabuki-za and then went with her to the first floor of a small, exclusive restaurant in Ginza. There were, however, already manoeuvrings for the girl to be wedded to another, and so Mishima did not take any further his romancing of the woman who is the current empress of Japan.

It was to be Atsuko Yuasa herself, the model for the central character in *Kyoko's House*, who was in March to inform Mishima of a promising candidate. The girl was Yoko Sugiyama, the eldest daughter of Yasushi Sugiyama (1909–1993), one of Japan's most famous traditional painters. Yoko was a 21-year-old college student – small and pretty, intelligent but not literary – who seemed to fulfil many of the criteria that Mishima was looking for. In an essay, 'My Arranged Marriage', he explained that he was seeking someone of

> marriageable age, without the slightest interest in literature; who likes housework; a kind and gentle, feminine person who would look after my parents; who even wearing high heels was shorter than me [Mishima was 164 cm/5 ft 4½ tall], a short girl with the round face I like; someone who would never interfere with my work, who would keep the house in good order, and by doing so indirectly support me.[7]

Mishima's mother's poor health speeded things along. She had a tumour and was advised to see a specialist as soon as possible. Two days later, Mishima accompanied her to a doctor, who initially smiled but immediately changed his attitude as soon as he saw her neck and called for his assistant. Together they felt her throat and pronounced on it in German – *gefahrlich* ('dangerous'), which Mishima understood but not his mother. The doctor then spoke to Mishima in private and told him that his mother had four months to live. As he rang to tell relatives, Mishima sobbed uncontrollably.

Shizue was hospitalized in early April and underwent an operation to remove the tumour on 1 May 1958. Mishima at least wished to give her peace of mind over the question of his marriage. He met Yoko for the first time on 13 April at the Ketel restaurant, with Atsuko in attendance. Afterwards he took her to another restaurant and then invited her to a nightclub, where he noted that her steps were clumsy while dancing and so approvingly concluded that she must have led a sheltered life. He took her home by car and the next day rang Atsuko, saying: 'It's looking good.' On 21 April he had a second date with Yoko, and Atsuko came along once more. On the day of Shizue's final test, Mishima declared he had made up his mind. Preparations for the wedding began to be made on 30 April. Ironically, the results of Shizue's operation the following day were that the tumour was benign. Hearing the news, Mishima screamed with delight, but his mother would later bewail the fact that, because of this, Mishima did not marry someone like his first girlfriend Kuniko or indeed Atsuko Yuasa instead.

On 5 May Mishima and Azusa invited the Sugiyamas to a Chinese restaurant and informed them of their intentions. Relations between the Sugiyamas and Hiraokas were rocky because both sides considered themselves to be doing the other a favour, and there was major conflict over Azusa's flat refusal to allow Yoko to continue her college studies. Mishima was brusque: 'I've started a 1,000-page book. Once I get into it, there's no way I'll be able to get

On his wedding
day, 1 June 1958.

married so I'd like to sort this out before I get too involved.'[8] On
9 May they were formally betrothed when Mishima and his father
paid the traditional husband's dowry.

At one point Yasushi Sugiyama asked Azusa if his son was a
homosexual and, having been told he was specifically getting
married to prove he wasn't, threatened to call off the wedding.
Yoko, though, was determined to go ahead. On 1 June the wedding
took place, with Kawabata and his wife acting as official match-
makers. There was a cocktail-party-style reception afterwards at
the International House in Tokyo, with guests free to wander into
the Japanese garden.

The happy couple departed on a honeymoon to Hakone, Atami, Kyoto, Osaka and Beppu, attracting press commotion wherever they went, particularly when they called in at Dai-ei Studios in Kyoto to watch Kon Ishikawa directing the film of *The Temple of the Golden Pavilion*. (The film, called *Conflagration* owing to the temple's protests, won a prize at the Venice Film Festival.) Mishima subsequently appeared to enjoy a warm and respectful relationship with his wife and included her on his trips abroad and evenings entertaining foreign friends. For the first eleven months of marriage they lived in the same house as Mishima's parents, but in January 1959, with Yoko now pregnant with their first child, Mishima declared he would build a new house for the whole family with a private wing for his parents. His younger brother Chiyuki, recently returned from four years with the Foreign Office in Rio de Janiero, attempted to dissuade him, fearing conflict between Mishima's wife and mother, but Mishima ignored him.

Explaining why he had married, Mishima referred to Kierkegaard's *Either/Or*:

> I gradually started to learn the life wisdom that to be truly free, you first have to shackle yourself.
>
> Get married and you will regret it. Don't get married and you'll regret it . . . I remember well the anecdote about how Flaubert in his later years would look at families pushing prams in the park and reminiscing, 'I too could have had such a life'.[9]

Mishima's new life would be symbolized by the house he was building, which he announced to the press, misleadingly, would be 'Victorian Colonial' in style, though it was better described as a fusion of Spanish and Italian influences: a two-storey white house overlooking a small garden with a sundial and a marble statue of Apollo. Mishima declared that if he had wanted a Japanese-style house, then the style of the Katsura Detached Palace in Kyoto could

At his newly built home in 1959.

not be surpassed, but that would hardly be comfortable. Instead he wanted a life of sitting on Rococo furniture in an Aloha shirt and jeans.

The house – designed in consultation with an irascible young architect and abstract painter called Yasuo Hokonohara, whom Mishima jokingly referred to as 'Emperor Hoko' – had no Japanese-style *tatami* mat rooms and visitors were not required, in usual Japanese fashion, to remove their shoes. Its combination dining-reception room was two storeys high, with a Louis XIV table and fourteen chairs, a variety of antiques (many of which Mishima bought in Madrid), miniatures and an ivory staircase. The upstairs

At his newly built home in 1959.

living room, containing a piano and a sofa adorned with Mishima's favourite stuffed lion doll from childhood, was used for cocktail parties and pre-dinner drinks. In 1965 Mishima added a third storey with a terrace looking out over Tokyo Bay and two completely modern, carpeted rooms with domed ceilings. One was decorated in sea blue, the other in scarlet, and they were used so the sexes could divide for a while after dinner. Mishima's parents, meanwhile, lived Japanese-style in a modest one-storey house with *tatami* rooms at right angles to the main house. They had two maids as well as their own Japanese garden and private entrance, though they were able to watch anyone approach the main house. It became Mishima's habit to drop in and see them every evening when he returned home.

Mishima had now created for himself a curious reproduction of his childhood set-up and found himself caught between the rivalries of his wife and mother, living separately but in close proximity, in the same way that he had once been subject to the emotional demands of his mother and grandmother. He remained a mummy's boy, referred to until his marriage as *boya*, or 'our boy' (confusingly, he was seldom referred to as 'Kimitake' by family and close friends, but using a different reading of the same characters was always called 'Koi-san' or the more familiar 'Ko-chan'). He also continued to show his mother all his manuscripts in progress and canvassed her opinion. Now, as then, he attempted to please both women and mollified his wife by acceding to her demands not to bring back to the house any friends whom she disliked and not to allow any interference in their private life from Shizue.

As a child, Mishima had reacted to the strain of an emotional tug of war between the two women in his life by retreating into his inner world of fantasy and imagination, but now he retreated into his austere writer's studio, a relatively small and spartan room with a metal desk piled with manuscripts, a low table and a couple of chairs, plus bookcases teeming with reference works, dictionaries, encyclopaedias and dozens of scrapbooks containing all his press clippings. The 8,000 books in his personal library were shelved in stacks across the hall from the study. Mishima's family started moving into the new house from April 1959, and Mishima now settled into the routine that he would maintain for the rest of his life: getting up at 1 p.m., looking at his mail over coffee, sunbathing for an hour or so, and then heading out to the gym to bodybuild or practise kendo, which he took up in earnest in late 1959 after an introduction to a *dojo* in the basement of the old occupation headquarters from the president of the Chuo Koron company. Late in the afternoon he would meet editors, have discussions with critics or attend rehearsals. He would rarely dine at home and did not usually return until 11 p.m., but would always be at work in his study by 1 a.m., when the night shift would begin.

Almost exactly one year after his wedding, on 2 June 1959, his daughter Noriko was born and in May 1962 his son Iichiro.

Mishima's lifestyle hardly seemed conducive to the rearing of children, and he could only spare a few days every month for them. From 1964 onwards he also spent every August with his wife and children at the Tokyu Hotel in the seaside resort of Shimoda, on the tip of the Izu Peninsula.

Mishima offered a modestly amusing assessment of himself as a newly married man, relating how he lorded it over his wife, dressed frivolously and feigned to have no interest in anything unless it was vulgar. He said he 'hardly ever read books' and was paying such attention to his health – by practising kendo and bodybuilding twice a week – that he hoped he would live to be 150. He remarked that he would hate to die of disease or the atomic bomb, though wouldn't mind being killed with a gun and thought about joining the SDF, but yet was not ready to die, even if the aesthetic of death was at the heart of all his books.[10] Meanwhile, he was busily engaged in rounds of drama productions (including a one-act Kabuki play, a dance drama and a Western play), essay writing, book reviews, *taidan* and group discussions. A weekly column he serialized between July 1958 and November 1959, called *Lectures on Unethical Education*, was turned into a film in December 1958, with himself saying a few words in both the prologue and epilogue; and over the space of four Saturday afternoons he dictated an entire book concerning his thoughts on myriad aspects of literary criticism.

Behind the scenes, while writing *Kyoko's House*, he also exhaustively read the works of the poet and literary anthropologist Shinobu Orikuchi (1887–1953), who had delved into the origins of Shinto, showing how it had been systematized in response to the introduction into Japan of Buddhism in the sixth century and investigating the original function of the emperor as a 'medium' communicating between gods and subjects. These ideas on Shinto spiritualism would be satirized in *Kyoko's House* (as indeed would Orikuchi himself in a later short story), but would come to have a significant bearing on Mishima's own concept of Japan and the emperor.

In 1959 he was commissioned by the state broadcaster NHK to write the love lyrics of a cantata, with music composed by Toshiro Mayuzumi, to celebrate the marriage of the crown prince to Michiko. On the actual wedding day, 10 April 1959, Mishima practised kendo in the garden. Having taken up a Japanese martial art that he had disliked as a boy (being put off by its group orientation and rowdy shouting), with his new bulked-up physique he now embraced it with a passion, saying that he realized that those shouts were the shouts of the true manly Japan of which the modern nation had become ashamed, that they represented the 'depth consciousness of the race'. In the afternoon he watched the wedding ceremony live on TV and like the rest of the nation was stunned when a young man – an opponent of the emperor system – ran up to the carriage of the crown prince and his bride and attempted to climb in. When the eyes of assailant and assailed met, Mishima described it as a moment of glittering drama more entrancing that anything in the ceremony itself.

In the space of two months in 1959, Mishima had moved home, celebrated an imperial wedding, had his first child and finished a major literary work. Had he found true happiness at last? Not if you read between the lines on any of the pages of *Kyoko's House*. Putting his own marriage to use in the form of the salaryman Seiichiro, who marries the deputy director's daughter, Mishima describes him as someone who thinks that his own marriage is something which has no connection to him. He soliloquizes:

Despite knowing that in the near future everything will be destroyed, why did you marry the daughter of the Deputy Chairman? . . . My completely numb daily life, my absurd existence starts now.

He sees his wife passed into the hands of a homosexual American man, a tacit admission that Yoko too would have to be prepared to tolerate Mishima's own discreet homosexual activities. 'I believe that a writer is ultimately never understood by his wife and that is fine by me', Mishima declared.[11]

Mishima seemed to be prepared to sacrifice his own life and marriage on the altar of art. He said:

> As a pelican is said to raise a child with its own blood, an artist atones for the existence of a work with his own blood. While bringing a work into existence, he actually is entrusting his existence to the work.[12]

So, in order to live, Mishima put his entire effort into the struggle with *Kyoko's House*, a child as precious to him as flesh-and-blood offspring. However, for the work to live, its import would have to be recognized by the readership: that was when Mishima would be able to reconfirm his sense of existence as a writer. But, although the sales were strong, with 150,000 copies sold in the first month, overall *Kyoko's House* was not critically celebrated. In the definitive year-end discussion of the novel published in *Bungakkai*, all five critics declared the novel a failure, complaining that its setting between 1954 and '56 was pointless and that all the characters were manifestations of parts of Mishima and schematized. The critic Jun Eto questioned whether he actually meant to reflect the outer world at all, as he was depicting his inner world. Mishima was stung by the criticism. In a *taidan* of 1968 with the film director Nagisa Oshima he said:

> With *Kyoko's House*, I'm ashamed to say, I really wanted to be understood by everyone. I was standing on a bridge about to throw a baby into the Imagawa River, expecting someone to stop me. But no one came to stop me. So, in despair, I thought,

ok, I'll throw the baby into the river and that'll be the end of it
. . . Although I was about to throw away the baby, nobody even
flinched. To say that sounds like I'm moaning, but that was my
acute feeling. After that I went completely crazy.[13]

Ominously, given that Mishima the artist had failed to achieve
verification of his existence, according to the divisions of his own
personality exemplified by the four characters in *Kyoko's House*,
this meant that Mishima would have to try one of the other
alternatives. Like Seiichiro, marriage did not bring fundamental
happiness, but represented a numb existence. He might follow
the path of the actor Osamu, first seeking self-verification in
bodybuilding and narcissism, then in the staged performance
of bloody death. Or else, like the boxer, he might be persuaded
to embrace right-wing extremism – calling for absolute faith in
the emperor, the outlawing of communism and rearmament –
as the means by which he could attain the rapture of death. Like
the boxer, he could don this mask not because he really believed
in any of these things, but because this was a convenient vehicle
that indulged fantasies of a glorious death. But, in the meantime,
he needed to write a big work to restore his reputation.

7

Seas of Controversy

The 1950s had marked a decade in which Mishima had attempted to transform himself physically, sexually and artistically. The inward looking, weedy homosexual of 1950, keen to give the public what it wanted, had been turned into the muscled, married writer, confidently at work on a broad social panorama, of 1959. But on all fronts Mishima had reached an impasse. Now that he had acquired a physical presence, he discovered that it was not enough to suppress existential angst. Marriage was not the final destination for his sexuality, but rather a trap, and his sexual odyssey needed to continue. *Kyoko's House*, his supposed 'social panorama', was widely hailed as a fake, nothing more than the projection of aspects of his own disturbing neuroses onto a variety of stereotypes. Where should he go from here?

Once more it was the pull of historical tides that provided the answer. In the spring and summer of 1960 Japan was overwhelmed by a storm of political tension as enormous mass protests were staged against the renewal of the 1952 Japan–U.S. Security Treaty. The treaty allowed for the stationing of U.S. bases on Japanese soil and many feared it might drag Japan into another war. Tens of thousands of students and workers were organized by left-wing activists and violent confrontations ensued with the police, yakuza thugs and right-wing extremists. Even after the treaty was finally ratified in June 1960, the rancorous divisions between left and right exposed by the treaty continued in the form of a wave of terrorist attacks. Mishima at first viewed this swirling melee of social and political ferment as a fascinated, disinterested observer. It was rather like the mass of riotous humanity he had witnessed in the *mikoshi*-pulling festivals as a child; but this terrifying sea of politicized humanity was beginning to call to him.

Before the final stage of chrysalis-into-fanatical-nationalist took place, though, came Mishima's emergence as an actor – one of the consequences of the critical failure of *Kyoko's House*. Mishima had already made various Hitchcockian stage appearances in his own plays, playing a gardener in *The Hall of the Crying Deer* and a soldier in his adaptation of Racine's *Britannicus*. He had appeared briefly in some films of his books and on stage in 1958 and 1959 in the year-end 'Literati Kabuki Play' (*bunshigeki*), with famous writers treading the boards, staged by the publishers Bungei Shunju. But he had never contemplated taking a lead part. The opportunity arose when Daiei Studios, who had agreed in October 1959 to make a film of Mishima's latest literary *Meisterwerk*, suddenly got cold feet after seeing *Kyoko's House*'s frosty critical reception. Instead, the Daiei chairman had the idea that Mishima should star in a film, to be released the following spring, and talked Mishima into it with a promise that he could play a yakuza. The press went wild, running headlines such as 'Introducing the Japanese Cocteau' (as the French director had himself recently starred in one of his own films). The only question was what the film should be about. Various scripts were rejected before it was agreed that he would appear in *Afraid to Die*, a gangster flick about a young punk (Mishima) recently released from prison after serving time for avenging the murder of his mobster boss father.

The role required that Mishima display both toughness and tenderness, and though putting on a front of machismo was his forte, he had trouble appearing loving to his female co-star. The fast-paced director Yasuzo Masumura, a contemporary of Mishima's at Tokyo University's Law Department, disgruntled that he had not been assigned a proper actor, felt unrestrained in expressing his frustration at Mishima's performance, demanding many retakes, and the whole experience soon became for Mishima both physically and mentally exhausting. To cap everything off, while filming the last scene at past midnight on 1 March at a department store in Sukiyabashi, Mishima, pressured to make his death scene look as realistic as possible, fell down the escalator and banged his head badly. There was little external injury, but he was admitted to hospital and his family stayed up all night nursing him before moving to a nearby hotel. Mishima remained at the hospital until he was discharged, still not fully recovered, nine days later. Filming was finally concluded, again past midnight, on 15 March. Mishima said to the press the next day that he had had his fill of appearing in films.

After all the effort, although the film was a talking point when released a week later, Mishima's performance was judged bland. He promoted the film enthusiastically, however, jazzing himself up in pinstripe suits and showing off his chest hair. More importantly, he remarked how appearing in a film offered the confirmation of existence he was looking for. Mishima said that he found that, paradoxically, he gained a stronger sense of existence by donning the masks provided by others, by being treated as a mere *objet*, than he did by expressing his own ideas on paper. Having often written the words spoken by actors, Mishima was now on the lookout for his own 'life script', a pre-written part that he could play and meld his angst-ridden identity into.

Mishima's first interaction with politics came in the seemingly innocuous form of his novel *After the Banquet*, which he started writing in November 1959 and which took ten months to finish. It was serialized in *Chuo Koron* between January and October 1960. A polished piece, it tells the story of an elderly, former statesman, Noguchi, who meets and marries the middle-aged, self-made owner of an exclusive *ryotei* called Kazu and then, with her help, runs for the governorship of Tokyo. Having 'failed' with *Kyoko's House*, this was Mishima's chance to reconfirm his position of pre-eminence as a writer and he was determined it would be a success. This time he was not 'writing blind' as he had done with *Kyoko's House,* but carefully monitored the novel's critical reception while it was serialized. And the reviews were good. Moreover, rather than wallowing in self-introspective nihilism, he employed all the tried and trusted elements that had made his works of 1956 so spectacularly successful. As with *The Temple of the Golden Pavilion*, he was basing his story on some real-life events from recent history and producing the type of political melodrama that had proved so wildly popular in *The Hall of the Crying Deer*. He added an analysis of nihilism only when the story firmly warranted it – after Noguchi had lost the election and Kazu closed her beloved *ryotei* – and resolved his heroine's crisis without resort to any blood and guts, but simply by reopening the restaurant that meant so much to her.

It seemed, then, that *After the Banquet* had all the ingredients for finely tuned success and would put Mishima's career firmly back on track. Unfortunately, however, this time another form of disaster was lurking in the wings and it was not the critics or the reading public who would cause it. What Mishima had failed to take into account was that, whereas with previous novels such as *The Age of Blue* and *The Temple of the Golden Pavilion* he was offering thinly disguised portraits of characters who had recently died, the person on whom the character of Noguchi was based was still very much alive. Moreover, Mishima had sketched unflattering portraits in *After the Banquet* of some of the most powerful conservative politicians in the country.

The central character Noguchi was based on Hachiro Arita (1884–1965), a foreign secretary back in 1936 who was subsequently reappointed in three more short-lived cabinets of the late 1930s. After the war he had devoted his efforts to defending the Peace Constitution and in 1953, as a widower of nearly 70, took as his third wife 47-year-old Terui Azegami (1906–1989), though their

association long pre-dated this. In 1955, Arita was put forward
by the Japanese Socialist Party as a candidate for the Tokyo
governorship and lost, but tried again in 1959. As in Mishima's
version, Azegami supported him in every way, selling one *ryotei*
and mortgaging her other *ryotei*, the Hannyaen, to raise election
funds. When she tried to sell the Hannyaen, pressure from the
very top of government, Prime Minister Kishi himself, caused
the negotiations to sell the restaurant to fail, and the conservative
establishment then used various underhanded methods (such as
anonymous documents relating to Azegami's colourful personal
history and posters about Arita being in a critical medical condition)
to ensure that he narrowly lost the election. Afterwards, saddled
with debts, the couple argued and finally divorced, but with help
from the conservative political establishment Azegami managed
to reopen the Hannyaen.

As ever, Mishima made a few alterations to the story where
it suited him (for example, having the couple marry shortly after
meeting), but the reading public had no trouble guessing who it
was about. Mishima took the trouble to visit Azegami beforehand
and read her own accounts of the election, but he had not directly
asked Arita's opinion. According to Mishima, he did receive from
Arita an autographed copy of a newly published book by him as
a sign of approval (this was a bone of contention at the trial, with
Arita denying he had ever sent it and the judge believing the former
cabinet minister, despite Mishima's lawyers actually producing the
book as evidence). Yet whatever the initial understanding, it was
surely not surprising that Arita would start to take offence when
he read not only descriptions of intimate bedroom scenes with
Azegami, but depictions of himself as the type of boor who
ultimately beat and kicked his wife. While it was being serialized,
he protested and made it very clear he did not want it released as
a book. Mishima, however, refused to give credence to Arita's
opinion, and after the serialization finished, Shinchosha published

it on 15 November 1960. The following year, on 15 March, both Mishima and Shinchosha were sued by Arita for invasion of privacy in the first case of its kind ever seen in Japan.

The legal proceedings were a disaster for Mishima, with far-reaching consequences. The case started on 20 April 1961 and ended in defeat for Mishima on 28 September 1964. What Arita was demanding – 1 million yen in compensation and a public printed apology – was a relatively minor matter, and the court ruled that Mishima should pay only 800,000 yen, without any need for a public apology. After Mishima appealed, the matter dragged on until eventually settled with Arita's family in November 1966 (following the old man's death in March 1965), with it finally being agreed that Mishima did not have to change a word of the novel.

But first and foremost, the proceedings meant that Mishima's big comeback novel ended up being regarded as a fiasco, eternally remembered not for its literary merit but in connection with the legal case it triggered and the trouble it brought the publishers. As well as placing a steady stream of psychological pressure on Mishima, the court case added to his sense of isolation by causing his ejection in November 1961 from the Potted Tree Group of artists. When the case started, the novelist Kenichi Yoshida, one of the mainstays of the Potted Tree Group, sided with Arita, who was friendly with Kenichi's father Shigeru Yoshida, the former prime minister (1946–7, 1948–54), who was himself depicted in *After the Banquet*. Before filing his suit, Arita had even requested, through Kenichi Yoshida, a meeting with Mishima, but had been haughtily turned down. Mishima was already seething in indignation at Yoshida *fils* for his savaging of *Kyoko's House*, when he had let slip that if this was the best Mishima could do, he should leave the Potted Tree Group.

Even more devastating in the long run was the fact that *After the Banquet* would ultimately, and for bizarre reasons, be the cause of

Mishima failing to win the Nobel Prize. Mishima had been concerned when the lawsuit started that the English translation of the novel, which had already been agreed with Knopf in America, would be cancelled and jumped for joy when informed by the translator, Donald Keene, that they were still happy to proceed. Mishima, meanwhile, petitioned Kawabata, as head of the PEN Club (the international writers' association) of Japan, asking that the club robustly support his right to freedom of speech during the trial. Kawabata was evasive but asked Mishima in return whether he would write a letter recommending the older writer for the Nobel Prize. This must surely have been mortifying for Mishima, given the fact that Kawabata had been so addled on sleeping pills over the previous two years that Mishima himself had mostly ghost-written his novel *The House of the Sleeping Beauties* (in a *taidan*, Mishima would cheekily refer to this as one of his 'favourite' Kawabata works; later he would secretly call Kawabata's most famous work, *Snow Country*, 'trashy patchwork'). Nevertheless, Mishima's recommendation would establish Kawabata as a firm rival to his glittering protégé when it came to the Nobel Committee deliberations in the late 1960s. In Sweden, where there was no expert in Japanese literature, the story goes that one member of the Swedish literati who had spent two weeks in Japan for a meeting of the PEN Club way back in 1957 now became an 'important adviser' to the Nobel Committee. The one book he had read by Mishima happened to be Keene's translation of *After the Banquet*, and seeing that it was about Noguchi, a candidate for the Reform Party, and the dirty tricks used against him by the conservatives, the 'expert' concluded that its author must be radically left wing. On account of this, at the height of the Cold War, the prize was awarded in 1968 to a writer of less controversial subjects such as traditional Japanese aesthetics: Yasunari Kawabata.

Comically absurd as it may now seem for the hapless Swede to have mistaken in 1968 an ultra-nationalist for a left-winger, back in the tumult of early 1960s politics in Japan, there would be many in Japan itself who would make the same error. Indeed the winter of 1960–61 would see Mishima implicitly involved in an incident heaping unspeakable insults on the imperial house, which led to him stalking his garden at night with a sword attempting to protect himself and his family from possible assassination attempts by *right-wing* extremists. The confusing swirl of mass protests and incendiary politics was starting to engulf the 'non-political' Mishima; we need to pick our way slowly through the melee, taking up the story in April 1960, shortly after the film *Afraid to Die* was released and when the political storm clouds finally broke.

Throughout 1960, political elements were beginning to creep more overtly into Mishima's writings, but at this stage they seemed little more than a backdrop to various unashamed manifestations of his sadomasochistic desires. As noted, Mishima later said that he 'threw the baby into the river' after the critical response to *Kyoko's House*. Previously, in all Mishima's works, there had been an ongoing battle with disturbing, barely suppressed desires that Mishima sought to control through the medium of writing itself. As an adolescent, he aspired to analyse his emotions coolly like Radiguet, or in *Confessions of a Mask* to structure all his experiences around the central theme of homosexuality. He could transform himself and mask these instincts entirely through embracing a 'healthy' Greek classicism in *The Sound of the Waves*, or create infinities of structured correspondence, as in *The Temple of the Golden Pavilion*. Even in the society-wide existential crisis of *Kyoko's House*, the artist recovers and does not sink into the nihilistic pit of the former boxer's embrace of extreme right-wing politics or the masochist actor's embrace of death.

But now, with the public rejection of *Kyoko's House*, Mishima seemed content to give free artistic rein to his sadomasochist desires. He justified this on intellectual grounds, arguing that when one has lost one's faith in God (or in Japan's case, lost the 'emperor as god'), one seeks out sensuality as a replacement. He returned to one of the seminal points of discovery of his own desires when he directed the Bungaku-za production of Wilde's *Salome*, which ran from 5 to 16 April 1960 with Kyoko Kishida in the lead role, and for which he personally designed the sets and costumes. In his private life, Mishima deepened his association with the seppuku (ritual suicide) expert Hiromichi Nakayasu and by October 1960 he published, under a pseudonym, a seppuku-porn story called 'Love's Punishment' in a supplement to the gay magazine *Adonis*. He also became attracted to the works of the French philosopher Georges Bataille (the 'Nietzsche of eroticism') and in 1960 reviewed the Japanese translation of Bataille's book *L'Érotisme*. But by far the most important manifestation of this new trend was his writing the short story 'Patriotism', which we shall return to shortly. In the meantime, however, came the long summer of political discontent.

Protests against the impending renewal of the U.S.–Japan Security Treaty by Prime Minister Kishi had been building since 1959. A new treaty was signed in Washington on 19 January 1960 and then submitted to the Japanese parliament for ratification on 5 February. On 19 May it was forced through a special committee out of a desire to hasten its progress through parliament ahead of President Eisenhower's scheduled visit to Japan on 19 June. Socialist Party MPs staging a sit-in protest were forcefully ejected by a combination of police and right-wingers mobilized as 'public secretaries'. The new treaty now had only one month to be debated by the upper chamber before being automatically accepted. Both press and public became concerned about the collapse of democracy, and demonstrators surrounded the parliament building, orchestrated by left-wing radical groups such as the nationwide union of students Zengakuren with the tacit support of the Soviet Embassy.

With the protests becoming ever more anti-government and anti-American in tone, Kishi dispatched the head of his 'Eisenhower welcoming committee' to meet Tokyo's gangland bosses secretly and recruit the manpower of over 20,000 yakuza and over 10,000 members of extreme right-wing organizations and furnished them with helicopters, trucks, vehicles, headquarters, rescue squads, food and 800 million yen ($2.3 million) in expenses. On 15 June the yakuza and right-wing thugs attacked the demonstrators, crushing a nineteen-year-old female student to death and leaving 1,000 injured. On 18 June, the final day before the treaty was automatically reinstated, hundreds of thousands of demonstrators besieged the prime minister's residence. Kishi, believing that, despite all the massive crowds swirling around him, he had the silent majority on his side, stayed inside the residence and allowed the treaty to automatically renew at midnight.

Three ex-prime ministers urged Kishi to resign and after Eisenhower's visit was cancelled, he finally did so on 23 June and was followed by his entire cabinet on 15 July. On both 15 and 18 June, Kishi had requested that the SDF be mobilized against the protestors, but the head of the Defence Agency refused. On 18 June, Kishi and his younger brother Eisaku Sato, the future prime minister at the time of the Mishima Incident, had resolved to kill themselves if necessary. Shortly before resigning, Kishi was attacked and suffered a near-fatal injury. On 12 October the chairman of the Socialist Party, Inejiro Asanuma, was stabbed to death by a seventeen-year-old member of the Great Japan Patriotic Party while delivering a speech. The genie of political violence had been let out of the bottle and was not going to go away; soon the political fanatics would have Mishima himself in their sights.

Mishima may, at the time, have been uninterested in politics per se, but all the political tumult was surely a factor in turning his mind to a major political upheaval in his childhood, the 26 February Incident in 1936, which was soon to dominate his thoughts and decisively turn him in the direction of ultra-nationalism. However, it was not politics but a minor episode that appealed to his now unfettered sadomasochistic instincts: Mishima got the idea for 'Patriotism', the first of a trilogy of works about this failed revolution, from *Seppuku* (1943), a book by Katsunori Wada. Wada's book briefly described the death of Lieutenant Kenkichi Aoshima and his wife, who killed themselves on the first night of the uprising fearing that Aoshima might be asked by the emperor to attack his rebellious army comrades the following morning. From this historical footnote Mishima manufactured a scene of eroticized seppuku that thrilled his imagination, but gradually he was to become increasingly engrossed in the historical significance of the incident himself. After all, if the mindset of the officers involved in the incident could produce exactly the kind of 'bliss' Mishima fantasized about, it was surely worth looking into this historical event in more detail.

At dawn on 26 February 1936, 21 officers leading nearly 1,500 soldiers attempted to overthrow the government by occupying key buildings south of the Imperial Palace in Tokyo. They attacked the prime minister's residence (located close to the Peers' School, where eleven-year-old Mishima was), and the prime minister only escaped with his life because he hid in a closet and the officers mistakenly killed his brother-in-law instead. Also targeted for assassination were six other powerful establishment figures, and the rebels managed to kill three of them, including two ex-prime ministers, who were shot in front of their families.

This was, however, a most unusual type of revolution. The officers were not attempting to seize power for themselves: rather they demanded a 'Showa Restoration'. The insurgents of 1936, disgruntled at political corruption, cuts in military funding and rural poverty, believed that their loyalty to the emperor would be recognized (they referred to themselves as 'His Majesty's Children') and that a new 'cleansed' government would be set up with the interests of the imperial nation, rather than corrupt factions, at its heart.

Yet, in a supreme irony, it was Emperor Hirohito himself who would have nothing to do with his most fervent worshippers. Furious that some of his most senior statesmen had been killed and that the Imperial Army had been embroiled in revolt, he demanded that the rebellious officers be treated as nothing more than mutineers. Many in the higher echelons of government and the army were secretly in sympathy with the rebels, and for two days advisers tried to dissuade Hirohito, but he would not budge and on 28 February reluctant troops were sent to surround the occupied zone. The officers now declared that if the emperor would send an imperial messenger asking them to lay down their arms they would do so and commit seppuku. Anxious to avoid a conflict between fellow army officers, the army's High Command urged Hirohito to acquiesce, but he again refused to do so, saying that the officers were no longer worthy to be called his subjects, that their atrocities were contrary to the code of *bushido*, the noble way of the samurai, and that they did not deserve such an honour. With that, the rebel officers announced that they would have no choice but to fight and let history judge their sincerity. On 29 February, after leaflets had been scattered from the sky demanding that the soldiers comply with the emperor's orders, the soldiers returned to their units and the officers were arrested. The army leadership, having seen that the rebellion had failed, now tried to rid themselves of the young officers as quickly as possible, advising them to commit suicide immediately. The officers refused and were instead tried in secret, with no defence lawyers or right of appeal. Fifteen officers were shot by firing squad that year and another two the following year, along with two civilians who were supposed to have provided the officers with their philosophical underpinning.

None of the incident itself is described in 'Patriotism'. Rather, Mishima attempted to capture the mindset of a couple who would be prepared to die together unflinchingly rather than be drawn into a conflict of loyalties. Whereas, in *Kyoko's House*, the boxer's transformation into a right-wing extremist is portrayed satirically, in 'Patriotism' irony is utterly absent. Everything is played out against a hanging scroll depicting two characters forming the word for 'absolute loyalty'. The lieutenant and his wife are depicted bowing to the emperor's portrait every morning and keeping fresh their shrine offerings to him. If Mishima fantasized about the same kind of death as the lieutenant in 'Patriotism', then slowly he would come to adopt the same belief system as a means of realizing that fantasy.

On 1 November 1960, Mishima set off on his third round-the-world trip, taking in Hawaii, North America, Portugal, Spain, France, England, Italy, Greece, Egypt, Pakistan, India and Hong Kong and not returning to Japan until 20 January 1961. This time he was travelling with Yoko, having promised her that this would be their long-overdue 'real' honeymoon. Highlights of the trip included visiting Disneyland in Los Angeles (which Mishima loved) and being introduced to Greta Garbo in New York, Jean Cocteau in Paris and the poet Stephen Spender and Arthur Waley (the famous translator of *The Tale of Genji* and other Japanese and Chinese classics) in London. In Rome, Mishima visited the sculptor Giovanni Aldini in his studio and, seeing him working on a replica of a statue of Apollo for the city of Rome, requested he make another one – which six months later Mishima installed in his garden in Japan. Mishima even had the pleasure in New York of seeing a production of some of his *Modern Noh Plays*, cancelling out some of the frustration he had felt about the failed production of 1957.

But by the time Mishima returned to Japan, he discovered he was at the centre of a storm of controversy. 'Patriotism' had been published in the January 1961 edition of *Shosetsu Chuo Koron* (a magazine specializing in fiction), although it was not this but another writer's story, published in the sister magazine *Chuo Koron* the previous month, that was to cause all the trouble. In contrast to Mishima's elegy to emperor worship, 'An Elegant

Dream' by Shichiro Fukazawa imagined a world in which a left-wing revolution has occurred and the emperor and empress have been executed. The narrator witnesses more decapitations of members of the imperial house, expressed by means of sentences such as: '[Princess] Michiko's head rolled along with a bumpity, bump, bump.' It naturally infuriated right-wingers and led to a campaign to bring down *Chuo Koron* and expel Fukazawa from Japan. Representatives of right-wing organizations visited the publisher and demanded a public apology, and helicopters hired by the Great Japan Patriotic Party dropped leaflets demanding that the publishers be tried by the people and sentenced to death. Even the Imperial Household Agency considered taking legal action, though informally it was decided that this would not succeed, so instead the chief editor was called to the agency to offer an apology. Meanwhile, on 30 January, a huge hate rally was organized by the Great Japan Patriotic Party and attended by over a thousand extremists, and two days later a youth attacked the home of the Chuo Koron company's president, Hoji Shimanaka. He was absent, but a maid was stabbed to death and his wife badly injured. Subsequently Fukazawa had to disappear from public view, resuming an itinerant lifestyle for four long years. Shimanaka, meanwhile, announced at a press conference that *Chuo Koron* had been wrong to publish the story and that the editor responsible had been dismissed.

Fukazawa had originally been a guitarist but had turned his hand to writing, and in 1956 his novel *The Tale of Narayama*, a folk tale about a mountain to which sons carried their aged mothers to die, won the inaugural *Chuo Koron* Literary Prize for New Writers. (The 1983 film version directed by Nagisa Oshima won the Palme d'Or at Cannes.) Mishima was a member of the judging committee that gave the prize to Fukazawa, and his praise for it subsequently turned it into a best-seller. As widely noted by the press, he had also collaborated with Fukazawa when, during the filming of *Afraid to Die*, he decided to sing the theme song and asked Fukazawa to set his lyrics to music and accompany him on the guitar. Now, in Mishima's absence, the rumour went around that it was Mishima who had recommended 'Elegant Dream' to the editors of *Chuo Koron*. As soon as Mishima returned to Japan he received death threats, including phone calls and letters which warned him to 'watch out for traffic accidents' and 'beware of fires', and after the Shimanaka Incident was assigned a police bodyguard who lived in his house and accompanied him everywhere until the middle of March.

Mishima bitterly resented that the publishers had not denied this rumour, which he believed was a ruse by Shimanaka to deflect attention away from himself. Mishima pointed out that a writer like Fukazawa who had already won the *Chuo Koron* prize hardly needed any recommendation to get his works published. However, Mishima was, as usual, not being entirely truthful. He had in fact read Fukazawa's story ahead of publication and suggested to an editor at *Chuo Koron* that it might be a good idea to publish 'Patriotism' and 'An Elegant Dream' in the same issue, presumably so that one could take the sting out of the other.

The effect of the Shimanaka Incident on Mishima was complex and difficult to disentangle. Despite his father Azusa's claim that Mishima 'enjoyed' all the excitement, other family members recalled that he had been terrified, with his younger brother even speculating that his drift into right-wing politics was partly motivated by a desire to overcome his fear of right-wing extremists. However, Mishima never forgave the established right-wing parties in Japan and refused all overtures from them, even after the formation of his private army in 1968. What this episode certainly did achieve, however, was to deepen Mishima's fascination both with contemporary political terrorism and with the events of the 26 February Incident.

His 1961 play *Out of Date* (*Toka no kiku*) started to make a link between the present-day world and the events of 1936 that increasingly absorbed Mishima's imagination. The play is set in 1952, sixteen years after the 26 February Incident, and is explicitly referred to by Mishima in the play as 'the year the Japan–U.S. Peace Treaty was put into effect'. The protagonist is a former finance minister who has been the target of assassination but narrowly managed to escape. He retires from public life, grows cacti and leads a purposeless existence, wishing that once more he could taste the terrifying glory of having a gun pointed at his head. But instead he carries on a desolate, corpse-like life in a world dedicated to peace. Written in the summer of 1961 to commemorate the 25th anniversary of the Bungaku-za theatrical company, the play ran from 29 November to 17 December and won the Yomiuri Drama Prize.

For Mishima, the focus was still on the nihilism of the individual and the inability to feel alive in a world where the thrill of death had been removed. But, little by little, the political turmoil in Japan and Mishima's ongoing contemplation of the 26 February Incident was nudging him in the direction of embracing the same values as the officers of 1936, seeing in political terrorism and direct action a means of transcending the anodyne sterility of post-war Japan. For the moment at least, however, the question of nihilism was still the primary concern. His novel *The Amusements of Beasts* (1961) was a psycho-sexual drama describing a dealer in porcelains who allows himself to be murdered by his wife and her lover. Mishima then took to reading Heidegger and being experimental, serializing in 1962 a science fiction novel, *Beautiful Star*, describing the confrontation between a family trying to achieve world peace and three men planning the destruction of mankind, though all turn out to be ruled by the souls of extraterrestrials. The novel was a culmination both of Mishima's longstanding interest in science fiction (Mishima read the novels of Arthur C. Clarke, wrote approvingly of the film *Godzilla* (1954) as a form of 'cultural critique' and even claimed to have spent evenings on his roof looking out for UFOs) and the worldwide angst about the threat of nuclear catastrophe. In commercial terms, however, *Beautiful Star* was a complete dud, selling only 20,000 copies – the lowest for any book he had ever written.

His literary novel *Silk and Insight* of 1964, based on the Silk Workers Dispute of 1954, won the Mainichi Prize, but was still regarded as a failure, with a total of only 18,000 copies published, a mere 12 per cent of the first-month sales of *Kyoko's House* only five years earlier. Notwithstanding that he was now earning $75,000 a year in royalties from his vast back catalogue, these were years of relative novelistic slump for Mishima. Although he was becoming increasingly popular abroad, Knopf would later pass on translating *Beautiful Star* and Mishima suffered the ultimate indignity of his new translator (and later biographer) John Nathan, whom he had courted in the hope of Nathan helping him win the Nobel Prize, refuse to translate *Silk and Insight* and go off to produce an English version of his arch rival Kenzaburo Oe's novel *A Personal Matter* instead. Mishima was mortified and never invited him to his home again. Worse, in 1966 Nathan would write an article in *Life* which remarked that 'reading Mishima was like going to an exhibition of glittering gold frames.' Although Mishima's potboilers aimed at the 'housewife' market still sold well, sales of his literary novels were only a fraction of his mid-1950s heyday, as students and young people now seemed to prefer reading the novels of Oe or Kobo Abe.

Mishima must have at least thought that he could rest on his dramatic laurels, completing in July 1961 a dramatization of Edogawa Ranpo's novel *Black Lizard*, and with a new production of his perennially popular *The Hall of the Crying Deer* opening in February 1962. But even his links with the theatrical world were about to undergo a revolution and an infusion of political strife. On 14 January 1963, the *Mainichi* newspaper carried the scoop that the Bungaku-za, the theatrical company with which Mishima had been associated for the last decade, was breaking up, with 29 of its 118 members, including many of its leading lights such as Hiroshi Akutagawa, heading off to form a new theatrical group. Despite his numerous collaborations with the Bungaku-za, none of the rebels had contacted Mishima beforehand and he only received a perfunctory invitation the day before the news broke. Mishima felt utterly betrayed and, fired up, put himself forward as a leader of a Bungaku-za revival, composing a three-point declaration of the group's aspirations. To demonstrate his commitment, he rewrote an existing translation of the play *Tosca* for a highly successful production in June 1962.

But the resurgence did not last long. In 1963 he penned *The Harp of Happiness*, a play written for Bungaku-za's New Year production. The play was, however, to bring the ailing Bungaku-za anything but happiness, embroiling them in another round of recriminations and splintering, this time led by Mishima himself.

The theme of the play was terrorism: police officer Katakiri finds out that terrorists are planning to derail a train on which the prime minister is due to travel and is sent by his superior, Matsumura, to the location, but the train is derailed and fatalities are incurred. Katakiri burns with anti-communist belief and is an ardent admirer of Matsumura, who has imbued him with this anti-communist sentiment, but little does he know that Matsumura is secretly a member of a radical wing of the Communist Party. Following Matsumura's instructions, Katakiri concludes that the ones who planned the incident were right-wingers, before Matsumura is arrested and the truth about him is revealed. Katakiri sinks into despair, finding solace only when he starts to hear the sound of a harp in his ear.

Many of the Bungaku-za, however, were both sympathetic to communist thought and, after a tour of China in autumn 1960, supporters of communist China; this, indeed, together with the unwieldy size of the company, had been a major cause of the break away from it. Rehearsals of *The Harp of Happiness* soon came to a standstill as members made requests that references to the 'Japan Communist Party' and 'Chinese Communist Party' be removed from the script. The national broadcaster NHK, learning of its content, turned it down for broadcast and the Workers' Theatrical Association, who had great influence on the ability to create audiences, denounced it. The Bungaku-za requested that the performance be postponed, but a disgusted Mishima insisted that it be cancelled altogether. Furious that, despite supposedly believing in 'art for art's sake', the Bungaku-za was rejecting the script for ideological reasons, Mishima said that he could not work with such a company and on 25 November resigned. Takeo Matsuura, who had often directed Mishima's plays, together with Mishima's old friend the dramatist Seiichi Yashiro, and a variety of actors, also walked out and in January 1964 formed the NLT (Neo-literature Theatre) Group. It was another devastating blow for the Bungaku-za.

The Harp of Happiness was finally performed from 7–30 May 1964 at the Nissay Theatre, where they were actively looking for a controversial work that would garner attention for the newly established theatre. But the play was not a success. The confrontational scenes lacked dynamism and the climax merely consisted of Matsumura stating his nihilistic ideas. The following year, Mishima wrote another play, *Love's Distant Sail*, to commemorate the first anniversary of the Nissay Theatre, but this was also a flop. Mishima the playwright seemed to be having no more success than Mishima the novelist.

Just to round things off, Mishima showed a considerable talent for suddenly cutting off personal friendships and in spring 1964 broke with his longstanding friend Toshiro Mayuzumi over a failed artistic project. The idea had been that they would write a three-act opera called *Minoko* together for the formal opening of the Nissay Theatre. Mishima had duly written the libretto, and went through it word by word with Mayuzumi and the theatre's manager, Keita Asari. But Mayuzumi, never having written an opera before, found it much harder than he imagined to compose the music and when he reached the agreed deadline begged for another month to finish it, despite an orchestra, chorus and singers having already been arranged. Mishima was furious and did not speak to him for another seven years. The opera *Minoko* was never performed.

To compensate, perhaps, for the fractious nature of many aspects of his professional life, Mishima became, by contrast, a host of lavish parties at his new home. Champagne and caviar were served by waiters in white gloves as Mishima sported a tuxedo and entertained with songs in English by the piano, tequila shots and high jinks. An 'Aloha Meet' in 1960, all the men were required to wear Aloha shirts and Mishima addressed the guests assembled around the statue of Apollo in his garden as 'the most beautiful ladies and gentlemen under heaven', before entertaining them with dancing to a popular singing trio. Or else there were cosy dinners for distinguished guests with Yoko serving up the finest French cuisine.

In the midst of a string of commercial failures in the early 1960s came one novel that, miraculously, succeeded: *The Sailor who Fell from Grace with the Sea* (September 1963). A sailor is looked up to as a hero, a man of the sea, by a young boy until he marries the boy's mother and attempts to leave the sea behind. Disillusioned by this, the boy and his friends plan a gruesome vivisection on the man. It was a comparatively short work, written with concentration in one go, and offered a modern reworking of many elements of the St Sebastian story that had always fascinated Mishima – the beautiful youth arriving mysteriously from the sea before being sacrificed in a sadomasochistic ritual. Yet now there was the new twist: the addition of an Oedipus complex. Mishima's own son was born in May 1962 and, if this novel was anything to go by, it seemed Mishima felt homicidal towards his own identity as a father.

Where once Mishima had written about alienated and rebellious young men, now he analysed protective patriarch figures. His literary novel of 1964, *Silk and Insight*, was originally going to be called *The Father of Japan* and was based on a workers' dispute at a silk factory some ten years earlier. It was serialized between January and October in the magazine *Gunzo* (*The Group*), with Mishima dividing his time between appearing in court over the *After the Banquet* privacy case, conducting research for the novel in Hikone and serializing another novel called *Music* in a women's magazine. In *Silk and Insight*, Komazawa, the owner of the silk factory, treats his employees like obedient children, providing them with money, lodgings and food, while believing he has the right to inspect their personal belongings. (In the real strike, the strikers put up placards such as 'Allow us the freedom to marry', 'Don't force religion on us' and 'Don't open our letters'.) Komazawa's business rivals plant a Heidegger-reading intellectual called Okano in order to incite a strike and the factory owner's 'insight' at the end of the novel, far from making him realize the error of his ways, is that the employees will finally come to see that their victory will only alienate them and leave them feeling lonely and distrustful. The novel was meant to represent the conflict between European individualism, represented by Okano, and traditional Japanese patriarchy, represented by Komazawa.

Mishima's unsparing analysis of patriarchs now inevitably fused with his longstanding interest in the nihilistic void created by the 'death of the emperor-as-god' as he moved towards becoming increasingly obsessed with the idea of the emperor as the ultimate compassionate father figure. By seeing the emperor as the ultimate father, Mishima could turn his back on the father and grandfather from whom he had always been so alienated, and reimagine historical time itself.

Having stepped, Apollo-like, out of the sea, that primeval Dionysian force, the hero must either return to the sea or give himself up to Bacchic dismemberment. For Mishima, the pressure was now on to blaze as a glorious Apollo, to produce one stupendous piece of art before he too returned to the sea. Growing old and seeing his artistic powers and physical prowess wilt was out of the question. All Mishima's thoughts now turned to the production of a monumental life work. He wrote:

> From 1960 onwards, I was thinking that I must eventually start writing a long, long, long novel. But however much I thought about it, I could not think of an epic novel with a completely different reason for existing than the big novels of Western Europe from the nineteenth century onwards. First and foremost I was sick of those chronicle-like novels that blindly pursue time. I wanted something where time would jump somewhere, where a separate time would fashion a separate narrative, and moreover everything would form a big circle. I wanted to write the 'world-explaining' novel I had continued to think about since becoming a novelist.[1]

His quest focused on to how to produce a massive novel that could transcend time and get to the very heart of the nature of existence. He had been thinking about it for years, had discussed it with his editor Hiroshi Nitta since 1963 and now in March 1965 announced to the press that he would next write a novel that would be 3,000 pages long and take six years to write. Serialization of the first part, *Spring Snow*, would start in September.

If the process of writing fuelled Mishima's existential crisis and cut him off from the reality of the world, then what he was about to attempt was suicide. The only way in which he could see himself through to the end would be by employing all those methods in his private life that fostered a sense of existence: acting out roles, indulging his sadomasochistic desires, finding something to believe in. If life was to be unflinchingly sacrificed on the altar of art, then the extreme artistic project onto which he was now embarking would demand that his own personal life be driven in extreme directions.

The first indication of this came in January 1965, when Mishima brought the idea of a film of 'Patriotism', with Mishima himself acting out his fantasy death, to old acquaintances Masaki Domoto, an avant-garde director and expert on Noh, and a producer at Dai-ei Studios called Hiroaki Fujii. The resultant 28-minute, 35-mm film in black and white had no dialogue but, acting on the advice of the film critic Donald Richie, used as a soundtrack the 'Leibestod' from Wagner's *Tristan and Isolde*. Mishima's dedication to the film was absolute: he walked the cold winter streets of Tokyo looking for uniforms and hats of the time; interviewed in a hotel lobby the actress who would play the lieutenant's wife Reiko; purchased the China figurines Reiko leaves as mementoes to friends; wrote the calligraphy for the scroll against which the action plays out; and personally wrote the subtitles in Japanese, English, German and French. In April Mishima borrowed the Okura Film Studios and filmed 'Patriotism' in two days at a cost of 1.25 million yen. Mishima played the lieutenant, with Domoto stage managing.

Mishima revealed nothing to the Japanese media, fearing that they would dismiss it as another Mishima stunt, and instead arranged for it to be shown at a private screening at the Palais de Chaillot in Paris in September 1965, one of his stops on his latest round-the-world trip (5 September–31 October). The film was cheered and Mishima was exultant, inviting everyone back to his hotel for champagne. In January the following year it was shown at the International Short Film Festival in Tours, France, where it came second but caused a big stir and, after months of tabloid frenzy in Japan, from 12 April was shown in two arthouse cinemas in Tokyo. It created a sensation as pigs' intestines were used for the seppuku scene and was so realistic that it caused some of the audience, in both France and Japan, to faint. In Tokyo, 2,332 people viewed it on the first day, a record midweek opening day for the two arts theatres.

What meaning did the film have for Mishima? For him, the whole thing was

> a religious ritual, the ritual of live sacrifice . . . resembling the magical rites of elevation, destruction and rebirth . . . from the instincts and fear that makes you want to cover your eyes, the viewer will together with the protagonist be reborn with the re-emergence of anti-civilization-like reality.[2]

Mishima decided that the title of the English version of the film would be *The Rite of Love and Death*, and the film indicated that his masochistic instincts were best realized not by words but physically, a development which would now lead him inexorably down the path to his own rite of love and death in 1970. By acting out the role himself he could become the mere *objet* he had mentioned with relation to his performance in *Afraid to Die*. Becoming an *objet* meant donning a mask, allowing one's impulses to be freely released, and he experienced a fierce sense of existence that expunged his nihilism. With this, Mishima found the energy to set to work on *The Sea of Fertility*.

Yet still there was time for diversions, social and professional. As well as being a prolific newspaper correspondent at the Tokyo Olympics of 1964 (Mishima noted in a letter to Keene that if literature gave out medals, he would clearly win gold[3]), Mishima also started learning French in the spring of 1965 for the specific purpose of translating Gabriele D'Annunzio's play *Le Martyre de saint Sébastien*, employing a young student of French to work with him on the endeavour and publishing it in the members-only quarterly *Criticism* before bringing out a deluxe edition, adorned with 50 pictures of St Sebastian from his huge collection.

Mishima's journeys to the West were also frequent. He had made a ten-day trip to New York in the summer of 1964, where he was reported to have been specifically on the lookout for gay sex,[4] and in March 1965 accepted an invitation from the British Council to visit the UK and met his publisher Peter Owen as well as his friend the Japanologist Ivan Morris. While in England, Mishima was a private lunch guest at the home of Margot Fonteyn, met Edna O'Brien and stayed with Angus Wilson. Later on in 1965, when he returned to Paris as part of his world tour with Yoko, he was treated royally by the publishers Gallimard, about to bring out the French translation of *After the Banquet*, and the Rothschilds. The trip also took in promoting the English translation of *The Sailor who Fell from Grace with the Sea* in New York and a trip to Stockholm, perhaps in anticipation of a forthcoming Nobel Prize announcement, before continuing to the ultimate destinations of Bangkok and Cambodia.

Mishima had meanwhile become friendly with a younger generation of avant-garde artists such as Eiko Hosoe (1933–), who photographed him against a variety of backdrops between 1961 and 1962 for the collection *Punishment by Roses* (1963), and befriended the painter Tadanori Yokoo (1936–) and the poet Mutsuo Takahashi (1937–). Among them, the French literature scholar and novelist Tatsuhiko Shibusawa (1928–1987) inspired Mishima to write *Madame de Sade* (November 1965), widely regarded as his greatest dramatic masterpiece. Mishima had first met Shibusawa in 1956, though had already been requested by him to write the introduction to his *Selected Works of the Marquis de Sade*. In the introduction to his play, Mishima wrote:

I read Tatsuhiko Shibusawa's *Life of the Marquis de Sade* with interest. What excited my novelistic interest the most was the enigma that despite Madame de Sade staying so chaste and being completely devoted to her husband while he was in prison, when Sade as an old man was freed for the first time, why did she suddenly separate from him? This play took this enigma as its starting point and attempted a logical explanation of this mystery.[5]

The play was performed from 14 to 29 November 1965 by NLT at the Kinokuniya Hall with Takeo Matsuura directing. In this play, the Marquis de Sade does not appear. Rather, it is through the words of his wife and the other women connected to him that the darkness of Sade the artist's interior life is revealed. The play was a major success and indeed in the inaugural edition of *Theatre Arts* in 1994, the play was chosen by critics as the best post-war drama.

The sheer fecundity of Mishima's artistic outpourings meant that, for all the failures, he could still produce in a five-year period masterpieces in the short story, novel and drama genre such as 'Patriotism', *The Sailor who Fell from Grace with the Sea* and *Madame de Sade*. But all these achievements were about to be eclipsed by the final act of Mishima's life and the production of an epic 'world-explaining novel' that would claim in blood sacrifice its author's own life.

8

The Faustian Pact

At the beginning of *The Decay of the Angel*, the final volume of *The Sea of Fertility* and the last novel Mishima ever wrote, we are transported to a world of ever-evolving seascapes. For page after page, there are descriptions of the sea and the sky, sometimes cloudy, sometimes clear, sometimes calm, sometimes windy, with a flickering of boats that come briefly into view and then disappear and then for long periods the sea, the embodiment of the cosmos, is simply empty, beyond time, devoid of all human life whatsoever. It is an extraordinary literary tour de force, perhaps only achievable by a writer who has known great fame and crushing disappointment, acted a variety of roles, been buffeted by the winds of history and tormented by existential angst – and who displays the very rare ability possessed by only the greatest artists to describe seemingly nothing and through it represent everything.

With *The Sea of Fertility*, Mishima's ambition was so vast that he quickly left many critics' understandings trailing in his wake. The novel is comprised of four parts, spanning 60 years from 1912 to 1975. The narrative leaps forward by jumps of twenty years into radically different historical periods, each time discovering a protagonist who seems to be a reincarnation of the protagonist from the previous part. Each one is fated to die at the peak of youth, at the age of twenty.

Everything about *The Sea of Fertility* was different. For one thing, Mishima's usual practice with a novel was to decide on the final line and work out the entire structure before starting to write. Indeed for the first two volumes this practice seems to have been followed, with Mishima filling over twenty notebooks with jottings on how the plot would proceed. In volume three Mishima was faced with the problem of how to work Buddhist ideas about reincarnation into the plot so as to lend the whole work profundity, but, exceptionally for Mishima, volume four was a blank slate, the plot left deliberately open.

Chikako Kojima, the editor at Shinchosha assigned to Mishima and the person who would call to collect the final manuscript on the day of his death, recalled him saying evasively: 'I've deliberately decided to leave volume four open because I want to insert all the contemporary vogues at the time of writing'.[1] However, the critic Takeshi Muramatsu recalled a conversation before he started writing in which Mishima declared that volume one would be about the Meiji period, volume two the right wing in the Showa period and volume three about a Thai princess, and that the three protagonists would all be reincarnations of the same person. 'What about volume four?' Muramatsu asked. 'Volume four will be the future,' Mishima initially responded. But by the autumn of 1967, Mishima's answer to the same question had been revised to: 'it will be the anti-Security Treaty riots of 1970; I'll die with a sword in my hand.'[2]

From the beginning, Mishima equated the conclusion of his life's work with a bloody and heroic finale to his own life. Urgency had always been a spur to Mishima's creative talent: his early writings were fuelled by the knowledge that he would probably die by the end of the war. Unfortunately there was no convenient war scheduled for Japan in 1970, even if times were troubled and turbulent, so Mishima needed action, an emergency, and if he could not find an emergency naturally, then he would engineer one, an emergency that would end his life in a blaze of glory, as spectacular as any he had written for the stage. For his life work, he needed a 'deadline' in the fullest sense of the word.

What emerged was an elaborate simultaneous plan. First he had to discover the key to his masterwork and found it in reincarnation. Then he had to find the key to the final action of his physical life and found it in an idealized version of emperor worship. His life now bifurcated into the life of his artistic masterpiece and his life in the 'real world'. Within the world of that masterwork, there would be no foolish politicking, no distortions, only the diamond absolutes of pure art. Outside that world, 'reality' became a matter of play acting, a constant provider of energy for his marathon literary outpourings.

For Mishima, the greatest reality had always been the world of the imagination, and it was precisely this that stoked his lifelong existential crisis and forced him to seek out 'real world' activities that gave him a sense of physical substance. Previously this had been bodybuilding, boxing, kendo and acting; now that Mishima had subsumed himself in an overwhelming artistic project, his quest for a sense of reality was rendered all the more acute, and he increasingly sought to embrace extreme politics, the life of a soldier and the quest for a glorious martial death. Mishima had made a Faustian pact in which he was prepared to give up his fragile hold on existence in exchange for writing a book of books, a book about everything, a 'world-explaining novel', a book that would conquer time itself. As he steadily turned himself over to it, he would do whatever was required in his 'other life' to keep feeling alive and keep going with his masterwork.

First, though, was the question of how to make *The Sea of Fertility* different to any book that had previously been written and overcome the practical problem of transcending historical time in a naturalistic way. The answer was to adopt the Buddhist theory of *yuishiki*, which teaches that all existence is nothing but illusions produced by the consciousness. In recounting his artistic methodology, Mishima observed:

> Fortunately I am Japanese and had, close at hand, the concept of reincarnation. But the concepts of reincarnation which I knew were extremely basic ones, so I had to study numerous Buddhist books.[3]

Mishima had initially been influenced by *The Story of the Hamamatsu Chunagon*, included in the 'Compendium of Japanese Classic Literature 77' published in 1964 and annotated by Satoshi Matsuo, one of his teachers from the Peers' School, who had requested that Mishima write an article about it. This late Heian love story describes a courtier learning in a dream that his father has been reincarnated as a son of the emperor of China and crossing to China in search of him. Many elements from the plot would be borrowed for *The Sea of Fertility*, together with the premonitory power of dreams.

However, the book which most influenced Mishima was Seibun Fukaura's *Outline of Reincarnation*, a pamphlet of less than 100 pages, which explained how the theory of *yuishiki* denied the existence of a 'soul' and yet, following the traditions of India, had accepted the concept of reincarnation. So, what was it that was being reincarnated? The theory divided the mind into eight layers, the five senses plus consciousness, added to which were the 'depth psychologies' of *manashiki* and *arayashiki* ('alaya consciousness'), and argued that it was the last which contained the 'karmic seeds' for all the objects in the world. What was being reincarnated then was 'alaya consciousness', constantly being born and destroyed in the depths of consciousness.

Mishima was also influenced by a book by Yoshifumi Ueda called *The Concept of Karma in Buddhism*, which explained that while the world was an illusion created in the depths of consciousness, this illusion itself produced new karmic seeds and with each passing second both the illusory world and alaya consciousness were being simultaneously created and destroyed in an infinity of 'reincarnations'. Time, in other words, was not something which actually existed independently in the outer world, but something created in the individual consciousness.

Meanwhile, there was Mishima's life in the 'real' world. Mishima started writing *Spring Snow* in June 1965 and finished it on 25 November 1966. He then immediately started volume two, *Runaway Horses*, and finished it on 23 May 1968. On 1 July he started *The Temple of Dawn*. Mishima's literary outpourings were not confined to *The Sea of Fertility*, however, and many of the other works that Mishima produced in his final five years were concerned with bolstering the ego-asserting agenda of his 'real world' persona. The first was *Sun and Steel*, serialized in ten instalments between November 1965 and June 1968, and is Mishima's lament against the oppression and unreality of words. He recounts how, since childhood, he has lacked a physical sense of existence and has come to feel the need to assert reality over words and flesh over spirit. He asks why it is we attempt to express in words what cannot be expressed in words and holds the reader guilty as an accomplice in a crime that causes reality to be distorted. Here, as in *The Temple of the Golden Pavilion*, it is imagination that destroys life, but this is now expanded to the general problem of imagination, including that of all readers. Only through the mediation of the sun and 'steel' (bodybuilding weights and swords) has Mishima learned the 'language of the body'.

Sun and Steel was preparing the ground for an embrace of a political cause that would provide the firm sense of 'reality' that words could never offer. The first overt representation of the newly politicized Mishima came in June 1966 with the short story 'Voices of the Heroic Dead'. The narrator attends a Shinto ceremony of spiritual possession and faithfully records the words of the spirits

Mishima
practising karate
in 1966.

of the officers executed after the 26 February Incident and the
tokkotai (suicide mission) units during the war. The spirits bewail
the materialistic degeneracy of post-war Japan and the fact that,
although they acted out of the purest devotion to the emperor,
he did not recognize them. Worse, the emperor's declaration of
humanity in January 1946 has rendered their deaths meaningless.
Mishima told his mother that he composed this piece in a hotel
room in one night, writing like a man possessed, as if the spirits of
the 26 February officers were speaking directly to him and he could
not stop writing even if he wanted.

By eerie coincidence, just before 'Voices of the Heroic Dead' was
published, Mishima was approached by one of the senior members

of his *dojo* and asked to look over his unpublished 1,200-page manuscript called 'Screams of the Heroic Dead'. Ordinarily Mishima would brush off such requests, but taken aback by the title's striking similarity to his own manuscript, he not only took it home and read it, but edited it down to a third of its original length and helped arrange for its publication, adding his own preface. The author, Hiroshi Funasaka, a tough kendo devotee who had never written a book before, was the owner of a bookshop that Mishima had frequented since childhood and a veteran of the Battle of Angaur, a tiny island on the Palau Archipelago, which in 1944 had seen 1,250 out of 1,286 Japanese defenders killed. He had compiled 3,000 pages of notes from interviews with surviving families and written his book as a testament to the nightmarish experiences of the many thousands of Japanese killed in the strategically insignificant battles of the South Pacific.

Ominously, as a thank-you to Mishima for his editing and for promoting his manuscript, when the book was published Funasaka invited Mishima to his home and showed him two Seki no Magoroku swords, offering to present him with one. Mishima was so entranced with them that he accepted the longer one, which bore a chip near the sword guard, a sign that it had seen battle service. The exact provenance of the sword is unclear (it was not the most precious first- or second-generation Seki no Magoroku), but it was sufficiently prized by Mishima that he had it adjusted so that it could be sheathed as a regimental sword. Mishima also subsequently began taking lessons with Funasaka's son in the art of *iaido*, the ability to draw a sword from a sitting position. One aspect of this sword training to which Mishima paid special attention was how a sword should be handled during *kaishaku*.

The radicalization of Mishima's thought in his final years was, however, gradual: in 1966 and 1967 he was still pouring out a huge diversity of short stories and criticism. As an interesting study in contrast, in the same month that 'Voices of the Heroic Dead' was published, Mishima wrote up his impressions of going to see The Beatles perform at the Budokan Hall in Tokyo – he was bemused by the screaming girl fans and remarked that the whole experience left him cold; he had been vastly more interested in a boxing match he had seen at the same venue a month earlier.

'Voices of the Heroic Dead', however, positioned Mishima as a new, distinctive presence in right-wing conservative thought, daring to ask questions about the response to the 26 February Incident and the emperor that had never been openly asked and inviting an avalanche of abuse and threats from the right wing for daring to criticize Emperor Hirohito. In the essay 'The 26 February Incident and I', published as the afterword to 'Voices of the Heroic Dead' and printed, together with 'Patriotism' and *Out of Date*, as *The 26 February 1936 Trilogy* in June 1966, Mishima wrote that he saw the officers of the 26 February Incident as mythical heroes whose purity, valour, righteous indignation and youthful deaths made them eternally beautiful.

From this point on, Mishima indulged in the creation of a kind of fantasy politics that willingly distorted history in order to arrive at the right 'aesthetic': an ideal worth dying for. Having been drawn to the 26 February Incident initially because of a single episode that strongly stimulated his masochistic desires, he now transformed the officers of the Incident into the types of beautiful young men about whom he liked to fantasize. Now he too wished to become one of them and for that Mishima needed to adopt their entire belief system. He would become devoted to the emperor as the embodiment of the *kokutai*, the time-transcending historical oneness of Japan.

As part of his research for *Runaway Horses*, in mid-June he visited the Saegusa Festival at Isagawa Shrine in Nara and returned to the city to stay for three nights at the Omiwa Shrine with Donald Keene

– both shrines occupy an important role at the beginning of the novel – before travelling to Kumamoto in the autumn. By now, Mishima had a new object of fascination: a group of rebellious fanatics from the early Meiji period known as the 'Shinpuren' ('League of the Divine Wind').

The Shinpuren were for Mishima the ultimate example of men in glorious revolt against the oppressions of historical time. A strong impulse for the Meiji Restoration of 1868 had been to throw out the foreigners and return to a veneration of the emperor, symbolic of everything unique about Japan itself. But when the shogunate had been overthrown, the country found itself instead opening up to the West at a dizzying rate. There were many revolts in the early Meiji period against this historical trend, some fuelled by political infighting and resentment against the factions who had seized control of the government. The Shinpuren were in extreme opposition to all forms of foreign influence, whether missionaries spreading Christianity or cables carrying electricity. They would only touch banknotes holding chopsticks; would not go under telegraph wires; and would scatter salt after meeting someone in Western dress. They were virulently opposed not only to all Western influence, but to 'foreign' beliefs such as Buddhism, which had been prevalent in Japan for a mere 1,300 years.

Based around Kumamoto on the southern island of Kyushu, the Shinpuren planned an attack on the government's military headquarters there, but it would be an attack eschewing all Western arms and only using traditional Japanese weapons such as swords, spears and halberds. Not only that, but they refused to time their attack according to when their enemy was weakest, and rather relied on divination instead. In 1874, when another rebellion had broken out nearby, the government had sent many of its troops from Kumamoto to crush it and left only 200 soldiers behind. It was the perfect opportunity for an attack, and the Shinpuren leader Tomoo Otaguro cast lots at a shrine, waiting to see if there was divine sanction. But instead the answer came back: 'no'. It would be two years later when the divination answered 'yes' and allowed the 170 men of the Shinpuren finally to launch a surprise attack. The defenders of the government headquarters were at first flummoxed and, unprepared, suffered some 200 casualties. But they soon regrouped and 2,000 modern solders attacked the Shinpuren with the latest weaponry. The result was inevitable: 123 men of the Shinpuren, including its leader, were killed or committed seppuku on the slopes of the mountain to which they fled; the remaining 50 were arrested.

Even at the time, journalists in Tokyo laughed at them as an anachronism, but to Mishima they appeared utterly splendid, the very embodiment both of 'Japaneseness' and purity of action. He wrote:

> When thought manifests itself in action, invariably impurities creep in. Inevitably tactics are considered and human betrayals come into play. There's the ideology, but in order to achieve the ultimate goal inevitably it becomes a question of choosing one's means. But for the Shinpuren . . . the means *were* the goal and the goal was the means. Everything was a matter of divine will, so it was impossible to have a contradiction between political objectives and means . . . I think this was the most fundamental, in some ways the most fanatically pure, experiment of the Japanese spirit.[4]

In Kumamoto, Mishima was met at the station by the foremost scholar of the Shinpuren, Seishi Araki, an acquaintance in his younger days of Zenmei Hasuda, and Mishima's erstwhile lover Jiro Fukushima, now an aspiring author who had resumed contact with Mishima in 1961. After the three men chatted in Mishima's hotel lounge, Araki left and Fukushima and Mishima repaired to his bedroom to have sex while Mishima proudly showed off his muscular physique. The following evening Mishima invited Araki, Fukushima and Zenmei Hasuda's widow, Toshiko, to a restaurant. Mishima reflected that he was 41, the same age as Hasuda had been when he killed himself, and that the Shinpuren leader, Otaguro, had been 42 when he committed seppuku. Mishima gloomily speculated that he would be 47 when he finished his life work, *The Sea of Fertility*, and so would be too late for a heroic death like them. He fretted over whether it was better to finish his life work or die a hero. But he consoled himself with the fact that the leader of the greatest samurai rebellion of the 1870s, Takamori Saigo, had been 50 when he died.

On 29 August 1966, a hot day, Mishima visited the shrine where Otaguro had made his divinations and loitered for an hour. When he returned to Tokyo he wrote to Araki that he felt he had now discovered his spiritual home because the Shinpuren had effected a revolution in spiritual history. He now had all the materials he needed to commence the serialization in February 1967 of *Runaway Horses*, the second volume of *The Sea of Fertility*, with its lengthy descriptions of the Shinpuren Rebellion. Engrossed both in his writing and in his real life with a revolt against macro-time, he remained as punctilious as ever when it came to micro-time, presenting Seishi Araki, the scholar of ahistorical rebels, with a gift of a modern German battery clock. In a *taidan* with Shuji Terayama six months before his death, Mishima remarked: 'I've only recently realized how much I like clocks. I often go to Ginza and find myself salivating in front of 1.2-million-yen or 800,000-yen clocks.'

Next, in March 1967, his essay 'The Theory of a "Moral Revolution"' appeared in the magazine *Bungei* at the same time as the publication of the previously unpublished papers of Asaichi Isobe, one of the ringleaders of the 26 February Incident. Mishima exhaustively examined the 'spiritual' significance of the Incident. According to his analysis, when the dazzling celestial light of the *kokutai* had been clouded over, the officers of 26 February 1936 had taken their swords to 'return clarity and purity', carrying out the emperor's will. The problem was that the emperor had rejected them. To navigate his way around this problem, Mishima employed his reading of Heidegger and claimed that there were in fact two emperors, the '*sein* emperor' (the emperor who actually exists) and the '*sollen* emperor' (the emperor who *should* exist), and it was this '*sollen* emperor' who provided the ideal worth dying for.

For all the grandiosity of Mishima's lofty theorizing, his public image was still that of an enormously talented dilettante. When the magazine *Heibon Punch* polled their readers in the spring of 1967 with the question 'Who is Japan's greatest dandy?', Mishima came first, polling nearly 18 per cent of over 110,000 votes cast. It was hardly surprising: Mishima was to be seen hobnobbing with the emperor (though it is unclear whether they ever spoke) at a garden party in November 1966 and then appeared as the 'poet's slave' in his own play, *The Arabian Nights*, the following week.

The next stage of Mishima's self-transformation into a 26 February Incident officer required that he too became a soldier. So in 1966, immediately after his Shinpuren research, Mishima applied to undergo intense training with the SDF. Usually such requests were to spend a couple of nights with Japan's military forces, but officials were startled to see that Mishima had asked to join for a full six months. At first the idea was firmly rejected, but strings were pulled and eventually Mishima was allowed to join for six weeks. From 12 April to 27 May 1967 Mishima entered Kurume officers' training camp in Kyushu before transferring to a camp at the base of Mount Fuji and finally moving to the Parachute Division at Narashino in Chiba. At the Mount Fuji camp, he stayed in exactly the same barracks where he had endured arduous military training as a weedy teenager over twenty years earlier, though wryly noted that they now had flush toilets and no bedbugs.

Not surprisingly given his adulation for the lowly officers of 1936, Mishima had tried to enlist as a 'lieutenant' but in the end entered as plain 'Hiraoka' without rank. Mishima got up at 6 a.m. each morning, went on a 2-mile run, wolfed down every meal and slept wrapped in a blanket on a metal bed. He wrote thrilled letters home to his parents declaring how wonderful it was to be holding a rifle again after twenty years. He learned how to drive a tank, took a class on tactics, jumped twice from a 10-m (33-ft) tower and repeatedly practised a 'marine crossing' on a rope slung across a cliff looking down over a river ravine.

An article describing his six-week experience was published in the *Sunday Mainichi* on 11 June 1967 and covered eight pages, featuring a series of questions and answers between their top journalist Takao Tokuoka and Mishima. When asked if the experience had caused him to believe in constitutional revision, Mishima said no, there was no need to amend the constitution. Mishima also remarked that there was no interest in the emperor in the SDF. Indeed, Mishima had closely questioned the officers in the SDF about their thoughts on the constitution, domestic security, conscription and civilian control – the captain assigned to look after him later realized that Mishima was trying to work out how the SDF would respond to the looming security crisis accompanying the renewal of the U.S.–Japan Security Treaty in 1970.

Unique as it was for a member of the cultural elite to be so involved with the controversial SDF, there was also something disquieting about him being pictured in a tin hat with a gun on his shoulder. In December 1967 he was even allowed onto an air base and taken up in an F-104 as part of his complete SDF experience. Lift off, he said, was like a moment of ejaculation. Ascending to 13,700 m (45,000 ft) and travelling at 1.3 Mach, he was airborne for nearly two hours and flew over Mount Fuji. Impressed by the combination of sea, clouds and red sunset,

Mishima thought the mountain looked like a Hokusai print and took notes, unconcerned by the g-force.

Yet there were much grander concepts at work. First and foremost was Mishima's desperate need to feel a sense of physical existence, so that he could keep writing *The Sea of Fertility*. If the central idea of that novel was the quest to transcend historical time, then Mishima in his personal life was also intent on transcending time, making up for his failure to join the military in 1945 and attain a glorious death. But Mishima's quest for a glorious death also meant that he must both live and die beautifully, making him turn once more to his favourite book, *Hagakure*, which advised that while preparation for a resolute death must be long, action must be sudden.

The emergence of Mishima the soldier was looked upon with curiosity by many in the journalistic and literary world, with one editor at the magazine *Shincho*, then serializing *The Sea of Fertility*, strongly opposing his training with the SDF. His 26 February 1936 trilogy had, however, already drawn him towards young right-wing radicals of the 'Folk Movement', which had sprung up in resistance to the left-wing student movement of the late 1960s. A key role was played by the veteran writer Fusao Hayashi (1903–1975), himself a *tenkosha*, someone forced to convert from communist to nationalist beliefs, in the early 1930s. Mishima had first met Hayashi in the immediate post-war era and went on to write an essay about him, published in February 1963, which would be his longest analysis of any literary figure. Now, on the dark, rainy afternoon of 19 December 1966, through Hayashi's introduction, Mishima received a visit from a young nationalist called Kiyoshi Bandai, a graduate of Meiji Gakuin University, who was one of the editors of a start-up publication called *Controversy Journal* and had come to Mishima looking for a star contributor. Mishima immediately agreed to help, beginning with their inaugural issue the following month. As fellow devotees of the emperor and critics of post-war

Japanese culture, both Bandai and his fellow editor Kazuhiko Nakatsuji made a big impact on Mishima, and he was soon transferring to them his own desires, speaking of their 'willingness to die in battle' and conflating them with his Shinpuren heroes, even though both of them were actually more interested in writing cultural critiques. He wrote:

> A group of young men, who don't belong to any party or faction, with purity of heart making up their minds to right Japan's wrongs, swearing a firm union and overcoming one obstacle after another – listening to this story, for the first time a strange thing occurred inside me. It seemed impossible for me to be moved by the interior life of young men, but suddenly I was moved. More than being surprised by Bandai's story, I was surprised at myself.[5]

Mishima started to envisage a heroic death being cut down (*kirijini*) in battle in an epic confrontation with the communists, but he was also becoming increasingly fascinated by the subject of seppuku. In the autumn of 1966 he had received a letter from Ryohei Kawaguchi, the medical doctor who had rushed to the scene on 27 February 1936 after Lieutenant Aojima had committed seppuku. Kawaguchi told him that he had read 'Patriotism' and Mishima now wrote back: 'I would like you to tell me about the details of his death, the passage of his final moments, and the manifestations of his pain.' Kawaguchi answered:

> When I raced to the scene, I judged it to be five or six hours after seppuku, but the lieutenant was still not dead. He had lost consciousness with his intestines bursting out of the wide gash in his stomach and was writhing . . . so long as there is no *kaishaku*, it is surprisingly difficult to die by seppuku.[6]

The association with *Controversy Journal* brought Mishima into contact with other young, right-wing student radicals. One was Hiroshi Mochimaru, a student at Waseda University with strong practical abilities who was a central figure in the newly formed Japan Student Alliance. Mishima contributed an article to the inaugural edition of the group's *Japan Student Newspaper*, published in February 1967 and, thanks to an introduction by Mishima, a sub-group formed at Waseda in April 1967 trained with the SDF in July. Inspired by this, Mishima started planning a civilian military organization called the 'Japan National Guard', whose purpose was to defend Japan's history and traditions from indirect invasion (a civil war prompted by foreign communist powers). The idea was that this civilian army would train for ten days to a month twice a year with the SDF, and Mishima sought immediately to train 20–30 students to form an officer corps. Mishima and his activist friends produced a leaflet sent to Japanese corporations, explaining how they would be able to send their employees for military training in exchange for meals, travel and uniform expenses.

A particular spur to action had been provided by political developments, especially opposition to the escalating war in Vietnam. The U.S. had started bombing North Vietnam in March 1965 and in June 1966 bombed Hanoi, triggering huge anti-war demonstrations in San Francisco and New York. By July 1967 the U.S. troop strength of 320,000 men in South Vietnam exceeded that of the South Vietnamese army. When asked by *Newsweek* in 1967 for his opinions on the war, Mishima said that America was 'doing the right thing', but the mood among Japanese youth was very different.

On 8 October 1967, Prime Minister Sato had set off from Haneda Airport for a tour of Southeast Asia, including South Vietnam, only to discover student protestors out in force. During this First Haneda Incident a student from Kyoto University was killed, echoing the student death in 1960 which had acted as a rallying call to discontent and mass protest. On 12 November, Sato left Haneda airport again, this time for the U.S., nominally to discuss the return of Okinawa, though also to affirm once more Japanese support of the war in Vietnam. Again there were student protests, with the protestors wearing helmets, masking their faces with towels and carrying thick timber poles to fight the security forces. Yet more left-wing student protests followed the arrival of the U.S. nuclear aircraft carrier *Enterprise* at the American base in Sasebo, Kyushu, on 19 January 1968. The carrier had already been involved in the Vietnam War and its arrival openly recognized Japan's support role. Student protestors commuted daily from university dormitories three hours away in Fukuoka and received the support of locals and the mass media in a strange cocktail of peacenik-ism and anti-U.S. nationalism.

With bloody political battles on Japanese soil now almost a reality, Mishima's fantasy of dying with twenty beautiful young officers by his side seemed almost within grasp, and on 26 February 1968, 32 years after the original 26 February Incident, he signed an oath in blood with about ten students at the offices of *Controversy Journal*. The pledge was that they would be the foundation of the Imperial Nation, and all cut their left thumb with a safety razor and dripped blood into a cup, then, using this, signed with a brush a metre-wide scroll. First to sign was Mishima, denoting himself as 'Kimitake Hiraoka'. Some of the students became nauseous and weak-headed, but Mishima proclaimed that while paper may be destroyed, their vow should live forever and so suggested that they all drink the blood. Jokingly enquiring first whether anyone had a venereal disease, he then mixed in some table salt as a disinfectant and they all took a sip. (The pact stayed in Mishima's memory and two years later, ten days before the Mishima Incident, Mishima contacted Mochimaru and arranged to meet him in Roppongi, where he asked about the scroll. The following day Mochimaru brought it to a theatre in Kanda and

Mishima, wishing to clear the slate ahead of his 'final action', burned it in front of him.)

The next week Mishima led 23 students, including Bandai, Nakatsuji and Mochimaru, for a month's military training. At the last minute some of those chosen had dropped out, so five students from Waseda University joined instead. One of them, Masakatsu Morita, was fated to be the man who would die with Mishima and his dedication immediately earned Mishima's respect. The students ate and slept with the army regulars, and although they drilled separately, so impressed their instructors that they were in tears when the students left.

Was a National Guard necessary? Even the right-wingers of the Japan Student Alliance questioned it, but Mishima still secured interviews with the head of the SDF Training School, the deputy head of the Defence Agency and the head of the powerful business consortium Nikkeiren to strongly petition his case. On 5 October 1968, after an 'evaluation meeting' following a second training experience with the SDF, Mishima announced to journalists the formation of a 'Shield Society' which would form the nucleus of 'Japan's National Guard'. The society would be formed of a 100-strong civilian officer corps, whose soldiers would be volunteers and receive no pay, but be provided with uniforms. Although *Heibon Punch* devoted a ten-page spread to the news, the press were mostly derisive, but even so there was a steady stream of student recruits from a diverse number of universities. In March and July 1969, Mishima again led groups of students for a month's training at the Mount Fuji training camp, and by March 1970, the time of the fifth and final training camp, the desired quota of 100 members had almost been reached.

It looked as if Mishima's 'civilian army' idea had borne fruit, but from Mishima's letters to various officials it can be seen that the reality was more complicated. To begin with, Mishima had envisioned the Japan National Guard as a state organization funded by the financial sector and had produced a detailed pamphlet entitled 'Why is a National Defence Unit necessary?' The student leader Mochimaru had experience of fundraising from his work on the committee of the Japanese Students Alliance and through an introduction from Fusao Hayashi had started visiting the director of the powerful business consortium Nikkeiren, Takeshi Sakurada. Now Mishima also visited. However, there was a considerable difference between Mochimaru in his student uniform meekly asking for money and a proud national celebrity like Mishima having to bow his head. Moreover, those who seemed to be sympathizers, when they learned the details of his plan, quickly distanced themselves. Takeshi Sakurada offered a measly 3 million yen and warned Mishima not to create a private army. Mishima was furious and further disappointed that there was not even any support in the SDF. So he determined to have an army free of all outside interference: the volunteers would not receive any pay, but would be provided with uniforms, battle fatigues and training expenses paid for by Mishima himself.

Behind the scenes, though, Mishima's pamphlet had yielded important consequences, having been passed to Kiyokatsu Yamamoto, head of reconnaissance training at one of the SDF academies. Yamamoto, an elite colonel and graduate of the pre-war officer school, had the responsibility of creating spies in the event of the army being mobilized to quell civil unrest. Various nightmare scenarios envisaged by both Mishima and Yamamoto were that, if a pro-Soviet Union faction gained the upper hand during the ongoing Cultural Revolution in China, and America lost the Vietnam War, there could either be a military invasion of Japan or else Chinese guerrillas could unite with Japanese socialists and create a civil war. If the police were unable to maintain peace in such an eventuality, the SDF would have to be mobilized, but did they even have sufficient personnel to maintain order? It was Yamamoto's job to ensure that the SDF were ready for such an eventuality. For this reason, Yamamoto was greatly interested in Mishima's proposal to train volunteer soldiers as civilian help.

By now, the student protests had set alight the campuses, and in May 1968 Yamamoto began his instruction to Mishima's cadres, lecturing in a discreet suburban *ryokan* on the fundamental knowledge needed to fight urban guerrillas. After the lecture, Mishima and some of the students went to a coffee shop, but unbeknownst to them, as an example of espionage, Yamamoto had secretly arranged with the Intelligence School to record their conversation and play it back to them the following day: Mishima was amazed. Next came actual city drills for which Mishima was asked to come in disguise. Mishima showed up sporting an absurd-looking moustache and appeared depressed when Yamamoto asked him if anyone had recognized him on the way there. Mishima said that a student had, indeed, asked him on the train if he was Mishima.

Applicants for the Shield Society, many recruited from the Japan Student Alliance and National Student Cooperation Society, were first screened by Mochimaru at the offices of *Controversy Journal* on the Ginza and then, if deemed suitable, were taken for a personal interview with Mishima himself. As stipulated earlier for his would-be wife, Mishima did not want anyone of a literary bent ('literary youth won't make warriors', he said), but looked for earnest young men prepared to fight for the emperor with no ties to any political organizations. When not in camp, the Shield Society met every month at the Ichigaya Hall, a building in Tokyo next to the head-quarters of the SDF, where Mishima would start proceedings with comments on current events, followed by a discourse on his political beliefs, then a discussion, a light lunch and a military drill on the roof or march around the base afterwards.

Mishima seemed to delight in the company of these uncomplicated young men, even if it also meant that they were soon calling round to his house at all hours of the day, forcing him to allocate an hour to them every Wednesday afternoon between 3 p.m. and 4 p.m. in a basement coffee shop called the Salon de Clair, in Ginza.

Yet soon there were problems within the Shield Society itself. From the time of the fourth training camp with the SDF, differences surfaced between Mishima and Bandai and Nakatsuji, who had requested financial backing for the cash-strapped *Controversy Journal* from the powerful right-wing extremist Seigen Tanaka, a move bitterly opposed by Mishima, who was furious at Tanaka's boasts that he had Mishima at his beck and call. In August 1969, Bandai, Nakatsuji and others connected with the journal left the Shield Society altogether. Then Mishima's right-hand man and first student captain, Hiroshi Mochimaru, turned down Mishima's offer to support him financially and devote himself to the Society. Mochimaru's monthly income had mostly come from Seigen Tanaka. Mishima had bitterly opposed Mochimaru's forthcoming marriage, believing that the leaders of the Shield Society, like the 26 February Incident officers, should remain unattached so they might spring into action at any time, offering up their lives without restraint. But Mochimaru had no wish to die, and despite Mishima relenting and even offering to put the newlyweds up in a flat, sensing the direction in which things were now moving, he too left.

In July 1968 Mishima published 'The Theory of Cultural Defence' in *Chuo Koron*. Having previously concocted his theory of the '*sollen* emperor', with the emperor as the embodiment of an ideal political state, Mishima now took things further by unveiling his notion of the 'cultural emperor', arguing that the fount of all Japanese history and culture was to be found in none other than the emperor and that, because of this, 'it is urgently essential to link with ties of pride the emperor and the military', demanding that the emperor inspect troops and hand out medals. The flaws in Mishima's logic were mercilessly exposed both by left-wing critics,

who pointed out its contradictions and referred to Mishima as
a 'dangerous thinker', and by the literary critic Bunzo Hashikawa,
an expert on such matters as the Shinpuren and *Hagakure*, who
had written a book on the Japanese Romantic School and was
regarded by Mishima as a close ally. Hashikawa remarked that he
failed to see why the emperor urgently needed to be linked to the
army and that Mishima was actually trying to force a link between
the idea of 'cultural defence' and his own training with the SDF.
Mishima was so affected by his 'defection' that he even published
a public letter to him, though it did no good. Meanwhile, Mishima
continued to peddle more easily digestible diatribes as part of his
intensely masculine 'writings of the sword', such as his essays
'Spiritual Lectures for Young Samurai', serialized in the magazine
Pocket Punch Oh! (a compact version of *Heibon Punch* intended
for younger readers), which now replaced his light offerings for
women's magazines.

Repeatedly, the opportunity for the Shield Society actually to
enter the fray seemed tantalizingly near, but then retreated once
more. When the student protests reached their zenith with the
International Anti-war Day of 21 October 1968, students not only
swarmed the campuses but undertook simultaneous guerrilla
actions in their designated 'liberation zones' of Shinjuku,
around the parliament building and the Defence Agency and
in Ochanomizu and Ginza. The response, from 12,000 men of
the security forces, involved shields and tear gas, and late in the
evening, in front of Shinjuku station – the centre of the rail network
transporting American material for the Vietnam War – an
armoured police vehicle was overturned and torched as protestors
burst into the station and brought commuter trains to a halt.
A riot was declared and the security forces moved to mass arrests
and rounded up 737 people.

Mishima, dressed in battle fatigues, a helmet and boots, had
been appointed a 'special correspondent' for the day by the *Sunday*

Mainichi and had been watching events unfold first in Ochanomizu, where students erected barricades and smoke from Molotov cocktails and tear gas made Mishima's eyes bloodshot. Moving on to Ginza, Mishima climbed on top of a police cabin and stood still, his whole body trembling slightly as he surveyed the carnage. Over 40 members of the Shield Society had been dispatched throughout the metropolis to collect information and, late in the day, excited at what they heard was going on in Shinjuku, Mishima and the Shield Society cadres wanted to go on the offensive, but were restrained by Yamamoto who, seeing that the SDF had not yet been mobilized, feared their becoming a target of the mass media. Mishima denounced him as too cautious, but Yamamoto realized that though the SDF were on standby, they would only be mobilized if the country descended into full-scale civil war, and that today's localized riot would have blown over by tomorrow.

Even after the Anti-war Day had passed, Yamamoto and Mishima still readied themselves for action, intensifying their preparations and ratcheting up the level of expectation. Mishima arranged for the use of business premises in a discreet location next to Shinagawa Station where, over four days, Yamamoto organized 32 hours of lectures on guerrilla warfare. On 18–19 January 1969, the Security Forces, dispatching 8,500 riot police equipped with water cannon and 10,000 gas grenades, stormed the main occupied building – known as 'Yasuda Castle' – on the campus of Tokyo University and after bitter resistance arrested 631 people. Mishima alternately complained that not a single student gave up his life in the battle, while also fretting that one of them might jump from the roof of the nine-storey Yasuda Hall, causing a media uproar that would both paralyse the riot police and make the left-wing students seem profoundly heroic.

The following month, with the cultish world of the Shield Society becoming progressively more extreme, Mishima organized another intense study camp, this time at a temple next to a SDF base. At the study camp, no contact with the outside world was allowed, nor any alcohol or cigarettes, and the cadres ate canned food and slept in sleeping bags in rooms with no heating and little water. They rose at dawn to exercise before lectures commenced at 8 a.m., with breaks to practise reconnaissance around the base.

On 28 April 1969, dubbed Okinawa Anti-war Day (highlighting the demand to immediately return Okinawa, where the U.S. had its largest military base, to Japan), there was another major disturbance, with 967 people arrested and police cabins in Shinbashi, Ginza and Sukiyabashi attacked and some set on fire. The protestors were attacked with tear gas and hosed with coloured water for identification even if they fled into the underground. Mishima burst into Yamamoto's house and demanded to know why he wasn't doing anything and took him out in a limousine to track the students. The following month, with close to half the universities in Japan on strike and their campuses barricaded, Mishima accepted the opportunity to debate with the student radicals at Tokyo University. He entered the back gate, but could not find the meeting place and then saw himself caricatured as a gorilla at the entrance: instead of an entrance fee, 100 yen to feed the animal was requested.

Like many of the events at the time, there was a mordantly humorous side, but also a very considerable danger – Mishima was under no doubt that he was risking his life by entering into such a hostile arena and, fearing a knife attack, wore a tightly bound cloth under his shirt to protect him. Surrounded by his intense intellectual enemies, Mishima coolly held his ground, noting that both sides agreed on the need for violence and that what he feared most was compromise. Mishima complimented the students by telling them they had smashed the nose of self-conceit at Tokyo University and floored them by famously pronouncing:

'If you would just say the word emperor once I would happily join hands with you . . . but you don't.'

However, cracks now began to emerge between Mishima and the intelligence guru Yamamoto. As Mishima grew ever more intense in his determination to be involved in some violent showdown, Yamamoto, whose sole interest was in keeping the peace, saw that extreme action would only be justified when communist guerrillas allied themselves with the students. Furthermore, Mishima, in his fanaticism, believing that a willingness to die was much more important than modern weapons, was now becoming far removed from Yamamoto's practicality. In June he invited Yamamoto and some others to a private room at a hotel restaurant in Tokyo and, promising to order food after the conversation was finished, locked the door and took out a piece of paper which had a three-point action plan on it. He pronounced first that it was his intention to form a suicide unit and defend the emperor to the death with a unit armed only with Japanese swords; Yamamoto was so shaken that he forgot what the other two points of the plan were. Yet to someone else, Mishima confided that what he actually wanted to do was kill the emperor in the imperial palace. Defend the emperor to the death or murder the emperor: increasingly there seemed to be little difference between the two.

The following month, Yamamoto was promoted to Vice-Principal of the SDF Reconnaissance School and so became unavailable for instructing the Shield Society. For Mishima, meanwhile, the cost of supporting his private army was now crippling. Mishima provided his recruits with both winter and summer uniforms, designed by Igarashi Tsukumo, who had also designed De Gaulle's uniforms. The summer uniforms were brilliant white, while the winter uniforms were mustard-coloured. Though Mishima was thrilled when he was complimented on them by taxi drivers and passers-by, as well as paying 120,000 yen a head for the uniforms of his 100 cadres, Mishima also incurred coffee shop expenses, training camp expenses, seminar expenses . . . In two years he spent at least 15 million yen (approximately $440,000 today), when his entire income for the magazine serialization (not including book sales) over five years of the 3,000-page *Sea of Fertility* was 4.5 million yen ($130,000 today). He grumbled to Atsuko Yuasa that his expenses were 'beyond a joke'.

What should not be forgotten throughout all this is that Mishima was still continuing relentlessly with *The Sea of Fertility.* Despite having originally intended not to release *The Sea of Fertility* as a book until the whole work was completed, disappointed by the lack of critical response and desirous of extra income, he authorized the publication of volumes one and two, which appeared in early 1969. Sales were spectacular, with *Spring Snow* (volume one) selling 200,000 copies in just two months, and within a year the book was turned into both a highly successful play and a television series.

In September 1967 Mishima and Yoko had travelled to India so that Mishima could conduct more research for volume three, *The Temple of Dawn*, accepting the invitation of the Indian government to visit the Ajanta Caves and be introduced to Mrs Gandhi. Mishima visited Bombay, Jaipur, Agra, Delhi and Varanasi, witnessed open-air cremations by the Ganges and walked round the temple in Calcutta where dozens of goats were routinely sacrificed to the goddess Kali: both of these practices would be described in detail in *The Temple of Dawn*. He spoke positively not only of India's bustle, colour and diversity, but of its stubborn resistance to modernization, believing that it offered in its spirituality an alternative to the blind faith in Western technology.

It was while he was in India that the Japanese press anticipated, yet again, that he might be declared winner of the Nobel Prize. Two years earlier, when Mishima had first visited Thailand and Cambodia at the end of his round-the-world trip with Yoko, there had been headlines in the *Asahi Shinbun* that Mishima was a candidate and on 15 October 1965 an article that he was on the final shortlist. (Before 1965, Japan had only one Nobel Prize-winner in any category, so press interest was intense.) Expectation about Mishima winning the Nobel Prize had indeed been building since December 1963, when a Swedish newspaper included Mishima in a list of nineteen of the world's greatest writers, many of whom had already won the prize, including Faulkner, Hemingway, Steinbeck and Camus. From May 1964, Donald Keene had also been tirelessly campaigning as a member of the U.S. delegation for Mishima to win the $10,000 Formentor Literary Prize, established in 1961 and already awarded to Beckett and Borges, though this prize too narrowly eluded him.

The same media circus ensued in 1966, with the Japanese press once more sure that he would win the Nobel Prize, and Mishima was asked in advance to prepare material for them. Suitably chastened, by 1967 Mishima wanted to avoid such an unpleasant experience. Yoko had returned home from India on 4 October, while Mishima continued on to Bangkok. There, the *Mainichi* newspaper telegraphed Takao Tokuoka, who six months earlier had interviewed Mishima after his SDF experience and was now stationed in Bangkok as back-up reporter on the Vietnam War, to stake out Mishima and prepare an article just in case. Tokuoka went to Mishima's hotel, but could not find him in his room and eventually tracked him down to the steak room downstairs, explaining to an American tourist in a baseball cap why Japan must change its constitution. The prize went to the Guatemalan novelist Miguel Ángel Asturias instead.

Deliberately avoiding a return home immediately after the announcement, and disappointed that he was refused access to the Thai court, Mishima instead secured an audience with the Laos king (through his brother Chiyuki, who was working at the Japanese Embassy at Vientiane in Laos). Mishima travelled to

Luang Prabang to meet him and after discussing Proust and other French literature for the best part of an hour with him began to regret not making Laos rather than Thailand part of the plot of *The Sea of Fertility*. The garden in his brother's house in Laos had chameleons and snakes and was verdant with papayas and bananas, which Mishima picked and ate before having a doze. He did not return home until 23 October. By then, the media circus had moved on for another year, more concerned now with the upsurge of protests by left-wing student radicals.

The following year there was one last round of frenzied speculation as it was now certain the prize would go to Japan. On 17 October 1968 (four days before the 'Anti-war Day' riots) Mishima spent the evening earnestly waiting for the news at the Publishers' Club with his editor Hiroshi Nitta and Munekatsu Date, a reporter from NHK television; at 7.30 p.m. came the announcement that Kawabata had won. Mishima immediately called to congratulate Kawabata, then wrote a glowing article for the morning edition of the *Mainichi* before going home, changing and driving down with Yoko to see Kawabata in Kamakura. Date recalls Mishima mumbling darkly that it would be another ten years before the prize came to Japan again.

In the autumn of 1969, Mishima's fantasy 'real world' reached a low ebb. With the departure of both Mochimaru and the *Controversy Journal* cadres from the Shield Society, Mishima briefly considered disbanding it, though somewhat embarrassingly had already sent out invitations to numerous celebrities and journalists for the first anniversary parade of the society. Bizarrely, if somewhat appropriately, this was to be held on the roof of the National Theatre, where Mishima was directing a new Kabuki play. The ceremony started with 83 Shield Society members from seventeen different universities facing the Imperial Palace and singing the national anthem, *Kimi ga yo* (May Your Reign Last Forever), before parading for fifteen minutes to the accompaniment of the military

Commemorating the 1st anniversary of the Shield Society, 3 November 1969.

band from the Mount Fuji camp. Afterwards, there was a reception in the theatre's grand dining hall and, following a speech in Japanese by a retired general, Mishima, dressed in white military uniform, spoke in English. Of the 100 guests invited, only 50 attended, the rest being put off by press scrutiny of the invitee list. Kawabata too made his apologies.

After a brief hesitation, and also after rejecting Mochimaru's own suggestion for someone to replace him as student captain, Mishima fatefully decided to appoint 25-year-old Masakatsu Morita to the post. Unlike those who had fled the society, Morita was someone who also shared Mishima's intense death wish. Born in July 1945 (his first name meant 'must win' and was given to him just days before Japan's catastrophic defeat in the war), Morita had lost both his father and mother in 1948 and had been raised by his elder brother. Possessed of a delicate, unstable personality, his childhood, like Mishima's own, was permeated with loneliness, existential angst and death longings. In a diary entry of 19 October

1962 he had written: 'I don't want to die, but I deeply admire death. If I was to just suddenly die, no one would be sad about it.'[7] Mishima had now finally found someone who was fully prepared to die with him.

The astonishing thing is just how extraordinarily prolific Mishima remained, both as a dramatist and a media celebrity, right up to the end, producing numerous plays while simultaneously writing *The Sea of Fertility* and recreating himself as a political activist. Most of his plays were fuelled by the concept of finding otherworldly transcendence through dedication to an ideal. In April 1968 Mishima, together with Takeo Matsuura, had left the NLT and formed the Romantic Theatre Company, and their first production was *My Friend Hitler* (premiering the night police stormed Tokyo University and performed until 31 January 1969), in which Mishima described the aesthetics of Ernst Rohm, who despite being brutally purged by Hitler, continues in his blind belief. Having assumed the persona of a 'dangerous right winger', Mishima was now milking it for all it was worth, though it should be pointed out that Mishima, while admitting to a fascination with Hitler (particularly after reading Alan Bullock's *Hitler: A Study in Tyranny*), never professed any liking for *der Führer*, and indeed was always sharply critical of the Nazis, arguing that what they lacked was the samurai virtue of 'self-sacrifice'. For all his obsessive talk about the emperor and the army, Mishima was unequivocal in his view that freedom of speech and parliamentary democracy must be retained.

After an eleven-year gap, Mishima also wrote a Kabuki play, *A Wonder Tale: The Moonbow*, performed from 5–27 November 1969 as the third-anniversary production of the National Theatre. It was based on a famous novel by the nineteenth-century novelist Kyokutei Bakin, with its protagonist Tametomo Minamoto (1139–1170) also shown as someone enduring in his devotion, this time to the emperor Sutoku. The play was dazzling in its set pieces, with a thrilling battle in the snow and a gory final seppuku

Promoting his play *My Friend Hitler*, 26 October 1968.

scene. Mishima insisted on designing not just the sets and costumes but also the garish posters and even demanded that the entire celebrity cast listen to a three-hour recording of him reciting all the parts. It was this play that Mishima was rehearsing on 3 November 1969, the same day that he welcomed a hundred guests to a banquet at the National Theatre celebrating the first anniversary of the Shield Society.

Both of these plays were essentially extensions of Mishima's 'real world' persona and interests, but much more revealing was the play *The Terrace of the Leper King*, the last modern play he wrote. Mishima was supposed to have drafted it in a single night after being inspired by a legend he had encountered on his trip to Cambodia in 1965 and wrote it up in April 1969. In the play, a handsome young king builds a magnificent temple while he fades away from leprosy. Mishima said it was 'a metaphor for the life of an artist who transfuses a work of art with his entire existence and then perishes',[8] an indication that Mishima was only too aware that he would be laying down his life in exchange for completing *The Sea of Fertility*.

A selection of Mishima's other diverse activities in 1968 and '69 could include conducting an orchestra at a pop concert in March 1968; writing an introduction to a collection of photographs of 'naked festivals'; being the sole editor of an edition of *Criticism* devoted to 'decadence'; and being elected as a director of the newly formed Japan Cultural Congress, intended as a 'philosophical bridge between East and West'. He premiered his own ballet, *Miranda*, and posed as a model for a series of photographs by Kishin Shinoyama called *Death of a Man*, with the sessions set to continue, appropriately, until just before his death. Mishima sat on committees for two important literary awards, including the Akutagawa Prize, and was constantly making field trips in connection with research for his literary works, whether travelling to Okinawa in July 1969 as research for *The Moonbow* or inspecting

Relaxing at home, December 1968.

the area around Gotenba in Shizuoka to find the right milieu for Honda's villa in *The Temple of Dawn*. Mishima also had a discussion with the secretary general of the ruling Liberal Democratic Party in July 1968 in which he proposed that the SDF be divided up into a force for national defence and a force that would contribute to a UN police reserve. Shortly afterwards the cabinet secretary asked him if he would consider running for office.

Mishima found time in May and June 1969 to star as the historical figure Shinbei Tanaka in the film *The Assassin*. As a terrorist devoted to restoring authority to the emperor in the last days of the Tokugawa shogunate, and who cut down a dozen targets before being arrested and committing seppuku, Tanaka was a man after Mishima's own heart. (Intriguingly, Tanaka was said to have died in the house of Mishima's ancestor Naoyuki Nagai, the magistrate of Kyoto at the time.) This time around there was none of the trauma of production associated with *Afraid to Die* and Mishima's performance even attracted positive reviews. A co-star on the film was the actor Tatsuya Nakadai, who had previously appeared in the film version of *The Temple of the Golden Pavilion*. One day they found themselves sitting next to one another on a flight to Osaka on their way to film in Kyoto. Making small talk, Nakadai asked Mishima why he was so devoted to bodybuilding despite his being an author. Mishima answered: 'Because I am going to die committing seppuku.' Nakadai said, 'You mean the seppuku scene in this film?', to which Mishima responded, 'Not at all. I mean when I actually die committing seppuku. I wish to be sure that my stomach will be pure muscle with no fat on it.'[9]

9

Battle against Time

The events of the last year of Mishima's life are so fascinating, dramatic and outlandish that entire books have been written in Japanese specifically about it. Almost as soon as Morita became student captain of the Shield Society, it seems that he and Mishima resolved to die together. Whether there were actual physical relations between the two is a matter of conjecture, though there is little doubt that both men felt strongly that they had found their soulmate. Mishima now groomed Morita both as his secret fiancé and companion in death, though Morita certainly needed no coercing. Mishima remarked that, while he was devoted to the emperor, Morita was devoted to him, and declared that Morita would be the man who would kill him. Bizarrely, he took Morita along with his own wife to expensive French restaurants or introduced him to friends, demanding that Morita recount his entire life story in front of them as a shining example of a noble and valuable life.

The question was, in what fashion could they now engineer their deaths together? Mishima had long dreamed of dying in an epic battle with left-wing demonstrators against the security treaty, or else falling, sword in hand, in an attack mounted with the SDF on the parliament building. When, on 21 October 1968, International Anti-war Day, Mishima had stalked the streets of Tokyo observing hundreds of people being injured or arrested during violent demonstrations, such a fantasy death seemed only too attainable. Everything appeared to be bubbling up nicely to the climax of 1970, the long-anticipated year of Security Treaty renewal that would surely provide Mishima the dramatic death he so desired.

But then came the disaster of 21 October 1969, the next International Anti-war Day, when the protestors had been overwhelmed by a vastly increased police presence of 32,000 men armed to the teeth with anti-riot gear. A week beforehand he gave a lecture at the Ministry of Finance – his old employers – predicting that the renewal of the treaty would provoke a crisis of identity in Japan. There would be those arguing in favour of super-nationalism, while on the other hand anarchists would appear. Towards this end, Mishima said that he was preparing his literature, thought and action: he was 'resolved'. Then, on 20 October, the day before Anti-war Day, the Shield Society members assembled at Mishima's house and decided which members would monitor which areas of protest, wearing fake 'press' armbands and carrying cameras to look as if they were part of the media. Mishima had even set up a large radio in his home to try and tap police communication. But the following day was a great disappointment. The Riot Act was not invoked, nor were the SDF mobilized. Mishima, wearing a leather jacket, dark glasses, a helmet and an armband from the magazine serializing his *Introductions to the Philosophy of Action*, set off in the evening to Shinjuku. There was tight security control and no mob, with shops closed and buildings shuttered down. Mishima called it a 'weird, nihilistic void'.

Suddenly, it looked as though the mass riots imagined for 1970 might not happen after all. Mishima despaired of the half-heartedness of his opponents and their feeble guerrilla tactics, their lack of 'purity of action'. Now the politicians would feel confident and all impetus to change the constitution would be lost. When the leaders of the Shield Society gloomily met ten days later, they fretted over what they should now do. Morita proposed that the Shield Society rise up with the SDF and surround the parliament, but Mishima answered that without weapons it would be pointless. He already knew that the SDF had no interest in joining such a rebellion. On 16 November 1969 there was one last major demonstration against the prime minister's trip to America, with an all-time record 1,940 people arrested, but with this the movement to prevent the Security Treaty's renewal was completely crushed. The barricade strikes at universities too all came to an end.

In December 1969, while he pondered his next move, Mishima made a trip to South Korea with his scholar friend Ivan Morris (the translator of *The Temple of the Golden Pavilion* and a founder of Amnesty International USA) to investigate North Korea's guerrilla activities in the South. Ironically, Mishima narrowly missed meeting exactly the type of emergency he had been on the lookout for: on 10 December he took an internal flight back to Seoul when the following day the same flight was hijacked by North Korean guerrillas.

In Japan, meanwhile, a sense that the age of protest politics was coming to an end was only more sharply signified by the elections of December 1969, when the Socialist Party lost 40 per cent of their seats. Mishima responded by setting up a study group on constitutional reform within the Shield Society.

The need for Mishima to die was becoming more acute as he edged closer to the conclusion of *The Sea of Fertility*. On 20 February 1970, Mishima gave the completed manuscript of *The Temple of Dawn* to his Shinchosha editor, Chikako Kojima. Mishima now suspended serialization for two months, the first break since serialization had started nearly four years earlier. Serialization of the fourth volume, *The Decay of the Angel*, commenced in July.

Pausing work on his masterpiece threw Mishima into an immediate crisis. He described being assailed by an indescribable unease:

With the completion of *The Temple of Dawn*, I confirmed the existence of two types of reality, and as the world of my artwork was completed and closed, the entire reality that existed until then outside my novel instantly became waste paper. Actually I didn't want it to become waste paper. To me, it was my life, an important reality. But with the hiatus after one year and eight months of being involved with volume three, the confrontation and tension between these two types of reality disappeared as one side became the artwork and the other side became waste paper . . . When the conclusion of volume three attacked like a storm, I could hardly believe it. I had bet on a reality where perhaps there would be no conclusion . . . But still one volume remained. The final volume remained. The words 'when this novel ends' are the greatest taboo to me now. I cannot imagine a world after this novel has finished. Imagining that world is both hateful and terrifying.[1]

Mishima's mind was entirely focused on the end of things, but for the rest of the population it was all about beginnings. The 1960s were over, the 1970s had begun and Expo '70 was the curtain raiser, proclaiming Japan's enormous economic success. The great mass of the population seemed to have tired of student protests, and under the police crackdown, left-wing groups splintered into extremist organizations like the Japanese Red Army, 53 members of which were arrested on 5 November 1969 for plotting an attack on the prime minister's official residence and the Metropolitan Police headquarters.

Yet again, Mishima appeared to have been tricked by 'macro-time' and seethed in indignation at opportunities lost. In the spring, Yamamoto suddenly received a visit from Mishima in Japanese dress and carrying a Japanese sword in a brocade scabbard protector. Mishima was taken into the living room and stood the sword on the wall behind the sofa: Yamamoto feared he might be slain. Mishima lamented that it was a mistake for Yamamoto to break away from him and accused him of leading Mochimaru astray, but eventually conceded that it was inevitable that Mochimaru would leave. Yamamoto's wife nervously referred to the sword and Mishima showed it to them before she placed it on the piano, remarking that they too must arrange to have their swords sharpened.

Mishima seemed to be itching to use that sword. His father recalled an occasion when the *New York Times* wished to take a picture of Mishima in an aikido pose, so a white sheet was spread on a stage at the National Theatre for a photo shoot. However, the sheet kept slipping so Mishima instructed his attendants to nail it down. The attendants were appalled at damaging the stage in this way and refused, whereupon Mishima pulled out a sword and threatened to cut their heads off, damaging the ceiling as he did so. Mishima warned them that, although this was a practice sword, it could still kill them, and that he had a famous sword at home.[2]

For the students in the Shield Society, meanwhile, serenely oblivious of the inner thoughts of their commander, the training became ever more gruelling. In March 1970, they practised parachute jumps and at the Gotemba base of the SDF underwent tough 'ranger' training in 30 cm (1 ft) of snow. They were made to march all day and night without food and, after two dropped out with exhaustion, were eventually given some uncooked rice and a live chicken with which to feed themselves.[3] After finishing an eighteen-hour march on 14 March, they went to a shop on the camp and watched the opening ceremony of the Osaka Expo on TV. They then returned to a sub-freezing room and composed Japanese-style poems (*waka*), which Mishima critiqued. By June, their 'refresher' training course involved not just the shooting of live ammunition, but instructions on the use of bombs.

To anyone paying attention, Mishima was clearly signing in his writings, too, that he intended to act soon, serializing in the magazine *Shokun!* his thoughts on the philosophy of *yomeigaku*, based on the principle of the unity of 'knowledge and action' and advocated by the Chinese Confucian scholar and military commander Yangming Wang (1472–1529). The roll call of tragic Japanese heroes who had been influenced by *yomeigaku* was a lengthy one and included such famous rebels as Heihachiro Oshio (1793–1837), Yoshida Shoin (1830–1851) and Takamori Saigo (1828–1877). Mishima was now very consciously positioning himself as the heir to this tradition of self-sacrificing, glorious rebellion.

Yet, far from the establishment detecting any warning signs, Mishima was considered such an authority on defence that on three occasions in 1970 he discussed the issue with the secretary general of the ruling Liberal Democratic Party and with the head of the Defence Agency, the future prime minister Yasuhiro Nakasone. When Nakasone was appointed head of the Defence Agency on 14 January 1970, Mishima had worried that the connection between the Shield Society and the SDF would be severed, as Nakasone had publicly dismissed the Shield Society as toy soldiers. Yet not only did Nakasone personally ring Mishima to apologize for his public remarks, but Prime Minister Sato also secretly offered to fund the Shield Society, offering a million yen (approximately $28,000 today) a month.

On 7 July 1970, Mishima published an article in the *Sankei* newspaper in which he railed against the hypocrisy and fraud of modern Japan. He remarked that he had thought such hypocrisy would die out with the end of the American occupation, but instead it had worsened. From the end of the war until 1957, he wrote, he was thought of as being a believer in 'art for art's sake' and passed through the world with a cynical grin, but finally had come to do battle with the cynicism inside him, tormented by the idea that he had unfulfilled promise. In this respect, he remarked, literature was neither here nor there. The following month, the critic Takehiko Noguchi speculated that Mishima was soon coming to the point where he would have to die in a political crisis or else stick his tongue out and declare that everything had been a charade. Mishima read the article and declared that it chilled him to the bone.

Mishima realized that all his activities in the 'real world', his political posturing and play-acting at soldiering, were nothing but attempts to grasp a tangible 'reality' that would crush his overwhelming sense of existential angst and provide the energy to keep going with the masterpiece. But should that masterpiece ever be finished, then that 'reality' would instantly collapse and Mishima's life in the 'real world' would have no meaning. Mishima remarked that while people might think it was pleasant to take a break from writing, in fact it was 'really, really, really unpleasant'. Mishima believed he could not live a day longer than it took to finish *The Sea of Fertility* and that his death must demonstrate 'purity of action' on the political stage, that it must be a Shinpuren- and *Hagakure*-style death.

At precisely this moment in March 1970, Mishima began to lay plans with Morita for a spectacular terrorist attack which would result in their joint deaths. At the end of March they decided to enlist the help of two other Shield Society cadets, both students aged 22. Masayoshi Koga, known as 'Tiny Koga', was all of 150 cm (4 ft 11 in) tall, and was asked by Mishima in the coffee shop of the Imperial Hotel: 'Are you prepared to join in a Final Action?' Masahiro Ogawa, the second young recruit, looked up to the slightly older Morita as a brother and was called to the Mishima home and asked the same question a week later. All four were ready to lay down their lives. The first scheme proposed was that they would force the Tokyo Ichigaya division to assemble by threatening to blow up their arsenal or by taking their supreme commander prisoner, then call up volunteers and occupy parliament. At their next meeting, on 13 June in Room 821 of the Okura Hotel, this was refined to inviting the supreme commander to the second anniversary parade of the Shield Society and seizing him there. By 21 June, at a meeting in Room 206 of the Yamanoue Hotel, Mishima announced that he had secured permission to hold the parade at the Ichigaya heliport, but they would have to take the supreme commander's subordinate, the 32nd Regiment's commander, instead because the former's office was too far away. It was also decided that the only weapons used would be Japanese swords. Finally, on 5 July in Room 207 of the Yamanoue Hotel, it was decided that the action would be in November on the day that the Shield Society met.

On 1 September, another young cadet, Hiroyasu Koga, known as 'Old Koga' (because of the character for 'old' appearing in his surname), turned three accomplices into four. A week later, at a French restaurant on the Ginza, Mishima told 'Old Koga' that probably no one in the SDF would rise up with them, but whatever happened Mishima had to die and the date decided was 25 November. 'Old Koga' was permitted to make one last trip back to his family in Hokkaido at the beginning of October and was given half his travelling expenses.

Meanwhile, Mishima started getting his worldly affairs in order. On the pretext that he was way behind schedule with *The Sea of Fertility*, he asked his editor Hiroshi Niita to forget about their plans for him to write a historical novel about the great court poet Fujiwara no Teika and suggested to his collaborators on the magazine *Criticism* that the next issue be the last. In June he invited out for dinner or a drink all his old friends, including the critics and writers he most admired, or made late-night phone calls that ended with the telling word 'farewell'. He transferred to his mother the copyright to *Confessions of a Mask*, still selling 100,000 copies a year, and *Thirst for Love*, his earliest literary works as a professional writer, published before he was married.

In August, he invited Donald Keene to the Tokyu Hotel in Shimoda, where Mishima was taking his annual family holiday, and showed him a pile of papers containing the final section of *The Sea of Fertility*, based on research he had conducted at the Enshoji temple in Nara at the end of July. Mishima had not yet finished the novel, but had already drafted it and was honing its extraordinary conclusion. Meanwhile, he was working furiously to ensure that the novel was finished by 25 November, the self-imposed 'deadline'. (Why this date? Because it would be exactly 22 years since he had promised his publisher he would commence writing *Confessions of a Mask*? Was this also the date on which he initially heard about his first love Kuniko's betrothal in 1945?) In any case he returned from his 'holiday' looking gaunt and exhausted.

On 25 September, at a meeting in a sauna, it was decided that any Shield Society members with links to the SDF, or who had already been offered a job after graduating, would be excluded from the November drill, and Mishima personally chose who to invite, signing each invitation. On 2 October, they decided on the details of the plan and Morita and the other three cadets went to the base to conduct research. On 19 October, Mishima, Morita and the three others had an old-fashioned, commemorative picture taken wearing their Shield Society uniforms, but on 3 November, in Misty Sauna, Mishima instructed the other three that there was a change of plan. The two Kogas and Ogawa were now not to die, but to guard the regimental commander and then, when arrested after Mishima's and Morita's deaths, were to make clear in court the aspirations of the Shield Society. 'Old Koga', having prepared himself for death, was most disappointed at being forced to live.

The following day saw the beginning of the final 'refresher' course for members of the Shield Society at Camp Takigahara near Mount Fuji. On the evening of the 6th, Mishima had his final meeting with them. He poured toasts for all 40 people present, drinking with each student, singing individual songs and reciting poems, and, unusually for him, got very drunk. Then, on 14 November, again

Studio portrait of Mishima and the 4 cadres chosen to embark on a 'final action'.

at Misty Sauna, Mishima read to his four accomplices the contents of his 'Declaration of Protest'.

For all his blood lust and shocking pronouncements, Mishima was not entirely convincing as a political terrorist. A right-wing 'extremist' who still believed in democracy and parliamentary representation, he also told the cadets at another sauna meeting on 19 November that, whatever happened, the hostage must not be harmed. Mishima was intent that nobody should be seriously hurt except himself and Morita.

In typical fashion, Mishima kept up an impressive array of other activities right until the end: writing an afterword to an anthology of Japanese writers, an essay on Tanizaki and one on manga, as well as the foreword to his wife's translation of the novel *Les Petites Filles modèles* by the Countess of Segur and even to his horseback-riding instructor's book, *The Equestrian Reader*. He posed for a life-size sculpture of himself and for the final shoots of the *Death of a Man* photo series (where he posed in a large number of outlandish 'at point of death' positions, whether as St Sebastian, drowning on a rock or committing seppuku). He even toyed with the idea of having himself tattooed, yakuza-style, ahead of his final action, while also spending hours at the open day at his son's school, chatting with the headmaster.

On 20 November, Mishima suddenly called all his family, including his brother, together for what was – unbeknownst to them – a final dinner. Throughout 1970, Mishima's mother had sensed something was amiss. Even back on New Year's Day, when the tradition was to take a family photo together, Shizue had a sudden intuition that this would be the last one. Distracted and unresponsive, in mid-August during a family dinner on the second-floor balcony of his home, Mishima sloped off and stared at the evening sun, making his mother feel lonely and want to say to him: 'Don't die!' By the end of August she thought he looked thin; he said that this was the last year he would go to Shimoda with the children and that in future he would stay and rest in Tokyo. Despite personally not liking dogs, he even suggested that his mother and father get another dog after their beloved dog had died four years earlier.[4]

At the meeting with the cadets on 19 November, the schedule for the day of action was also discussed: twenty minutes for the army to assemble; thirty minutes for Mishima's speech; five minutes each for the speeches of the four others; five minutes for instructions to the Shield Society, which was to be disbanded that day; then three cheers for the emperor. Mishima's manifesto was also approved without emendation. However, on 21 November everything was thrown into chaos as it became clear when Morita visited the base that the regimental commander would be away that day, so the designated target was changed back to the supreme commander, General Mashita. Mishima immediately rang him and made an appointment to see him at 11 a.m. on the 25th, and the next day they purchased their materials for the day: rope to bind him, pliers and wire to secure the doors and fabric from which to fashion banners, as well as plastic bags, bandages, a flask and brandy. On the way home, Morita asked 'Old Koga', a trained swordsman, to act in his place should he be unable to carry out the *kaishaku*.

From the 23rd until the following day, they rehearsed in Room 519 of the Palace Hotel, with Mishima playing the general. They wrote out their banners, prepared their headbands and agreed that when Mishima offered to show the general his splendid Seki no Magoroku sword he would ask Tiny Koga for a handkerchief to clean the blade. This would be the prearranged signal for Tiny Koga to move behind the general and put his hand over his mouth while Ogawa and 'Old Koga' restrained him. They practised the manoeuvre eight times. Meanwhile, Mishima rehearsed his speech with the television on so that he could not be overheard and also surprised Morita by producing some cotton-wool padding for them both to insert under their anuses lest they void their bowels during seppuku. Worryingly for a man about to act as Mishima's beheader, Morita asked to be shown where the carotid artery is.

During the afternoon of the 24th, in true samurai tradition, they each wrote poems taking their leave of the world, with Mishima brushing up the others' efforts where necessary. They left behind in the hotel room the beginnings of a play to make it look as if that was what they had been working on. In the evening they had a farewell dinner at a *ryotei* in Shinbashi with Mishima making light conversation about films and saying nothing about the following day. He remarked that he thought he would feel more sentimental when it reached this point, but that it was actually others looking back at them in the future who would become sentimental. Mishima then went home, observing to the others in the car: 'It's a shame because the supreme commander is a fine man. When I kill myself in front of him, hopefully he will understand' and 'If the soldiers come on to us before we get into the supreme commander's room, there's nothing for it but for all five of us to bite our tongues and die.'[5]

At 10 p.m., Mishima popped in to see his mother and father for a final time and waited with his father while his mother returned from a relative's wedding. Surprised when she got back at the unusual time he had called, she asked if he had finished his work. He remarked that he was feeling exhausted and she advised: 'You're working too hard. The best thing to do is to get some rest.' He bid goodnight to his father, who grumbled that his son was smoking too many Peace cigarettes for his health. In his study Mishima then put his final papers in order and asked the maid to wake him at 8 a.m. He left a note on his desk which read: 'Human life is limited, but I would like to live forever.'

10

Time and Mr Mishima

When all was said and done, though, what exactly had the Mishima Incident all been about? It certainly represented Mishima's attempt to transcend time and grasp the glorious destiny he had missed at the end of the war, fused with his sadomasochistic fantasies linked to the 26 February Incident. But, ultimately, what was at the heart of the Mishima Incident was not the faux politicking, nor the playing at soldiers nor the love suicide with Morita. What was central was not the Seki no Magoroku sword, nor the theatre of headbands and banners nor the cries to the emperor. The crucial elements were rather two things: the watch he took off his wrist as his very final act before death and the single envelope, containing the final instalment of his manuscript, which Mishima left quietly behind in the hallway of his home. Once he had sealed that envelope, as Mishima well knew, he was living on borrowed time.

From that envelope an entirely different drama unfolded on the morning of 25 November 1970. As well as ringing two journalists the day before the Incident, Mishima had also rung his editor Chikako Kojima and asked her to collect the manuscript at 10.30 a.m. When she arrived, ten minutes late, at 10.40 a.m., she was surprised that Mishima was not there. Kojima was instead handed the manuscript by the maid. There was nothing unusual in this, but previously the envelope had always been left open, not thickly sealed as if to prevent it being checked on site. She was tempted to open it on the train back, but when she did so back at the office, discovered that there were three layers of envelopes, all stapled down four times. She wrote:

> Feeling something was not quite right, when I opened the manuscript it said *The Decay of the Angel* (Final Part). That was unexpected. When I turned the final page, it formally recorded over two lines:
>
> The End of *The Sea of Fertility*
>
> 25 November 1970.
>
> That was a complete surprise. While it was clear that completion was drawing near, I had not heard it was going to be this month and imagined it would be in another two or three months . . . What was going on? I felt it was incomprehensible, or perhaps I should say mystifying.[1]

For all those who strained to make any sense of the Incident, Mishima had already publicly provided the answer. From 12 to 17 November, just one week before the Incident, a 'Yukio Mishima Exhibition' was held at the Tobu Department Store in Ikebukuro. Mishima promoted it himself saying:

> This is my personal complete works, a complete edition of 45 years of contradictions . . . constructed so that the four rivers of 'writing', 'stage', 'body', 'action' would converge in *The Sea of Fertility*.

For Mishima, *The Sea of Fertility* was not just the culmination of his *writing* career, but the end point of *all* his other activities as well. They were like rivers feeding into a vast sea and once they reached the sea they fused with infinity. This was Mishima's final in-joke, a river of life that took in everything from pictures of him as a baby to some of the shots from the *Death of a Man* series. On the wall of the exhibition, a meandering black river a metre wide was interspersed with life-size portraits. Mishima's mother described going to see this exhibition and observing seven floors of escalators brimming with university students.[2]

Yet, despite Mishima making it clear that the ultimate destination of everything in his life was *The Sea of Fertility*, when critics later reflected on the meaning of this exhibition, they invariably turned all their attention to the 'river of action'. By insisting that he appear in his coffin in his uniform and that only the word for warrior (*bu*) appear in his posthumous name, it might seem as if Mishima was finally determined to shake off his identity as a writer, that Mishima the man of action had finally triumphed over Mishima the artist. Yet exactly the reverse was true. The fantasy life of 'Mishima the soldier' lasted for only a couple of hours and every embodiment of that existence was placed in a coffin and burned like so much useless waste paper. Mishima the artist, on the other hand, fully intended to live forever.

Incomparably his greatest artistic achievement, *The Sea of Fertility* was ultimately everything Mishima aspired to as an artist. Its impact would be profound and diverse, whether being read by Francis Ford

Mishima at the Yukio Mishima Exhibition, November 1970.

Coppola in the jungles of the Philippines during the filming of *Apocalypse Now* or inspiring a complete change of direction in the writings of Shusaku Endo, the writer who took over from Mishima, in the eyes of the West at least, as the greatest Japanese writer in the 1970s.

One of the many paradoxes of Mishima's life was that, for all his eccentricities and absolute uniqueness as an artist, he was always strangely in tune with the zeitgeist, even in his final years, when he managed to visit India the year before The Beatles and be serializing *The Sea of Fertility* in the run-up to the Moon Landing. Similarly, within the world of Japanese literature, Mishima seemed both to effortlessly collect the literary baton from the nihilistic Dazai in 1948 and also pass it on in 1970 to the Christian Endo. In later works such as *Scandal* (1986), Endo would continue *The Temple of Dawn*'s exploration of alaya consciousness as well as the lascivious degeneracy of old age; *Deep River* (1993) saw Endo too taking his characters to Varanasi in search of the fundamental meaning of religious faith. By strange coincidence, Kenzaburo Oe, the other great Japanese writer of the age and the future Nobel Laureate, was actually in Varanasi when he heard news of the Mishima Incident.

By the 1980s, wherever you lived in the world, you did not have to seek Mishima out, he was pretty much hard to avoid. The photos of him posing with bulging muscles, sword aloft, bandana in place and with a steely glare had burned into the world's consciousness forever. As one of the first writers adept at manipulating the media and stage-managing his image in an age of celebrity, he was the one Japanese writer everyone in the West had heard about, albeit not always for the best reasons. Mishima appeared to embody every cliché of Japan – swords, samurai, seppuku – at which anyone who is more familiar with the country inevitably rolls their eyes. Indeed it became increasingly exasperating that this was the only face of Japan with which so many in the West were familiar.

Mishima with a sword and wearing a headband with the samurai declaration 'Seven Lives for the Nation'.

From the mid-1990s, though, things began to change. Mishima was gradually displaced by Haruki Murakami as the one Japanese writer of whom everyone was cognisant in the West. Intriguingly, Murakami's novel *A Wild Sheep Chase* begins on the day of the Mishima Incident, as if signalling that Murakami's Japan begins on the day that Mishima's ended. There was no obsession with

Japanese culture or militarism or the death aesthetic. Murakami was born in 1949 (the year *Confessions of a Mask* was published) and knew nothing of the trauma of the war or the shock of American occupation. Quite the opposite: as a child of the 1960s, he embraced the Americanization of Japanese culture and through it created a new form of writing which was readily accessible to people around the world.

Those who think, though, that with the advent of the age of Murakami, Japan has left behind its schizophrenic lurching between the values of the past and an embrace of a globalized, interconnected future would do well to take a look at the current bestsellers in Japan. Books advising the nation to break with America and return to first principles, the ethics of *bushido*, sell in the millions; samurai adventure stories top the fiction lists. Mishima is not just an embodiment of the psychological trauma Japan has lived through in the modern age, but representative of something with which people in all countries, in some form or other, are always struggling: knowing how far to stay in communion with the past and how thoroughly to reinvent oneself for the future.

In Mishima's fiction, the place of ultimate escape from the oppressions of historical time is the sea, a place where time is meaningless. Time, indeed, only acquires meaning when the sea reaches the shore. Thus, in the final part of *The Sea of Fertility*, the protagonist, the coordinator of docking ships, gazes constantly at the sea and yet is utterly ruled by time. When ships emerge from the sea they must wait for a berth. Time imposes itself upon them. In *The Sailor who Fell from Grace with the Sea*, the sea is linked with the infinity beyond time itself, with the narrative breaking off in the middle of the book as the sailor sets off to sea for the final time. Sailing into timelessness is the ultimate vision of beauty. The ship sailing out to sea gleams in the sun and seems, in an allusion to *The Temple of the Golden Pavilion*, like a 'pagoda of steel' rising upward to heaven. The point at which the ship leaves the shore

– the moment of parting – reduces time to the instant and from there the ship breaks free of time.

In the end, Mishima succeeded in the impossible – in stopping time. When news of the Mishima Incident spread across the nation, everyone stopped, open-mouthed, and stared at televisions. The shock and disbelief were immeasurable: this was to be not only the moment that twentieth-century Japan became frozen in eternal memory, but also arguably the day that Japan finally became a modern nation. Ironically, the only other person to have achieved such a time-freezing feat was the emperor himself with his radio broadcast that brought the Pacific War, the great catastrophe of modern Japanese history, to an end. But in the case of the emperor, the script had been written by others: he was history's servant. In Mishima's case, everything was self-generated: he was the master of time.

Rereading the various biographies of Mishima – such an intensely Freudian writer – written in the 1970s by men who knew him, it is interesting how each of them had the same experience of Mishima overwhelming them, invading their sleeping and waking thoughts. His Japanese biographer, Takeo Okuno, said he had nightmares about Mishima 200 or 300 nights in a row. His English biographer Henry Scott Stokes dreamed of Mishima visiting his home in Glastonbury and of murdering Mishima with a mattock. Mishima's loud, guttural laugh would echo in their dreams. He was a force of nature from which they could not escape.

As a distillation of history as well as a force refluxing and reprocessing both personal history and world history into a profusion of literary masterpieces; as a master of prose in every conceivable form; as a model of both how to live and how not to live; as the supreme analyst of the interaction of time and consciousness, Mishima's presence in the world of twentieth-century letters is monumental. It seems likely he will be invading our collective dreams for quite some time to come.

A Note on Japanese Names

Japanese names in this book are generally presented in Western order: personal name followed by family name. In Japanese the order of these names would be reversed – thus Hiraoka Kimitake rather than Kimitake Hiraoka. But matters are complicated by the frequent adoption of pseudonyms or stylistic literary names known as *go*. In Kimitake Hiraoka's case, he adopted a completely new literary name – Yukio Mishima – and the fake surname, Mishima, became the name by which he is most commonly known. Similarly, writers who use their real names (for example, Junichiro Tanizaki, Kenzaburo Oe and Shusaku Endo) are commonly known by their family names (Tanizaki, Oe, Endo).

Traditionally, however, many writers assumed a single literary name that replaced his/her given name and followed the family name. For example, the writer Natsume Kinnosuke adopted a literary name, Soseki; he published as Natsume Soseki, and he is often referred to simply as Soseki. For writers with literary names, the Japanese sequence of family name followed by literary name has been left intact in English in this book to indicate that it is the literary name rather than the family name by which these writers are best known. Famous examples include Mori Ogai, Nagai Kafu and Masamune Hakucho, all better known by their literary names – Ogai, Kafu and Hakucho – rather than by their family names of Mori, Nagai and Masamune.

There are a profusion of variations. Some writers such as Edogawa Ranpo (a play on Edgar Allan Poe) adopted a pseudonym based on a Western name, with Ranpo acting as his literary name. The poet Sakutaro Hagiwara, like numerous others, used his real name but is better known by his personal name, Sakutaro; while Matsumoto Seicho adopted a literary name, Seicho, that was a variant reading of his given name.

References

1 Japan in the Age of Mishima

1 Kazuaki Yoshida, *Mishima* [1985] (Tokyo, 2007), pp. 18–19.
2 Ibid., p. 19.
3 Yusuke Nakagawa, *Showa 45-nen 11-gatsu 25-nichi* (Tokyo, 2010), p. 36.
4 Donald Keene, *On Familiar Terms* (New York, 1994), p. 150.
5 Nakagawa, *Showa 45-nen*, p. 141.
6 Naoki Inose with Hiroaki Sato, *Persona: A Biography of Yukio Mishima* (Berkeley, CA, 2012), p. 670.
7 Yoshida, *Mishima*, p. 35.
8 Ibid., p. 30.
9 Ibid., p. 32.
10 Yukio Mishima, 'Todai o dobutsuen ni shiro', in *Wakaki samurai no tame ni* (Tokyo, 1969), pp. 111–12.
11 Yukio Mishima, 'Bunburyodo to shi no tetsugaku', in *Wakaki samurai*, pp. 202–3.
12 Ibid., pp. 207–9.
13 Mishima, 'Todai o dobutsuen ni shiro', pp. 113–14.
14 Yukio Mishima, 'Makeru ga kachi', in *Wakaki samurai*, p. 150.
15 Mishima, 'Bunburyodo to shi no tetsugaku', pp. 171–2.
16 Masayasu Hosaka, *Mishima Yukio to tate no kai jiken* [1980] (Tokyo, 2001), p. 21.

2 Macrocosm and Microcosm

1 Naoki Inose, *Perusona: Mishima Yukio-den* (Tokyo, 1995), p. 56.
2 Ibid., p. 84.
3 Ibid., p. 180.
4 Ibid., p. 173.
5 Azusa Hiraoka, *Segare: Mishima Yukio* [1972] (Tokyo, 1996), p. 34.
6 John Nathan, *Mishima* (Boston and Toronto, 1974), p. 10.
7 Hiraoka, *Segare*, pp. 35–6.
8 Ibid., p. 39.
9 Kazuaki Yoshida, *Mishima* [1985] (Tokyo, 2007), p. 83.
10 Hiraoka, *Segare*, p. 46.
11 Takashi Inoue, *Mishima Yukio: Hojo naru kamen* (Tokyo, 2009), pp. 27–8.
12 Yoshida, *Mishima*, p. 92.

3 A Mask Facing Inwards

1 Yukio Mishima, 'Radige ni tsukarete – watakushi no dokusho henreki' ('Entranced with Radiguet – My Reading History'), *Nihon Yomikaki Shinbun* (2 February 1956), see *Mishima zenshu* (Tokyo, 2000–2005), vol. XXIX, p. 147.
2 Kazuaki Yoshida, *Mishima* [1985] (Tokyo, 2007), p. 93.
3 Yukio Mishima, lecture, teach-in at Waseda University, 3 October 1968, see Takashi Inoue, *Mishima Yukio: Hojo naru kamen* (Tokyo, 2009), p. 42.
4 Yukio Mishima, 'Issatsu no hon – Radige *Dorujeru Haku no Butokai*' ('One Book – Radiguet's *Count Orgel's Ball*'), *Asahi Shinbun* (1 December 1963), see Inoue, p. 52.
5 Yukio Mishima, 'Wa ga miseraretaru mono' ('Beguiling Things'), *Shinjoen* (April 1956), see *Mishima Yukio no essei* (Tokyo, 1995), vol. I, p. 179.
6 *Literary Culture* (July 1938), see Inoue, *Mishima Yukio*, p. 58.
7 *Literary Culture* (January 1942), see Inoue, *Mishima Yukio*, p. 58.
8 Naoki Inose, *Perusona: Mishima Yukio-den* (Tokyo, 1995), p. 211.
9 Azusa Hiraoka, *Segare: Mishima Yukio* [1972] (Tokyo, 1996), p. 95.
10 Zenmei Hasuda, *Literary Culture* (September 1941), see Jiro Odakane, *Hasuda Zenmei to sono shi* (Tokyo, 1970), p. 464.

11 Yukio Mishima, '*Hasuda Zenmei to sono shi jobun*' ('Introduction to *Zenmei Hasuda and his Death*'), *Mishima zenshu*, vol. XXXVI, pp. 60–63.

12 Inoue, *Mishima Yukio*, pp. 65–6.

13 Yukio Mishima, 'Watashi no henreki jidai' ('My Wandering Years') (1964), see *Mishima Yukio no essei*, vol. I, p. 98.

14 Naoki Inose with Hiroaki Sato, *Persona: A Biography of Yukio Mishima* (Berkeley, CA, 2012), p. 95.

15 Mishima, 'Watashi no henreki jidai', p. 99.

16 Ibid, pp. 98–9.

17 Donald Keene, *Dawn to the West: Japanese Literature in the Modern Era* (Boston, 1984), p. 1176.

18 Hiraoka, *Segare*, pp. 70–71. Translation from John Nathan, *Mishima* (Boston and Toronto, 1974), p. 55.

19 Yukio Mishima, 'Hachigatsu jugonichi zengo' ('Around 15 August'), quoted in *Mishima zenshu*, vol. XXVIII, p. 527.

4 Sentenced to Live

1 John Dower, *Embracing Defeat* (New York, 1999), pp. 189–90.

2 Ibid., pp. 123–32.

3 Yukio Mishima, 'Shumatsukan kara no shuppatsu, Showa nijunen no jigazo' ('Setting out with a Feeling of Apocalypse: A Self-portrait in 1945'), *Shincho* (August 1955), see Takashi Inoue, *Mishima Yukio: Hojo naru kamen* (Tokyo, 2009), pp. 74–5, *Mishima zenshu* (Tokyo, 2000–2005), vol. XXVIII, p. 516.

4 Yukio Mishima, 'Hachigatsu nijuichinichi no aribai' ('21 August Alibi'), *Yomiuri Shinbun* (evening edn, 21 August 1961), see Inoue, *Mishima Yukio*, p. 74.

5 *Taidan* with Takashi Furubayashi, see Kazuaki Yoshida, *Mishima* [1985] (Tokyo, 2007), p. 104.

6 Yukio Mishima, 'Shumatsukan kara no shuppatsu', see *Mishima zenshu*, vol. XXVIII, p. 516.

7 Yukio Mishima, 'Watashi no henreki jidai' ('My Wandering Years') (1964), see *Mishima Yukio no essei* (Tokyo, 1995), vol. I, p. 103.

8 John Nathan, *Mishima* (Boston and Toronto, 1974), p. 84.

9 Mishima, 'Watashi no henreki jidai', pp. 104–5.

10 Naoki Inose with Hiroaki Sato, *Persona: A Biography of Yukio Mishima* (Berkeley, CA, 2012), pp. 149–50.

11 Mishima, 'Watashi no henreki jidai', p. 105.

12 Ibid., p. 109.

13 Kazuki Sakamoto, '*Kamen no kokuhaku* no koro' ('The Time of *Confessions of a Mask*'), *Bungei* (February 1971), see Yoshida, *Mishima*, p. 119.

14 Yukio Mishima, letter of 2 November 1948 to Kazuki Sakamoto, see *Mishima zenshu*, vol. XXXVIII, p. 507.

15 *Mishima zenshu* (Tokyo, 2004), vol. XXXVIII, pp. 513–14.

16 Mishima, 'Watashi no henreki jidai', p. 124.

17 Yukio Mishima, note on *Confessions of Mask*, see *Mishima zenshu*, vol. II.

18 Inoue, *Mishima Yukio*, p. 90.

19 Tsuneari Fukuda, '*Kamen no kokuhaku* ni tsuite', see Yoshida, *Mishima*, p. 119.

5 Mishima à la Mode

1 Naoki Inose with Hiroaki Sato, *Persona: A Biography of Yukio Mishima* (Berkeley, CA, 2012), pp. 198–9.

2 Yukio Mishima, letter of 16 December 1949 to Tokuzo Kimura, see *Mishima zenshu* (Tokyo, 2000–2005), vol. XXXVIII, pp. 490–91.

3 Yukio Mishima, 'Watashi no henreki jidai' ('My Wandering Years'), (1964), see *Mishima Yukio no essei* (Tokyo 1995), vol. I, p. 139.

4 Ibid., pp. 144–5.

5 Inose with Sato, *Persona*, pp. 230–31.

6 Mishima, 'Watashi no henreki jidai', p. 147.

7 Ibid., pp. 146–7.

8 Ibid., p. 147.

9 See Shoji Shibata, *Mishima Yukio: Sakuhin ni kakusareta jiketsu e no michi* (Tokyo, 2012), pp. 58–68.

10 Yukio Mishima, 'Kyodokenkyu, Mishima Yukio no jikken kabuki' ('Combined Studies of Yukio Mishima's Experimental Kabuki'), *Engekikai* (May 1957), see Takashi Inoue, *Mishima Yukio: Hojo naru kamen* (Tokyo, 2009), p. 109.

6 *Nihil*

1 See Kazuaki Yoshida, *Mishima* [1985] (Tokyo, 2007), p. 126.
2 See Takashi Inoue, *Mishima Yukio: Hojo naru kamen* (Tokyo, 2009), pp. 116–20.
3 Naoki Inose, *Perusona: Mishima Yukio-den* (Tokyo, 1995), p. 307.
4 Yukio Mishima, 'Chosha no kotoba' ('A Word by the Author') (November 1957), see Inoue, *Mishima Yukio*, pp. 140–41.
5 Donald Keene, *On Familiar Terms* (New York, 1994), p. 206.
6 Interview in evening edn of *Minami Nippon Shinbun* (29 October 1959), see Inoue, *Mishima Yukio*, p. 154.
7 Yoshida, *Mishima*, p. 134.
8 Inose, *Perusona*, pp. 333–4.
9 Yukio Mishima, 'Ratai to isho' ('Nudity and Clothing') (1959), see Yoshida, *Mishima*, p. 136.
10 'Juhassai to sanjuyonsai no shozoga' ('Portrait at Eighteen and Thirty-Four'), *Gunzo*, XIV/5 (May 1959), see *Mishima zenshu* (Tokyo, 2004), vol. XXXI, pp. 225–7.
11 'Sakka to kekkon' ('The Writer and Marriage'), *Fujin Koron* (July 1958), see *Mishima Yukio no essei* (Tokyo, 1995), vol. I, p. 197.
12 '"Yukoku" no nazo' ('The Mystery of "Patriotism"'), *Art Theatre* (April 1966), see Inoue, *Mishima Yukio*, p. 160.
13 'Fashisuto ka kakumeika ka' ('Fascist or Revolutionary?'), *Eiga Geijutsu* (*Film Art*) (January 1968), see Inoue, *Mishima Yukio*, p. 161.

6 Seas of Controversy

1 Yukio Mishima, '*Hojo no umi* ni tsuite', evening edn of *Mainichi Shinbun* (26 February 1969), see Takashi Inoue, *Mishima Yukio: Hojo naru kamen* (Tokyo, 2009), p. 188.
2 '*Yukoku* eigaban: Seisaku ito oyobi keika' ('The Filming of *Patriotism*: Production Design and Execution') (April 1966), see *Mishima zenshu* (Tokyo, 2000–2005), vol. XXXIV, pp. 35–64.
3 Donald Keene, *On Familiar Terms* (New York, 1994), p. 257.
4 See Henry Scott Stokes, *The Life and Death of Yukio Mishima* (New York, 1974), p. 150.

5 Postscript to *Sado Koshaku fujin* (Tokyo, November 1965), see Inoue, *Mishima Yukio*, p. 194.

8 The Faustian Pact

1 Chikako Kojima, *Mishima Yukio to Dan Kazuo* [1989] (Tokyo, 1996), p. 51.
2 Takeshi Muramatsu, *Mishima Yukio no sekai* [1990] (Tokyo, 1996), pp. 423, 505.
3 Yukio Mishima, '*Hojo no Umi* ni tsuite', *Mainichi Shinbun* (evening edn, 26 February 1969), see Takashi Inoue, *Mishima Yukio: Hojo naru kamen* (Tokyo, 2009), p. 188.
4 *Taidan* with Fusao Hayashi, see *Mishima zenshu* (Tokyo, 2000–2005), vol. xxxix, p. 634.
5 Yukio Mishima, 'Fuyu no ame no kurai gogo' ('A Dark, Rainy Afternoon in Winter'), *Controversy Journal* (September 1967), see Naoki Inose, *Perusona: Mishima Yukio-den* (Tokyo, 1995), pp. 388–9.
6 Kazuaki Yoshida, *Mishima* [1985] (Tokyo, 2007), p. 162.
7 Inoue, *Mishima Yukio*, p. 227.
8 John Nathan, *Mishima* (Boston and Toronto, 1974), p. 251.
9 Yusuke Nakagawa, *Showa 45-nen 11-gatsu 25-nichi* (Tokyo, 2010), pp. 178–9.

9 Battle against Time

1 *Shosetsu to wa nani ka* (Tokyo, March 1972), see *Mishima zenshu* (Tokyo, 2000–2005), vol. xxxix, pp. 710–21.
2 Azusa Hiraoka, *Segare: Mishima Yukio* (Tokyo, 1972), pp. 229–30.
3 Toyoo Inoue, *Hatashiete inai yakusoku* (Tokyo, 2006), p. 68.
4 Hiraoka, *Segare*, p. 194.
5 Ibid., p. 243.

10 Time and Mr Mishima

1 Chikako Kojima, *Mishima Yukio to Dan Kazuo* [1989] (Tokyo, 1996), pp. 10–11.
2 Azusa Hiraoka, *Segare: Mishima Yukio* (Tokyo, 1972), p. 188.

Select Bibliography

All of Mishima's works listed below in Japanese are contained in the capacious 42-volume set, the *Complete Works of Mishima* (*Mishima zenshu*) (Tokyo, 2000–2005). All of the novels and most of the plays, short stories and essays are also available in compact paperback editions (*bunko*).

Novels in Japanese

All published in Tokyo

Tozoku (*The Thieves*, 1948)
Kamen no kokuhaku (*Confessions of a Mask*, 1949)
Ao no jidai (*The Blue Period*, 1950)
Ai no kawaki (*Thirst for Love*, 1950)
Junpaku no yoru (*The Immaculate Night*, 1950)
Natsuko no boken (*Natsuko's Adventures*, 1951)
Kinjiki (*Forbidden Colours*, 1951, 1953)
Shiosai (*The Sound of Waves*, 1954)
Shizumeru taki (*Sunken Waterfall*, 1955)
Kinkakuji (*The Temple of the Golden Pavilion*, 1956)
Nagasugita haru (*The Overlong Spring*, 1956)
Bitoku no yoromeki (*The Wavering Virtue*, 1957)
Kyoko no ie (*Kyoko's House*, 1959)
Utage no ato (*After the Banquet*, 1960)
Kemono no tawamure (*The Amusement of Beasts*, 1961)
Utsukushii hoshi (*Beautiful Star*, 1962)
Gogo no eiko (*The Sailor who Fell from Grace with the Sea*, 1963)
Kinu to meisatsu (*Silk and Insight*, 1964)

Haru no yuki (*Spring Snow*, 1969)
Honba (*Runaway Heroes*, 1969)
Akatsuki no tera (*The Temple of Dawn*, 1970)
Tennin gosui (*The Decay of the Angel*, 1971)

Plays

All published in Tokyo

Yoru no himawari (*Sunflowers at Night*, 1952)
Iwashi uri koi hikiami (*The Sardine Seller's Love Net*, 1954)
Wakodo yo yomigaere (*Young People, Resurrect Yourselves*, 1954)
Kindai nogakushu (*Modern Noh Plays*, 1956)
Rokumeikan (*The Hall of the Crying Deer*, 1957)
Bara to kaizoku (*The Rose and the Pirate*, 1958)
Yorokobi no koto (*The Harp of Happiness*, 1964)
Sado koshaku fujin (*Madame de Sade*, 1965)
Wa ga tomo Hittora (*My Friend Hitler*, 1968)
Chinsetsu yumiharizuki (*A Wondertale: The Moonbow*, 1969)
Raio no terasu (*The Terrace of the Leper King*, 1969)

Short Stories

All published in Tokyo

'Hanazakari no Mori' ('A Forest in Full Bloom', 1944)
'Misaki nite no monogatari' ('A Tale at the Cape', 1947)
'Yoru no shitaku' ('Preparations for the Evening', 1948)
'Manatsu no shi' ('Death in Midsummer', 1953)
'Radige no shi' ('Radiguet's Death', 1953)
'Hashizukushi' ('The Seven Bridges', 1958)
'Yukoku' ('Patriotism', 1966)
'Eirei no koe' ('Voices of the Heroic Dead', 1966)

Essays

All published in Tokyo

'Aporo no sakazuki' ('Apollo's Cup', 1952)
'Shi o kaku shonen' ('The Boy who Writes Poems', 1956)
'Ratai to isho' ('Nudity and Clothing', 1959)
'Hayashi Fusao ron' ('Essay on Fusao Hayashi', 1963)
'Watashi no henreki jidai' ('My Wandering Years', 1964)
Hagakure nyumon (*Introduction to Hagakure*, 1967)
Taiyo to tetsu (*Sun and Steel*, 1968)
'Bunka boeiron' ('The Theory of Cultural Defence', 1969)
Wakaki samurai no tame ni (*For Young Samurai*, 1969)
Kodogaku nyumon (*Introductions to the Philosophy of Action*, 1970)

Works by Yukio Mishima in English

The Sound of Waves, trans. Meredith Weatherby (New York, 1956)
Five Modern Noh Plays, trans. Donald Keene (New York, 1957)
Confessions of a Mask, trans. Meredith Weatherby (New York, 1958)
The Temple of the Golden Pavilion, trans. Ivan Morris (New York, 1959)
After the Banquet, trans. Donald Keene (New York, 1963)
The Sailor who Fell from Grace with the Sea, trans. John Nathan
     (New York, 1965)
Death in Midsummer and Other Stories, trans. Edward Seidensticker et al.
     (New York, 1966)
Madame de Sade, trans. Donald Keene (New York, 1967)
Forbidden Colors, trans. Alfred H. Marks (New York, 1968)
Thirst for Love, trans. Alfred H. Marks (New York, 1969)
Sun and Steel, trans. John Bester (Tokyo, 1970)
Spring Snow, trans. Michael Gallagher (New York, 1972)
Runaway Horses, trans. Michael Gallagher (New York, 1973)
The Temple of Dawn, trans. E. D. Saunders and C. S. Seigle (New York, 1973)
The Decay of the Angel, trans. Edward Seidensticker (New York, 1974)
Mishima on Hagakure, trans. Kathryn Sparling (New York, 1977)
Acts of Worship, trans. John Bester (New York, 1989)
'A Forest in Full Bloom', trans. Christopher Rich (Ann Arbor, MI, 1997)

Silk and Insight, trans. Hiroaki Sato (Armonk, NY, 1998)
My Friend Hitler and Other Plays of Yukio Mishima, trans. Hiroaki Sato
(New York, 2002)

Books Wholly or Partly about Yukio Mishima

Ando, Takeshi, *Mishima Yukio no shogai* (Tokyo, 1998)
Fukushima, Jiro, *Mishima Yukio: Tsurugi to kanbeni* (Tokyo, 1998)
Hashimoto, Osamu, *'Mishima Yukio' to wa nanimono datta no ka*
(Tokyo, 2002)
Hiraoka, Azusa, *Segare: Mishima Yukio* (Tokyo, 1972)
Hosaka, Masayasu, *Mishima Yukio to tate no kai jiken* (Tokyo, 1980)
Inose, Naoki, *Persusona: Mishima Yukio-den* (Tokyo, 1995)
——, with Sato, Hiroaki, *Persona: A Biography of Yukio Mishima* (Berkeley,
CA, 2012)
Inoue, Takashi, *Mishima Yukio: Hojo naru kamen* (Tokyo, 2009)
——, *Maboroshi no isaku o yomu: mo hitotsu no 'Hojo no umi'* (Tokyo, 2010)
Inoue, Toyoo, *Hatashiete inai yakusoku: Mishima Yukio ga nokoseshimono*
(Tokyo, 2006)
Keene, Donald, *Dawn to the West*, 2 vols (Boston, 1984)
——, *On Familiar Terms* (New York, 1994)
——, with Tokuoka Takao, *Toyu kiko* (Tokyo, 1973)
Kojima, Chikako, *Mishima Yukio to Dan Kazuo* (Tokyo, 1989)
Mishima Yukio to sengo, collection of essays on Mishima by various
authors, special edition of *Chuo Koron* (Tokyo, 2010)
Muramatsu Takeshi, *Mishima Yukio no sekai* (Tokyo, 1996)
Nakagawa, Yusuke, *Showa 45-nen 11-gatsu 25-nichi* (Tokyo, 2010)
Nathan, John, *Mishima: A Biography* (Boston and Toronto, 1974)
——, *Living Carelessly in Tokyo and Elsewhere* (New York, 2008)
Nosaka, Akiyuki, *Kakuyaku-taru gyakko* (Tokyo, 1991)
Okadane, Jiro, *Hasuda Zenmei to sono shi* (Tokyo, 1970)
Okuno, Takeo, *Mishima Yukio densetsu* (Tokyo, 1993)
Piven, Jerry S., *The Madness and Perversion of Yukio Mishima* (Westport,
CT, 2004)
Ross, Christopher, *Mishima's Sword: Travels in Search of a Samurai Legend*
(London, 2006)

Scott Stokes, Henry, *The Life and Death of Yukio Mishima* (New York, 1974)

Shibata, Shoji, *Mishima Yukio: Sakuhin ni kakusareta jiketsu e no michi* (Tokyo, 2012)

Tokuoka Takao, *Gosui no hito* (Tokyo, 1999)

Yamamoto, Kiyokatsu, *Jieitai 'Kage no butai': Mishima Yukio o koroshita shinjitsu no kokuhaku* (Tokyo, 2001)

Yuasa, Atsuko, *Roi to Kyoko* (Tokyo, 1984)

Acknowledgements

Most of the research for this book was conducted in the incongruous surroundings of the Art of Tea café in Didsbury, Manchester. My thanks to the staff for maintaining the essential supply lines of soup, latte and carrot cake, and to Dr Robert Gutfreund-Walmsley, proprietor of the adjacent Didsbury Village Bookshop, for casting an ever-quizzical eye over my 'translations of Murakami'. My thanks too to his able assistant Chris Cohen for patiently breaking off from his readings of Dickens, Marlowe and American literature while I assailed him with a tsunami of thoughts on Mishima and world literature. My gratitude is also due to Andrew Clare, translator of Mishima, Shusaku Endo and Matsumoto Seicho, for reading through an early draft of this book. My greatest thanks are to my partner Karen, who both read and refined the manuscript, and quelled domestic chaos so that I could write it: she laughed when I told her about the next book. You can read more about that and my other literary adventures at damianflanagan.com.

Photo Acknowledgements

© Corbis: pp. 6, 218, 233 (Bettmann); © The Mainichi Newspapers: pp. 195, 220, 222, 239; courtesy of Mitsuo Fujita: pp. 35, 40, 42, 46, 47, 58, 69, 71, 89, 95, 115, 120, 124, 129, 130, 132, 137, 141, 143; courtesy of Shinchosha: pp. 122, 155, 157, 158; © Kishin Shinoyama: pp. 55, 241.